D1532236

YOU JUST DON'T DUCT TAPE A BABY!

YOU JUST DON'T DUCT TAPE A BABY!

TRUE TALES AND SENSIBLE SUGGESTIONS FROM A VETERAN PEDIATRICIAN

Norman Weinberger, M.D. with Alison Pohn

WARNER BOOKS

A Time Warner Company

Warner Books, Inc., 1271 Avenue of the Americas, New York, NY 10020

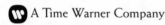 A Time Warner Company

Printed in the United States of America

First Printing: April 1997

10 9 8 7 6 5 4 3 2 1

Library of Congress Cataloging-in-Publication Data
Weinberger, Norman.
You just don't duct tape a baby: true tales and sensible suggestions from a veteran pedia-
trician / Norman Weinberger, with Alison Pohn.
p. cm.
Includes index.
ISBN 0-446-51965-0
1. Parenting--United States. 2. Child rearing--United States.
I. Pohn, Alison. II. Title
HQ755.8.W42 1997
649'.1--dc20   96-21476
                                                        CIP

Book design by Maura Gibbons

To my wife, Susan
N.W.

To Lexie, who makes every day an adventure, and
to Jack, who makes every day paradise.
A.P.

CONTENTS

There are only two lasting bequests we can give our children. One of these is roots. The other is wings.
—Hodding Carter

ACKNOWLEDGMENTS

• My patients, who have provided the opportunity for me to interact with them and their families. They have enabled me to teach them and learn from them.

• My children, Gordon and Lisa, for allowing me the opportunity to parent them.

• Dr. Bertram Grossman, my partner and colleague for twenty-four years.

• Dr. Donald Medearis, who taught me the science of pediatrics; Dr. Charles Wood and Dr. Jack Rinehart, who taught me the humanity of pediatrics and the importance of family-focused pediatrics.

• Maria Maisano, Woody Allen devotee, who recognized my story-telling and encouraged me to record stories on tape.

• Bruce Michel, who urged me to write a book.

• My staff, for their support and for putting up with me.

N.W.

• Kathy Atlass, a most wonderful, inspirational teacher and friend was the first one to tell me I was a writer—without her I very well might have become a lawyer! Thanks!

• Jeffrey Pohn, brother, confidant, advisor, and friend—thank you for making me get out there and do it. Thank you for always believing in me.

• A tremendous thank you to my sisters, Julie Blumenthal and Lisa Levy, and my sister-of-the-heart, Julie Keywell, who were always there to pull me back from the brink of despair and share a little Sunday brunch.

• My oldest and dearest friend, Susan Ocasek, helped me to view every setback as simply a lesson to be learned and a step closer to achieving my goals and potential. Thank you, Sue.

• I am forever grateful to Dr. Jean Carney—teacher of perseverance and power—miracle worker.

• My thanks and devotion to my tenacious and talented agent, Denise Marcil, without whom I would not have been part of this wonderful project.

• Every day of this project I thanked God for putting me in the hands of our editor, Betsy Mitchell. Her kindness, support, and wonderful wit made this project a beginning author's dream-come-true. Thanks.

• And finally a huge thank you to Norman and Susan Weinberger. I often wondered what karma would suddenly throw together a Connecticut pediatrician and a budding Chicago writer, but it resulted in a wonderful growing experience for me and, I hope, a lifetime friendship for us all.

A.P.

YOU JUST DON'T DUCT TAPE A BABY!

PROLOGUE

It All Begins

That August morning, in 1971, we woke up to a big, deep blue Montana sky. The sun was barely up, but the temperature was already above 100 degrees. Two airmen attempted to make the final inspection of our now empty house as six-year-old Gordon and four-year-old Lisa chased each other around in excited circles. Monty, our German short-haired pointer, jumped and barked frantically, confused by all that was going on.

I went to headquarters to sign off and be released. I received my final paycheck and the reams of paperwork necessary to say nothing more than the Air Force no longer owned me. I had fulfilled my obligation.

Early on in medical school I had applied for and was accepted by the Berry Program. This was a government deferment program that ensured that enough medical students would be properly trained in their specialties rather than drafted. In return, once you completed this training you would serve the military as a doctor/officer for two years.

When we first arrived at Malmstrom Air Force Base in

Great Falls, where I had been assigned as a pediatrician, I had been apprehensive, worried about what this strange new place would be like and determined not to let myself become too "militarized." But Susan, my wife, insisted this was a wonderful opportunity for our whole family to be together and take advantage of this magnificent part of the country. She was right. Not only did I have more time with the children than I would have outside the military, but we also formed an extended family among the friends we made on the base. The very urban Weinbergers became outdoorsmen and -women, hiking, fishing, and reveling in the national parks. It had been a wonderful experience, but now I was more than ready to begin a new chapter of our life.

I returned to find that Susan had already packed the kids into the back seat and was in the process of trying to force Monty, who was a hundred pounds of frenzied, high-strung muscle, into the wayback of our Ford station wagon. Dark green, with fake wood, it was our first car. We had bought it when we arrived in Montana two years earlier.

With Susan at the wheel we headed off the base for the last time. I saluted the gate guard and then, in a fit of euphoria, pulled my uniform off and let it fly piece by piece out the car window into the hot Montana wind. Susan turned to me screaming, "You're crazy, Norman. You're nuts!" The kids shrieked joyfully at the sight of my uniform blowing away against the brilliant blue sky.

We were on our way.

About six months earlier, with the end of my Air Force career approaching, I had traveled to the East Coast to look at—and be looked at by—several pediatric practices. I was intent on finding a good fit to start my life as a private practicing pediatrician. Despite the love we had developed for Montana, Susan and I had chosen to return to the East Coast, to raise our family close to her home in Boston and my home in Pittsburgh.

So in March, I flew to Allentown, Pennsylvania, for a brief visit with my brother, sister, and their families. Then, armed with my list of ten pediatric practices, culled from the pediatric journal classified ads, I flew to Hartford, Connecticut, rented a car, and set out on my search. I felt alone and a little scared. Here I was, thirty-one years old, with a wife, two children, and a dog, trying to find a new life in a new land—sort of like Moses, but not nearly as wise.

I knew that I wanted to be part of a practice where we cared about families and their children, a practice where I could use what I had been taught to enhance their lives. And I was looking for someone to practice with who shared these views. For my family I wanted a place where we all could be part of the community.

As the days passed, I became more and more frustrated. I couldn't seem to find a practice where I clicked. None of the doctors I was meeting seemed to share my philosophies. None seemed to want to take the time with their patients and their families to really get to know *who* they were treating, rather than what they were treating.

There was a four-man practice I felt good about until the junior partner confided to me the reason he was leaving. The senior partner had been stealing from the practice. I quickly crossed that one off my list.

More frustrated than before, I called my friend and mentor Charlie Wood to discuss my dilemma. Charlie Wood was a well-known pediatrician who had taught at Baby's Hospital, Columbia Presbyterian while in private practice in New York. He then moved to Pittsburgh's Children's Hospital to run the outpatient department. My first contact with him was as a medical student and he was there throughout my pediatric training. Charlie was a warm, compassionate pediatrician— well-read, knowledgeable, thoughtful, and wise. Plus he seemed to know everyone in pediatrics. He contacted a friend of his, Dr. Neal Lebhar, in Westport, Connecticut, and, while Dr. Lebhar wasn't in need of an associate, he knew of a pediatrician in a neighboring town who was looking for help. So I added Dr. Bertram Grossman of Norwalk to my list.

I made my way through Connecticut, and by Thursday night of that long week I was in Norwalk. The next morning I found myself in the compact, no-frills offices of Dr. Bert Grossman, a white-haired man of medium, athletic build—a Jewish Ivy League preppy in rep tie, tortoiseshell glasses, and immaculate starched white lab coat.

After brief introductions, I was immediately caught up in the whirlwind schedule of Dr. Bert Grossman. Things went well as I spent the day in his office, looking over his shoulder, seemingly being tested and tried by Bert. I was impressed with the mutually warm relationship he obviously shared with his patients and staff, and I liked the way they ran an efficient but caring office. I liked that Bert had very up-to-date information and was very skillful in imparting it to his families in a friendly, informative, and nonthreatening way. It all felt right.

That night Bert took me home to meet his wife, Bea, and their four young daughters. We shared a casual meal of Bert's all-time favorite food, hamburgers. Although Bert told me straight out he had been looking for someone of Italian descent to complement the Norwalk population, it was apparent we had clicked. His practice had grown to the point where he had to bring in a new doctor, and I could tell that he felt, at the very least, that I would do.

Later that evening Bert's daughters came into the living room to say good night. When I watched them kiss their parents, I mentioned how much I missed kissing my two children good night. To my delight, each of the girls came over and gave me a good-night kiss. Bert was grinning from ear to ear. It seemed I had just received the ultimate seal of approval. We agreed that I would join the practice.

The next morning I got into my rental car and began the one-and-a-half-hour drive back to Hartford. I suddenly became aware that the steering wheel was shaking, and I was freezing although it was fifty degrees. I turned the heater on full blast—no help. I finally realized it was fear causing my shivers. What was I doing? I wished Susan was there with me making this decision. I returned to Montana still feeling shaky. Susan and I spent the next several days going over the trip in great detail and my decision to enter Bert's practice.

We still had a few details to take care of, like checking each other's references. But all went well and before I knew it I had a one-year contract typewritten on a yellow piece of paper. It was a done deal. Now suddenly our family was contemplating a move to a place we had never lived, where we had no family or friends; a place where I would be working in close quarters with someone with whom I had spent less than twenty-four hours.

I was happy and excited, but the anticipation was tempered with fear and uneasiness. Suddenly the decision seemed hastily made and I spent the spring and summer overwhelmed by uncertainty, one minute thrilled, the next apprehensive. But there was no turning back now.

We had been traveling several hours, Susan at the wheel the whole way. The car seemed uncomfortably warm and humid, although the air-conditioning had been running on high. I turned to look at the back seat where my children sat damp and quiet and flushed. Beyond the children and the dog and the suitcases, I could see white smoke streaming from the back of the car.

"Susan," I said, trying to sound as calm as possible, although I was sure that the car would suddenly explode, "we should pull off the highway at the next exit and find a service station."

"We've got plenty of gas," Susan responded. Then she saw my face. "What? What's wrong?" I nodded my head in the direction of where the smoke was still streaming out of the car. I tried to be as subtle as possible so that the kids wouldn't notice. But they were immediately alerted by Susan's voice. "Norman, my God! Is the car on fire?" The children started screaming and bouncing up and down trying to see out the back window.

"No," I replied, trying to convince myself. "Just get off at the next exit. I see a gas station sign."

We quickly left the highway and pulled into the service station, kids yelling, dog barking, and Susan and I imagining every conceivable mechanical failure. We rushed the kids and dog as far from the car as possible, just in case.

A very young man named Eddie (at least that's what it said on his grease-stained coveralls) strolled over to the car. "What's the problem?" he asked pleasantly. I explained the smoke to young Eddie, trying not to sound totally mechanically ignorant. He nodded knowingly, poked around under the hood for a few minutes and confidently diagnosed an overworked air conditioner. He added coolant and declared the car to be in fine working order.

This was somewhat anticlimactic for those of us who were expecting major mechanical failure, fires, and floods. Not quite trusting the young man, I drove the rest of the day with both hands clenching the steering wheel, one eye on the rearview mirror, keeping a vigil for smoke, flames, or falling car parts.

We pulled into a motel that evening, tired and cranky. While the kids were, for the most part, good travelers, often sleeping or playing games, Monty was another story altogether. Each bathroom, gas, or food stop had to be planned with the precision of a military invasion. Who would hold Monty when the door opened? Who would remove him from the car, far away from the gas pumps, so he didn't terrorize the attendant? Who would wrestle him back into the car? How would we calm him down when he saw something he didn't like, or worse, did like, along the highway?

The morning's euphoria had long since worn off. It was hard to imagine several more days of this. Then the children saw the motel swimming pool and let out a cheer. With their spirits rising, ours did too. We all played happily in the pool for a long time, the children conveniently wearing themselves out, while Susan and I felt refreshed and energized.

That evening, as Susan and I relaxed by the motel pool in the still-hot sun, keeping an eye on Lisa and Gordon, Susan asked, "What will life be like in Norwalk?"

I knew this question had been on her mind more and more as our move approached. It had certainly been on mine. It was hard to imagine going to a place where we knew no one, where there was no ready-made support system like there had been during the first seven years of our married life in Pittsburgh with my family, or even the two years in the Air Force where we had a ready-made family of people who shared our same situation.

"It will be like we make it," I told Susan, although I wasn't at all sure what that meant. And so we began a discussion that continued as we traveled the country. We talked about what each of our jobs would be. How I would have to devote most of my time to build my practice, and that Susan's job would be to take care of the family and to establish all of us in the community.

We talked about staying as close to the children as possible. We had long ago decided that one of the most important aspects of a family was to sit down to dinner together on as many nights a week as possible with Friday night, Sabbath dinner, being a must to spend together. We also felt reading was important. So we pledged to continue to read daily to the children. We hoped that by doing this we would instill in them the importance and joy of books and reading—something that would be valuable to them throughout their lives.

Our conversations went on to include what my goals were for my practice. When I was a resident at Children's Hospital in Pittsburgh, from 1966 through 1969, the emphasis there—as in most training programs of the time—had been on diagnosing and treating childhood disease. We spent very little time trying to understand how the children felt about their illnesses or how families coped with the stress of their children being ill. We spent even less time on wellness, on the normal developmental milestones of children and their normal behavioral aspects. In fact, residency seemed to me to be all about diseases and not at all about children and their families. At best, families were peripheral and the relationship was a formal one; at worst the relationship was an adversarial one.

That is, until psychiatrist Dr. Jack Rheinhart began holding sessions with some of us in the residency program. Dr. Rheinhart was a child psychiatrist who, when he wasn't seeing patients, worked with the medical students and house staff, teaching us about the behavioral, developmental, and psychological aspects of pediatrics. He gave us an understanding of how each child is unique, and how each is the same. And in time, I began to view Jack as a mentor who made me aware that dealing with children's feelings and addressing family issues was critical to providing comprehensive care. Although this was not quite a revolutionary approach, Jack Rheinhart was certainly ahead of his time. Now this approach is not only widely accepted, but considered to be a cornerstone of modern pediatric practice.

Dr. Rheinhart taught us interview techniques that showed us how to ask open-ended questions that couldn't be answered with just one or two words. He taught us how if you really took your time to talk with families rather than just questioning them, you could quickly establish a mutually respectful relationship. By listening to their questions as well as answering them as completely as possible, the families knew you were interested in them, their concerns and their fears. He gave us the ability to seek out family strengths and resources that would help them deal with their children.

As an Air Force pediatrician I had, for the first time, the opportunity to put into practice what I had learned from Dr. Rheinhart. The practice of pediatric medicine was not just diagnosing and treating. It was about helping parents to recognize how they could raise their children to be healthy, whole, socially responsible, functioning adults. In order to help families, it is necessary to understand the parental role in guiding children from infancy to adulthood.

The two years in Montana showed me that without integrating these aspects into my practice, I would be giving less than families required. I felt that I had an opportunity—a challenge—to provide a family-centered approach to the practice of pediatrics.

Over the past twenty-five years that I've practiced pediatrics, I have seen this concept evolve—both in our practice and in pediatrics in general. Some of that evolution has been the result of necessity. Being a parent and raising children today is a far different and, in many respects, a far more difficult process than it was when I was parenting my own children. And it is surely far different from the process my parents went through raising me.

When my generation were children, most of us grew up with our families intact. Not only did we have two parents, but a whole extended family (also known as the connected nuclear family) lived within shouting distance of each other.

Aunts, uncles, grandmas, grandpas, and cousins could be counted on in times of need, whether it be illness, for baby-sitting, or as an extra hand. In times of joy or sorrow, there was your family with a unified idea of what was right and wrong—a belief system of how children should be raised passed from one generation to another. Some of these belief systems may seem arcane or even comical in light of present information, but these families trusted their "family truths" and felt sure that if they adhered to them, all would be well.

This overriding sense of well-being and certainty has all but disappeared in this far more complex day and age. Many factors have contributed to the uncertainty and confusion that seems to reign these days: the dissolution of the connected nuclear family, both parents having careers, child care dilemmas, divorce, single parenthood, the effects of too much information, advertising, and marketing, and the prolonged absence of fathers and mothers, as commuting times and business travel increase. I see the family-focused pediatric practice as a necessity to help families and children cope as we enter the twenty-first century.

This all may seem oh-so-serious but, in fact, the most rewarding aspect of this approach is the humor and fun that families have and are willing to share. This book is intended to help families by sharing my experiences both as a father and participant with my wife in the journey of our children to adulthood, and as a professional called upon to guide families through this wonderful, painful, funny, and treacherous trip.

Our cross-country trek continued: appeasing crazy Monty to minimize the noise and aggravation, swimming in motel pools to ease the uncomfortable combination of lethargy and built-up energy from riding in the crowded station wagon, planning and replanning our future to keep anxiety at bay, and keeping an ever-wary eye out for the white smoke that could herald disaster.

"Look, Daddy! Smoke!" Gordon said excitedly, pointing at the steel mills in the distance, thankfully not at the back of our car. It was mid-afternoon of day five on the road. I felt a surge of pure happiness at suddenly being surrounded by the familiar outskirts of Pittsburgh. I had lived my whole life there, prior to my military stint, and Susan had called it home since she left Brookline, Massachusetts, after high school to attend Carnegie Mellon University.

"Those are what's left of the steel mills. There used to be a lot more smoke," I told him, enjoying the familiar sight of smoke rising endlessly in the sky. How different this was from the broad open expanse and clean, clear air of the "Big Sky Country" of Montana. Here in Pittsburgh smoke and pollution were a sign of prosperity and abundance—a quickly fading prosperity, a dwindling abundance.

We drove over the Monongahela River across the Homestead High Level Bridge, and as the car climbed steep West Avenue, my spirits soared as well. In a matter of minutes my whole family would be together for the first time in two years. We entered the suburb of Homestead Park where my parents lived, and as we pulled into the driveway my mother came running out of the house, so excited and happy that she was clearly beside herself. Following closely behind her was Mrs. Taylor, whom we fondly called T. She had been hired to work for my family a lifetime ago when my mother started working with my father in his pharmacy. It was hard to remember a time when T wasn't ruling our home.

There was the happy reunion in our driveway; a jumble of hugs and kisses and "how big you've gotten" and "how beautiful you are" all punctuated by Monty's excited barking and Gordon's demand for the bathroom.

Later I left my family in the kitchen cooking my favorite summer Sabbath dinner to go to the pharmacy to pick up my father. By the time we returned the rest of the family had arrived to greet us. The house was filled with the excitement of our all being together again and the buzz of a never-ending conversation.

It was as if time had somehow reversed and I had never left this safe and wonderful place. My mother lit the candles and my father said the blessing over the wine and the bread. Then we feasted on my favorite dinner of Southern fried chicken, potato salad, coleslaw, and homemade apple pie.

T's Kosher Southern Fried Chicken

I guarantee that you and your family will love this. It's my most treasured summer dinner because it always brings back a rush of memories. Enjoy!

> 1 or 2 frying chickens, quartered
> salt and pepper
> pinch of sage
> flour
> 3 eggs, gently beaten
> bread crumbs, preferably from leftover challah
> Crisco shortening

Wash chicken and pat dry. Mix salt, pepper, and sage in with the flour. Roll chicken in flour mixture until well coated, then roll in beaten eggs, then bread crumbs. Refrigerate for at least two hours.

Melt Crisco in a large frying pan and heat to 375° F. If you don't have a cooking thermometer, test shortening temperature by putting a one-inch cube of bread in oil. It should brown, without burning, in one minute.

When the temperature is right, fry the chicken in small batches, leaving plenty of room between pieces. Chicken is done when golden brown and crispy. Drain on paper towels.

Special tip: This chicken is especially good on a hot summer evening when served at room temperature with potato salad. Delicious!

As usual the children were put to bed after dinner, while the adults moved to the living room to talk and have coffee and perhaps another slice of pie. Just when it truly began to feel like I had never left, the phone rang.

"Norman, I'm glad I was able to reach you." It was Bert Grossman. Something was wrong. I could hear it in his voice even though I didn't yet know him well.

"My father has died and I have to go down to Florida to take care of the arrangements. Do you think that you could possibly be here on Monday?"

I assured Bert that that would not be a problem—although I was a little ashamed that disappointment over cutting my family reunion short was competing with my sympathy for Bert.

"Just come straight to my house. My wife has the keys to the house I rented for you. She'll have everything you need."

I returned to the living room. "Bert's father has died and he has to go to Florida. I'm starting work on Monday."

"This Monday?" my father said. "You've only just got here."

"Sorry, but it can't be helped."

"Imagine that. The doctor is so confident in Normie that he's leaving him in charge and he hasn't even officially started yet," my mother said proudly. All the relatives nodded reverently.

I sat down next to Susan on the sofa. She had said nothing, but I could see she wasn't happy. "We'll just have to fit the whole trip into one day," I said, putting my arm around her.

The next morning I took Susan and the kids and the dog on my "this is your life" tour. We went to my elementary school, junior high and high schools, visited my father's pharmacy, Mt. Washington, the University of Pittsburgh Medical School and Children's Hospital, where I spent my days in medical training. It was getting late. We hurried home to get dressed for the big get-together that my parents had planned. The house was full with all of Susan's and my friends and family. We partied late into the night, celebrating my release from the military.

Early Sunday we got up, repacked the car, the kids, and Monty, who had worn out his welcome by eating his way through the door of my father's study. We sadly said our good-byes and set off for the nine-hour trip to Norwalk and our new home.

Without too much trouble we found Bert's house in Westport. As promised, Bea was waiting for us with keys and directions and instructions. With only a few wrong turns we found the house on Homer Street that would be ours for the next year.

The moving truck had beaten us there by an hour. We started to settle in. But around nine o'clock that night, knowing my poor sense of direction, I decided that it would be a good idea to find both the office and the hospital so that I would have no problem the next morning. It was fairly easy, even for me. Our house, the hospital, and the office were in a small triangular pattern with just a few miles between each place. This would make life fairly easy. Bert had done a good job in choosing our house.

Returning from my explorations, Susan and I quickly got the kids and the dog settled so that we could go to bed ourselves. I planned on an early start the next morning. However, I found that between my own excitement and the stifling heat of a bedroom without air-conditioning, a fan, or cross ventilation, I could hardly breathe let alone sleep. So I lay in bed, listening to Susan breathing next to me, trying to decide if I was more worried or relieved that I would be starting this first week in the office alone, without Bert.

The next morning, running almost entirely on nervous energy, I confidently found the hospital. However, once inside, I immediately got lost. Sometime later after asking directions, I found my way to the nursery, where I introduced myself to the nurses and went on to examine a couple of Bert's newest patients. All right, I thought, this is going pretty well. There had been nothing out of the ordinary, nothing that I couldn't handle.

I was a little more apprehensive as I walked from the newborn nursery down the hall to the maternity floor. I knew that these mothers expected to see Dr. Grossman and I hoped they wouldn't feel let down by a new doctor. I saw them as a tougher audience than the infants had been, but I managed to bumble through.

My confidence was building as I made my way to the pediatric floor, only getting lost once. I reviewed the charts, examined the patients, made notes, and wrote orders. I took the time to meet the parents and get to know them, their concerns and needs, as they began to get to know me.

I drove on to the office feeling somewhat elated. Pat, Bert's nurse, and Edith, his secretary and practical nurse, were already there. I had met them during my visit in March. Pat greeted me politely, but I could feel a restraint, a coldness from Edith that put me a little on edge, made me a little uncomfortable. There was no time to dwell on the feeling, though, because the waiting room was quickly filling up and the phone was ringing, and I immediately was thrown into an initiation-by-fire—the life of a thriving private pediatric practice.

It was like that the rest of the day . . . the rest of the week.

As I hustled from hospital to office, from examining room to examining room, took phone calls, throat cultures, and talked and listened and examined, one thought kept running through my head: *I am so lucky to have come into a practice that is this busy.*

1

Go to Sleep, Go to *Sleep!*

*"We put her to bed and she comes right back out, say-
ing she needs a glass of water, or has to go to the bathroom, or she's afraid."*

Bert returned from Florida and we slowly settled into practicing pediatrics together. Of course, it wasn't just Bert and me
in the office. I realized quickly that I had not just joined a
practice, but a family—a very close-knit family.

There was the nurse, Pat Kermis. She was an attractive
woman, with a pleasant smile, good with the children and
more than competent in her job. She was polite and accom-
modating but, at the same time, seemed to have no feelings
one way or the other toward me or my joining the practice.

Then there was Edith Cochran, who ran the office. Edith
was a bit of a character, jingling up and down the hall at
Christmastime with bells sewn onto the hem of her skirts and
wearing outrageous costumes on Halloween. The mothers
loved her. She was a big robust woman with a hearty laugh.
She had the ability to calm anxious parents and allay the fears
of frightened children. I, however, grew to view her as Bert's
private watchdog, her bark worse than her bite—but only
marginally so. She adored Bert and he, her. I immediately suspected that she viewed me as an intruder. I knew that I had to

prove myself to Bert, but I hadn't figured on having to prove myself to Edith—an even more formidable task. If I asked her a question I was given a cool but efficient answer. If I asked her to perform a task that was not part of the routine she had set up with Bert, I was thrown a glare punctuated by a barely audible "humph." As far as Edith was concerned, I was the black sheep of this family, if I was considered family at all.

One of our first confrontations occurred on my second day in the office. On the first day, when I arrived from making hospital rounds, I asked if there was any coffee. Edith looked at me as if I had broken a holy commandment. "We don't have food in the office," she said, giving me a look of disdainful incredulity.

"Okay," I said to her, but to myself I added, "but coffee's *not* food." The next day I brought in a little six-cup coffeepot, some coffee, and three mugs. With Edith looking over my shoulder disapprovingly, I made the coffee and went into Bert's little consultation office to drink it in private. As the morning wore on, I found myself between patients and went back to get a second cup of coffee. To my amazement I found the pot empty and unplugged. The two other mugs were in the sink with telltale coffee in the bottom of each. Round one: Norman.

Adding to the problem was the physical size of the office. It was all of seven hundred square feet. The waiting room seemed to bulge at the seams with crying babies, running children, and harried parents. The reception and bookkeeping areas could only comfortably hold one person at a time. The rest of the rooms seemed to be in miniature as well. There was Bert's office, a laboratory/storage room that doubled as a minor surgery room, two examining rooms, and a tiny bathroom. It might be comfortable for one doctor, but it was totally impractical for two. But, with Bert back, I wasn't all that busy. In fact I was spending a portion of each day in the consultation office that I now shared with Bert, reading journals and magazines, trying to keep busy while waiting for my patient base to build.

Bert decided that he wouldn't take any new patient families for himself, in my first year, to help me build my practice. Then Dr. Thayer Willis, the oldest pediatrician in town, retired. He turned his patient records over to us. It was a natural fit, since Bert had always covered Thayer's practice when he was away. His patients were, for the most part, comfortable and familiar with our practice. This was the perfect opportunity for me to quickly expand my practice and start carrying my own weight.

While I was in the office reading medical journals and trying to stay out of Edith's way, Susan was getting our house and children settled. Since it was August when we arrived, one of the first things we needed to do was register Gordon for school. When we went to enroll him in the first grade at Tracey, our neighborhood school, the principal, Edith Vogel, greeted us at the door and asked Susan if she would be volunteering at the school. We later learned that no one ever said no to Edith Vogel. On our return visit with the paperwork for Gordon's first day, Miss Vogel remembered Susan and Gordon by name. We had a good feeling about this school.

Then we set about finding a preschool for Lisa. There were many to choose from. Some allowed children to socialize in a safe, supervised, cheerful, and friendly environment. Some focused on developing the skills necessary to make the first years of elementary school easier and more productive. And some taught foreign languages and calculus. We decided what we needed was the cheerful, friendly environment—a place where Lisa could learn through play and exploration. Aside from that, the most pressing requirement was a preschool that picked up and delivered. We wanted bus service. So Lisa was enrolled at the Norwalk Jewish Community Center Nursery School.

On the first day of school the house was buzzing with excitement and tension. The sheer anxiety of starting first grade in a new school had drained the summer color from Gordon's thin face, while Lisa hopped wildly about the house, chanting, "I'm going to schoooool, I'm going to schooool," the ever-present Monty barking as he leaped after her through the house.

I sighed with relief when I finally got to the office that morning. I've always contended that working a full-time-outside-the-house job is much easier than staying home with the kids. Furthermore I believe (although they would never admit it) most fathers know this. With both children safely and somewhat happily deposited at school, "Now," I felt, "we are truly members of the Norwalk community."

A little later that morning I was examining a baby when a call came through.

"Yes?" I said to Edith.

"Your wife is on the back line," Edith said with her usual clipped efficiency.

"What's up, Sus?"

"Norman, I am so embarrassed." Her voice was shaking.

"What happened?" I said, sitting down.

"I just got a call from Gordon's school . . ." I immediately tried to think of something that Gordon could have done in one short morning to warrant a call home and Susan's being so upset. I couldn't imagine Gordon drawing even the slightest attention to himself—especially not today. If he could have phoned in his first day of school, he would have. He was a slow-to-warm-up child—never liked changes or new experiences. We knew this would be a child who would never want to go to sleep-away camp.

"What did he do?"

"It's not what he did. It's what you did!" Her voice was suddenly sharp with accusation.

"What did I do?"

"Gordon is not up-to-date on his inoculations. They wanted to know if we have a private physician or if the school should take care of it. Norman, do you know how this looks; the new pediatrician's son not being up-to-date on his shots?"

I thought it was funny, like the cobbler whose children have worn-out shoes. However, it was clear that Susan didn't find this amusing. "Tell the school that he'll be up-to-date by tomorrow, and I'll bring home the immunizations he needs and give them to him tonight."

So despite some resistance from Gordon, he was fully and completely inoculated that evening—no longer a health menace to the other children.

The whole family quickly made friends throughout the neighborhood and school and we fell into a comfortable pattern of home and work and school. Susan found that, in addition to taking care of the house and the kids, she wanted to do some volunteer work. She decided it was time to go out into the community and find some organizations that could use her. First, she became a member of the Women's Auxiliary of the community-based Norwalk Symphony. She so enjoyed her work with the symphony that she then joined several other organizations, each demanding more and more of her time.

A week before our first Norwalk Halloween, Edith stopped me in the hall between patients.

"You know *we* dress up for Halloween," she said in a somewhat threatening tone.

"Really?" I replied. "I don't." And I quickly ducked into the examining room.

"It's Halloween," Edith said later that same day. "The kids will be disappointed if you're not in costume."

I just shook my head. But Halloween morning as Gordon and Lisa ran around pulling together the last details of their costumes to bring to school, I had second thoughts. Maybe Edith was right. Maybe I should go in costume.

Rummaging through the garage, I found a pair of white coveralls. In the attic I found a pair of white arctic boots left over from my stint in the military. Mixed in with the winter clothes I found a white knit hat that pulled down to become a face mask.

"What the heck are you?" Edith, in complete clown garb, asked, obviously startled as I walked in.

"Can't you tell?" I said.

Edith shook her head.

"I'm the abominable snowman," I said proudly.

"Oh yeah, now I see it," she said sarcastically and then started laughing. "You'll take a little training, but at least you're in costume," she said triumphantly. Round two: Edith.

I found that I was spending less and less time in the office reading journals. My practice was building. It was time for me to go out into the community. Dr. Robert Appleby, one of the pediatricians in our coverage group, had recently opened up the Children's Medical Center in South Norwalk, a low-income area.

He had raised the money to buy a building and hire a full-time pediatric nurse-practitioner. The nurse-practitioner worked during the day with Dr. Appleby as backup. In the evening it was staffed by volunteer pediatricians. Fees were set on a sliding scale, with every patient paying something, so that families felt like they were taking responsibility for their care rather than receiving charity.

I was excited about the clinic and the prospect of being able to give something to this community that had so readily accepted me and my family. And I was proud to be able to supply medical care to children who might otherwise not have it, so I happily started spending Tuesday evenings at the center.

With Susan doing community work and me immersed in my practice, it became clear that our plan to spend the evenings with the children was on the verge of falling apart. It was time for a family meeting. We took out a calendar and marked off those nights when I was on call or working at the clinic, and the nights when Susan had board meetings scheduled. From then on, if something came up, we would check our calendars before accepting. This ensured that one of us was home every night.

Having dinner together as a family was a priority, but the meals had to be strategically planned to be nutritious, interesting to the kids, and take no more than ninety minutes from first entering the kitchen to leaving it with dishes washed and all cleaned up. So pasta, salads, chicken and fish, fresh vegetables, and bread became the mainstays of our dinners. And the grill was in constant use.

By 7:00 P.M., while one of us was finishing up in the kitchen, the other would be helping Gordon with homework or Lisa with an art project. More often than not, Lisa spent her time doing something art-related. She amazed us with her artistic talent. I would get the kids bathed, teeth brushed, pajamas on. Then it was time for a story and at 8:00 they were each in their own room. From this routine the children quickly learned that the evening, before 8:00, was their time. After 8:00, it was ours.

The rule was clear—they had to stay in their rooms. If they wanted to read, finish homework, or, in Lisa's case, draw, fine. But under no circumstances were they to come out of their rooms. During the day our attention was focused on our children. Dinner, the time when we were all together, was entirely about them: their day, their problems, their accomplishments, their stories, their needs. After 8:00 P.M., it was adult time: the time for Susan and me to talk, share problems, concerns, or go back to work or to meetings. Aside from giving Susan and me much needed adult time, this routine also ensured that Lisa and Gordon would get enough sleep each night.

Around this time one of my first patients, four-year-old Danielle Marx, came in for her yearly exam. The yearly exam provides the physician with the opportunity to integrate with the family the biomedical, developmental, psychosocial issues and behavioral aspects of their child. In other words, let's take a moment and see how your kid is doing.

Danielle sat on the examining room table, her curly reddish-brown hair framing her beautiful little face like the halo on an angel. Looks can be deceiving.

"Moooommmyyyy, I want to leave noowoow," Danielle whined to her mother.

"Now, Danielle, it will be just a few more minutes. I need to finish talking with Dr. Weinberger."

"But I want to leave NOOWOOW," Danielle insisted in a voice that could break glass.

"Sometimes the things she eats make her a little difficult and demanding," Mrs. Marx said to me apologetically. "I haven't been letting her have sugar, wheat, peanuts, grapes, or chicken," she counted off. "I think that she must be allergic to those foods."

"Why? What happens when she eats those foods?" I asked, thinking what a strange assortment of foods to restrict.

"Her behavior becomes just atrocious."

We both looked down at Danielle. She had climbed down off the table and was opening the door. "I'm leaving NOW," she said forcefully, as she opened the door, looking up at her mother to see her reaction.

"Okay, Danielle, you can go into the waiting room and play until Mommy and I are done talking," I told her.

"I'll be done in a minute," Mrs. Marx assured her, and Danielle went on to the waiting room.

"So, her behavior becomes atrocious. Can you describe it to me?"

"She's just out of control when she eats those things, and I can't do anything with her. She just doesn't listen."

"When you keep her off those foods and you give her other things like eggs and matzo balls and grilled fish, then her behavior is okay?"

"Oh yes! She has no problem then." Mrs. Marx paused and thought for a moment. "Actually she's still a problem," she finally admitted with a huge sigh.

In talking to her further, I discovered that the food allergies were an excuse, something on which Mrs. Marx could try to blame her daughter's out-of-control behavior. But it was clear to me and even to Mrs. Marx that foods were not the problem. After some judicious probing I got Mrs. Marx to admit that there was really no difference in Danielle's behavior, no matter what she ate. Danielle was simply running the house, the family, the whole show, and Mrs. Marx had no idea what to do about it.

"Tell me about her sleep habits."

"That's a real problem," she responded. I was not surprised. Bedtime was often the first thing parents lose control of. "She doesn't go to bed until ten or eleven o'clock. There's nothing we can do to make her stay in her room. We put her to bed and she comes right back out, saying she needs a glass of water, or has to go to the bathroom, or she's afraid and wants the lights on. Then she'll insist that one of us stay in the room with her. Sometimes she'll want us to lie on the bed with her and sometimes she tells us to lie on the floor next to the bed. I can't find anything that works.

"Finally, she'll fall asleep out of sheer exhaustion at about ten or eleven. She'll just drop on the floor wherever she happens to be. But that's not the end of it. She keeps getting up and waking us up too. At about four or five in the morning she'll get into our bed and that's really the only sleep we get. It's really getting to us. You know we're not as young as we were when we had Alyssa." Thirteen-year-old Alyssa was their other child. "I'm forty-four and my husband is forty-six and we really need our sleep." Mrs. Marx seemed more than a little embarrassed to be sharing their disturbing nighttime ritual with me.

"Wait a minute! You mean to tell me that this four-year-old child is running your house and you believe there's nothing you can do about it?"

Mrs. Marx was shocked by my directness. She tried to defend herself. "Believe me, we've tried everything and there's absolutely nothing that works." It was clear that Mrs. Marx had all but given up. Danielle had won.

"Let me ask you a question. When Alyssa was this age did you have the same problems?"

"No. She went to bed quite easily."

"Why do you think that was?"

"Alyssa knew that we wouldn't tolerate any of this craziness."

"Then why do you tolerate it from Danielle?"

"You know my husband and I both have to get up for work and Alyssa has to get up for school. We all need our sleep."

"But you're not getting any sleep the way things are now."

"No, I guess not."

"Have you considered this—first of all, Danielle was born into a different family than Alyssa was."

She started to protest but I stopped her. "I know, you're the same people, but then again, you're not. You even pointed that out. You're older and have a very busy, very adult-oriented lifestyle. You stayed home with Alyssa until she was in first grade, but with Danielle you went back to work after a few months." Again, she started to protest. "I'm not saying one is right and the other is wrong. I'm just saying that they're different. Danielle has had to fit into a very set lifestyle, while with Alyssa, changes and compromises were made around her needs."

Mrs. Marx nodded her head. "We let Danielle have her way when we're with her because we feel guilty that we're not with her enough. We all have such busy schedules. Our jobs are so demanding and then there are all of Alyssa's activities that we have to chauffeur her to and from . . ." It was clear that she was no longer feeling defensive.

"I know. That's not at all uncommon. Also look at the kind of child she is. Danielle is nothing like Alyssa. Their basic personalities are like night and day. Alyssa is quiet, compliant, and easygoing. Danielle is more of a tough cookie. She likes to test the limits, see how far she can go. Children like that need more limits and structure, not less. Danielle is absolutely begging you for some limits. It's very scary for children to feel that they're the ones in control, that they're the boss."

She looked at me hopefully. "So, what should we do? Can you give me some practical, concrete things that my husband and I can try?"

"Of course. First, let's stop blaming what she eats and start setting some limits. Bedtime is a great place to start. It would be helpful if you took the time, each and every night, to have bedtime rituals."

"Bedtime rituals? What do you mean?"

"You do the same things each night during the time leading up to bed. For example: about a half hour before bedtime give Danielle a nice, warm, relaxing bath. Then read her a quiet story. Give her a choice of two or three books so that she feels like she has some control over this, and then lie down with her on her bed and read to her for fifteen minutes to a half hour. This will relax and prepare her for sleep, and she'll come to associate the bath and story with bedtime. Then she'll be prepared for bed. Make sure to keep the evening hours between dinner and bedtime a quiet and peaceful time. You don't want to get her worked up."

"That's difficult because it's such a hectic time in our home."

"I know. It is in a lot of homes, but just try to keep it more low-key."

Mrs. Marx nodded, but I could see that she wasn't quite buying this.

"Now you tell Danielle, 'There's a new rule. At eight o'clock each and every night you're in your room. Now, your room is *your* room. It's your sanctum sanctorum. It's your holy of holies. It's your very special place. You can do whatever you want to do *in* your room, but after eight o'clock, when we're done with story time and leave your room, that's the time when you may not come *out* of your room.' "

"There's no way! You don't know Danielle well enough. What are we supposed to do? Shut the door and lock her in her room?"

"Well that's extreme, but it's not out of the question. It is her room, her special place. If you can't shut her door, then I recommend you buy a solid-core door. Have it cut so that two thirds of the door is on the bottom and one third is on the top, then hang it, in place of her bedroom door, like a Dutch door. When it's bedtime, you lock and bolt the bottom part of the door from the outside. Light, air, whatever, can come in through the open top part of the door. But the bottom half will keep her in her room."

Mrs. Marx looked at me with a mix of astonishment and horror. But I continued. "Now, you say to Danielle, 'It's eight o'clock. Time for you to be in your room and since you have trouble staying in your room on your own, we're going to help you by locking just the bottom of your special door.' "

"How can I say that?"

"Just like that."

"Well, I've never heard of such a thing. Who would lock their child up?"

"I would. In fact, I did. That's what we did with my son, Gordon. When he was about two years old, and we were going through the same thing you're going through with Danielle. There was no way that I was going to put up with it."

"So you locked him in?" She looked at me in disbelief.

"I sure did. I went to the lumberyard, got what was needed, and hung the door. I gave him a chance to stay in his room but he wouldn't. So I locked the door with a dead bolt so it would make a loud, serious CLINK of authority when I locked it."

"And your wife went along with this?"

"She was worried there would be a fire. I told her that if she wanted to stay up and be on fire watch it was up to her, but that we weren't putting up with his behavior."

"What happened?"

"At first he screamed and cried. After fifteen minutes we talked to him from the hallway, giving him reassurance. And after that he was fine. Within a week he was going right to sleep, and we no longer had to lock the door because he knew we meant business. He understood who the boss was and, guess what . . . ? It wasn't him. More importantly he redeveloped the normal sleep patterns we all have."

She continued to look at me in disbelief. I reassured her. "Really, this has worked for several families. I suggest you try it. There are other ways. You can do this gradually by telling her you'll be right outside her door and then, after a while, telling her you'll be back to check on her in ten minutes and so on until she's weaned. But I don't think that method will work with Danielle. She needs more immediate structure. I think if you take a stand, it will give Danielle the clear message that you are taking control back."

"I must be desperate because I'm actually considering it."

"Great! Do it and stick to your guns. It could be tough. She'll probably scream and cry, but she'll stop when she realizes that you mean business. Now what's also important is that you spend more time with her. Let her help you cook dinner, or go with you when you're taking Alyssa to her activities. She'll enjoy doing whatever you're doing if you include her. That's what most kids want, just time with their parents."

Mrs. Marx left the office looking a little shaken, Danielle whining by her side. I could only hope that she would take my advice.

Several months later Mrs. Marx brought Danielle to the office for a throat culture. There was definitely something different about Danielle. At first I thought that her calm demeanor and polite manner might be because she wasn't feeling well, but then Mrs. Marx took me aside and thanked me. "Dr. Weinberger, I've been meaning to call you and thank you. After talking it over with my husband we went ahead with your door idea. He was willing to try anything for a good night's sleep. It took almost two weeks of yelling and screaming and carrying on, but then something seemed to click with her and now, even though she occasionally regresses, she knows what she has to do and she does it. Not only is bedtime easier but everything seems easier. We started to include her more and she's become, well, really a pleasure. We not only have control again but actually enjoy being with her now."

"That's great," I replied. "I hope things will stay this way—at least until she hits puberty!"

While Danielle was one seriously out-of-control kid, the problems that the Marx family were dealing with were common. Bedtime, in particular, is a tough time for parents of children of almost all ages. This is a time of day when parents have to really take control and put their foot down. Yet, often parents find this hour, when they have to separate from their children, and their children from them, to be one of the most difficult times to exercise control.

Rita and David Barnett were both attorneys, on the fast track. Rita took off less than a month's maternity leave for the birth of each of her children, Julia, four, and Ryan, two. Then it was back to work. Luckily, the Barnetts had found a wonderful housekeeper, Thelma, shortly after Julia was born. Thelma would arrive at the Barnetts' at 6:45 each morning so Rita and David could catch the 7:05 train to the city. She was responsible for the children, the house, the shopping, and the laundry. She made dinner for the family each night and then would return, no doubt exhausted, to her home.

About three weeks after Julia started preschool, I was surprised to get a call, not from Thelma, but from Rita. "Dr. Weinberger, I'm afraid something's terribly wrong with Julia. Three or four times now, Thelma has gotten a call from the school, asking her to come and get Julia. They insist that she's ill, but she says she feels fine, just a little tired. Apparently she's falling asleep at school." Rita was very upset.

"She has no other symptoms—headaches, sore throat, fever?"

"No. We've asked her a million times, but she says that she's just tired. Could it be that school is too strenuous for her?"

"I doubt it. She's just in a morning program, right?"

"That's right—from nine till noon."

"How's she been sleeping? Is she up a lot during the night?"

"No. Once we put her to bed she's down for the count."

"What's bedtime?"

"It depends on what time David or I get home. One of us has to be home by seven so that Thelma can leave, but the other one might not get home until ten or eleven. The kids are asleep when we leave in the morning, so the evening's our only time with them."

"You mean you're keeping the kids up till ten or eleven and you can't figure out why Julia's falling asleep in preschool?" I asked incredulously.

"She's never fallen asleep during the day before," Rita replied defensively.

"Yes, but what time was she waking up before? Was she allowed to sleep as late as she wanted or was Thelma getting her up?"

There was silence on the other end of the line.

"Hello? Rita? You still there?"

"Yeah. I can't believe how dumb I am. The kids are asleep when we leave for work Monday through Friday and on the weekend they're not supposed to wake us. This is embarrassing—I have no idea what time they wake up."

"If you ask Thelma, I bet you'll find that Julia was sleeping until nine or ten on a regular basis."

"Thelma did say that she was having trouble getting her up, but I thought it was just part of the mystery illness."

"There's no mystery here. You just need to be putting the kids to bed at a reasonable hour."

"I think it's too late for that. They're both used to staying up and playing. There are nights when we're ready to go to bed before they are, they're so keyed up."

"Nighttime isn't the time for them to get riled up, especially now that Julia is in school. It's really not the time for active play at all. If you keep Julia and Ryan quiet and peaceful from dinner on, then you get them to bed no later than eight or eight-thirty, I think Julia will do fine staying awake during school."

"Eight o'clock! Then when will we have our family time? With the hours we keep, we'll never see the kids."

"I don't know what to tell you, except that the kids need a reasonable and consistent bedtime. You're asking them to fit into a schedule that might make sense for you, but is all wrong for them. The fact is, this is just going to get worse as the kids go on to kindergarten and then grade school. They have to have their sleep to function properly and stay healthy."

"So what do I do now? I can't come home tonight and just put the kids right to bed, out of the blue. They wouldn't even see David, and I would only have an hour with them."

"Maybe you should think about restructuring *your* schedules. Could you bring work home and do it after the kids go to bed, or just take turns with the kids in the evenings? Lots of families are in your situation and I know there's a solution that will work for all of you. But the kids are at an age where they're no longer going to be able to fit into your schedule. You and David are going to have to compromise if you want to have time with the kids, or you're going to have a couple of cranky, unhappy, and sick children."

"Okay, I hear you. I'll talk to David and see what we can do." Rita suddenly brightened. "I know! What if Julia takes a nap in the afternoon. Then she'd have enough sleep and she'd still be able to stay up late."

"Rita, come on. You know that's a temporary solution. You're just putting off the inevitable, and it will be that much more difficult if you put this off another year."

"I guess you're right. I'll see what we can do," she said, sighing.

About two months later Thelma brought three-year-old Ryan in. He had stuck a bead up his nose and couldn't get it out. I easily removed it, thanks to a very cooperative Ryan.

"How are things going with Julia at school?" I asked Thelma. "Is she still falling asleep?"

"No, not since you talked to Mrs. Barnett. They started

putting the kids to bed earlier, and now they get up without a fuss every morning. It sure makes my life easier."

"Hey Ryan!" I said. He stopped playing with the extracted bead and looked up.

"Yeah?" he said.

"What do you think of your new bedtime?"

"I don't like it," he said, sticking his lower lip out. "Now I don't see Johnny Carson anymore."

Joan Perlow brought in her nine-month-old daughter, Tina, for her checkup. Tina was perfectly healthy and normal. Everything seemed fine until I asked Joan how Tina was sleeping.

"She's still getting up several times during the night crying."

"How do you handle that?" I asked her.

"One of us goes in and rocks her. If that doesn't do it, we get her a bottle. The problem is she's usually up again in a few hours. So all three of us are exhausted and she's a little crab all day."

"You know, by nine months of age there is no physiological reason that a baby shouldn't be sleeping for ten to twelve hours without being pacified or fed. By going in every time you hear her, you're training her to get up, not allowing her to settle herself back to sleep. Of course she'd rather be cuddled and eat than sleep. During the day if you play with her and feed her and cuddle her and play with her some more, there's no reason why she can't be left alone at night. You need the nighttime for yourself and your husband to recharge your batteries."

"So what do I do?"

"Well, there's one method where you gradually . . . over a period of time . . . bit by bit . . . withdraw from her, each time she wakes up. Or you can try the Weinberger method," I said with a smile.

"I'm afraid to ask what that is," Joan said, holding Tina close.

"It's simple. When Tina wakes up at night, you let her get

herself back to sleep. It's really important she learn to do this, or you're going to be dealing with this throughout her child-hood."

"How does she get herself back to sleep?" Joan asked.

"I'd guess that the first few nights she'll probably cry. But she'll learn very quickly that you're not coming in, and she'll go back to sleep. No doubt it will be more painful for you than for her, but you'll get through it. She also might wake up and just play in her crib for a while. That's all right too. You shouldn't go in every time she wakes up. Then in the morning lavish her with affection, but during the night she needs to learn to sleep, and she won't if she knows that you're going to come in and play with her and feed her."

Joan and Tina came in three months later for Tina's one-year exam. "How's she sleeping?" I asked.

"We took your advice and we were amazed that it only took two nights for her to learn that we weren't coming in. Since then she's been sleeping through the night and she's a differ-ent child. She's sweet and easygoing. She's a pleasure. Frankly, I'm a lot nicer now too, since I get a full night's sleep."

I found that many parents, like the Perlows, need only to be reassured that they're not doing their child any harm when they leave them alone and that, in fact, they're helping their child take the first tentative steps toward being a separate and independent person, by letting them sleep through the night.

Sherwin and Kim Grover were having the same problem with their eighteen-month-old son, Richard. He had never been a great sleeper, and since the birth of his brother four months ago he had been up almost every night. They thought they had tried everything to get him to sleep. But they hadn't tried the Weinberger method.

"Trust me," I told them. "It's perfectly all right for you to read him a story, tuck him in, say good night, and leave him in the room crying for fifteen or twenty minutes. Just see what will happen."

A week later I got a call from Sherwin Grover. "I just had to tell you what happened last night. Richard fell asleep in my lap. I picked him up and carried him into his room and laid him gently in the bed. He woke up and started crying. I kissed him good night once more and left the room, per instructions for the Weinberger method. Richard cried for fifteen minutes. Then there was silence. We waited another ten minutes and then snuck a peek. He was sound asleep. This was the fourth night in a row that we had tried this. A half hour later there was a knock on the door. We were shocked to find that it was the police. Apparently they were called by our downstairs neighbors, who claimed that I was abusing my son.

"Luckily the policeman had children of his own so he was very sympathetic. But just in case, I told him that I had been following the directions of Dr. Norman J. Weinberger. I gave him your number and told him if there were any more complaints he should just contact you directly."

Nathaniel Ullman was a cute, rambunctious, and intelligent three-year-old. He was in for a checkup with his mother, Cheryl.

"He's perfect," I told Cheryl. "Are there any concerns or problems?"

"One night, about a month ago, he had a nightmare so I let him sleep with us. Since then, he's been in our bed almost every other night."

"How are you handling that?"

"I tell him to go back to his room, and he says that he's had another nightmare. But I can tell he's just saying it so he can sleep with us. Sometimes one of us takes him back to his room. Other nights we're too tired and we just let him sleep with us, but then none of us gets enough sleep."

"So is it an issue for you? Do you definitely want him in his own bed?"

"Well yes. Why do you ask?"

"Because some families are very comfortable with the idea of the family bed and for them it's fine. But if it's not your cup of tea you need to be consistent and firm about returning him to his room. As soon as he comes into your room one of you needs to get up and tell him that he belongs in his own bed, then quietly, without any conversation, and as little contact as possible, walk him back to his room. If he comes in again, you walk him back again. It won't take long for him to get bored with it, as long as you don't give in and let him stay. If you do that, you're back to square one."

"What if he really does have another nightmare?"

"Then you go into his room and comfort him there."

"How many nights do you think this will take?" she asked, looking very skeptical.

"Usually not many, once he knows that you mean business."

Cheryl called me two weeks later. "I didn't believe that your strategy would work but it sure did. It only took two nights before our nightly visitor stopped coming around. I was sure we would see him again after a day or so, but so far he's either been sleeping through the night, or getting himself back to sleep. Either way we're finally getting a decent night's sleep."

The Ullmans' story is a common one. Most families experience sleep problems at some point in their children's development. Most of these problems can be corrected the way the Ullmans did, but there are those more unusual cases where children have sleep issues because of some very real and concrete fears.

Darryl Grady was one of those children. At the age of five an electrical fire started in his room one night as he slept. Luckily, he and his family escaped without serious physical injury but Darryl was left with an emotional scar—an inability to sleep alone. This became extremely acute when the house was rebuilt and Darryl was back in his own room. His fear of another fire starting in his room was so severe he was unable to sleep. After a discussion with the family I recommended they take Darryl to a child psychologist. Through his work with the therapist it was discovered that his inability to sleep alone was caused not only by fear but out of a sense of guilt. Even though Darryl clearly had no part in setting the fire, he felt that somehow it was his fault since it had begun in his room. He was greatly helped by therapy and eventually even his sleep issues disappeared.

Every Friday Bert would spend the day at Baby's Hospital at Columbia Presbyterian Hospital in New York. He would spend part of the day making rounds with the attending physician to increase his knowledge and stay sharp, and the other part of the day teaching in the outpatient clinic. This meant that on Fridays I was on my own.

On Thursdays Bert would brief me on his patients who were in the hospital, and I would check on them during rounds. ". . . And I admitted Lara Malinger today so we could administer fluids intravenously. She has mono and is having a tough time of it," Bert finished, giving me my instructions.

I made a note of it and first thing the next morning, I stopped in to see Lara. Her mother looked very surprised and not too thrilled to see me. "How come you're here?" she inquired—tactlessly, I thought.

"I'm making rounds and stopped in to see how Lara's doing," I replied.

"There's no need for you to check on her. Dr. Grossman will do that."

"I don't think so. He's off today but I'm sure he'll be in tomorrow."

"No, I'm sure he's going to be in today," she insisted.

"Well, if you and Lara don't mind, I'll take a look at her anyway, as long as I'm here," I replied, realizing there was no point in debating Mrs. Malinger.

I examined Lara and made a notation on the chart, chatted for a few moments, and left to finish my rounds and get to the office.

That evening I stopped by the hospital to do evening rounds and, once again, went in to see Lara, fully expecting a tirade from Mrs. Malinger on the whereabouts of Bert.

But both Lara and Mrs. Malinger were resting comfortably. I picked up the chart to make my notations and saw a notation, following my morning one, from Bert. I thought it best not to ask Mrs. Malinger about this.

The first thing I did when I got home was call Bert. "How come you went to see Lara Malinger today?" I asked. "You're never around on Fridays."

"I know," he replied, "but I knew that Mrs. Malinger would be disappointed if I didn't stop by. So I just dropped in on my way back from Columbia."

"Well," I thought to myself, "I really did do a good job picking a practice. You can't get much more caring and involved than that."

2

The Witching Hour

That time when children turned into animals just as their parents' reserve of patience was ebbing. The time when dinner still had to be made and the bath and bed and homework scramble was still ahead.

It had been almost a year since I had been in practice with Bert. Pat, who had long ago accepted me, had to move away because her husband was transferred. Edith continued to look at me as the silly young doctor who did silly things. Yet she ran things at the office as well for me, on Bert's days off, as she did when Bert was there. She was a true professional.

I heard screaming coming from one of the examining rooms, followed by Edith's calm—but forceful—voice reassuring the child. A moment later the door opened and Edith came out. "It's Megan Davis, she's cut her chin open. It looks like it's going to need some suturing."

"Megan Davis," I thought out loud. "I don't think I've met her yet."

"No, but you're about to," Edith said.

We went into the examining room together. The mother looked up at me with a mixture of surprise and anxiety. It was clear she expected to see Dr. Grossman.

Edith must have noticed her apprehension too. "This is Dr. Norman Weinberger, Dr. Grossman's associate. He can do the job just perfectly," she said with a confident smile. I tried to hide my surprise while Megan's mother seemed to immediately relax and gave a nod of approval.

Later that day I stopped Edith in the hall. "Hey, thanks," I said.

"For what?" she asked, then hurried down the hall without waiting for my answer. But I'd swear she had a little smile on her face.

Having apparently made inroads with Edith I now found myself faced with another challenge. Doctors are traditionally known as poor businessmen. A sweeping generalization, I know, but one that I readily admit to. So, I felt that I was in unknown territory as I went about negotiating my renewal contract with Bert. I was thrilled that we both wanted a contract—that it was evident that this was a mutually good situation and one we wanted to continue beyond the initial one year we'd agreed upon. But beyond that fact, I was at a loss.

Along with negotiating our contract we were also negotiating with dentist Al Frank, the landlord from whom we were renting our meager office space. Al had decided to expand his building. Now it seemed like a good idea to stay where we were and simply take a larger space.

Al and Bert debated back and forth over how much space we would take, what kind of rent we would pay, and who would be responsible for what. There was a lot more than I had imagined to negotiating an office lease—more choices, more debate, more compromises.

Although I was part of the proceedings, I felt like an outsider looking in. This was because I was acutely aware that the office expansion was ultimately Bert's responsibility—his "little red wagon." ("Little red wagon"—translation: a Bertism meaning one's total and complete responsibility.) Due to my somewhat bleak fiscal situation, the financial burden for the office expansion would fall squarely on Bert's shoulders. So, although it was well against my basic nature, I felt that I had to keep my mouth shut. This was true whether we were talking about the amount of space or the color of the hallway carpeting.

From the window of Bert's consultation office I had a bird's-eye view of the new building going up. The very window that I was looking out would soon be bricked in to become the wall of our new waiting room. I could see our new office slowly taking shape. I wondered what it would be like, how it would feel to be practicing in this new space.

It ended up being beautiful, bright, and warm, and much more spacious and patient-friendly than the old office. Now I had my own examination rooms and consultation office.

Still, I was feeling stressed. Office space and contract negotiations were a part of practicing pediatrics that I hadn't given much thought to—a part that I found I loathed. I was negotiating my contract for employment feeling that I didn't have the know-how to forge the optimal deal for myself and my family. But at last Bert and I came to an agreement. I was signed, sealed, delivered and well on my way to buying into a very successful and wonderful practice.

Apparently, I was not the only one feeling stressed. Around this time I noticed a pattern developing. Almost every afternoon around four, Susan would call.

"Hi, Sus," I'd say. "How you doing?"

"When will you be done . . . stop that, Gordon, don't push your sister . . . what time will you be home?" I could hear screaming, crying, and barking in the background. I knew it wasn't the TV.

My stomach immediately tied into a knot. Beads of perspiration broke out on my back. "I'll be home as quick as I can," I tried to assure her.

"What time?" she demanded, needing to know exactly when she had hope of rescue.

"In an hour?" I guessed, not knowing exactly, but not wanting to leave her hanging.

I hurried through my afternoon patients, dreading what I

knew I would find at home. Sure enough, when I arrived the kids were fighting, and Susan was playing referee, and I would walk into this situation already tense with apprehension, not being able to add anything soothing or constructive.

This scenario, or some version of it, had been going on for some time when the Cooney family came in for their yearly checkups. Sally, a harried but attractive woman in her late twenties, sat with two-year-old Stuie hanging over her lap like some sort of boneless creature, moaning in a halfhearted, annoying way. Four-year-old Owen, stripped to his underpants, was sitting under the examining table singing. He was rolling a large fire engine back and forth while working the very realistic-sounding siren. Five-year-old Katie was lying flat on the examining table wearing a princess dress-up outfit, her hand draped dramatically over her eyes. She was apparently exhausted from a day of dealing with her brothers.

"How is the Cooney clan today?" I greeted them.

Sally gave me an exhausted smile. "I'm never making another late-afternoon appointment again. It's hard enough just to be home in front of the TV with them at this time, but to get them organized and out the door—forget it."

It was 4:15. I was expecting my late-afternoon Susan-call at any moment. "You have trouble this time of day too?" I asked her rhetorically. She threw me a dirty look.

"No, really, we do too. My wife should be calling any minute. Tell me," I said, pushing Katie's legs to the side and sitting down on the end of the examining table, "what do you do to get through it every day?"

"I was going to ask you that," Sally responded.

"Let me think about this and get back to you on it," I told her.

For the next few days I polled my families, asking the parents what their worst time of day was. Debbie Dragonetti, a petite, curly-haired dynamo, confessed to me laughingly that getting out of the house was the sole reason that she worked in the evening, teaching English as a second language to adults. "You know it hardly pays anything," she said. "My compensation is that I'm out of the house from four-thirty to nine-thirty. It's perfect because the twins get crazy right around then and Elizabeth just falls apart. On some days I'm standing at the door in my coat waiting for that sitter." Debbie was the mother of extremely energetic three-year-old twin boys and a sensitive five-year-old daughter.

"The best though," Debbie continued, "was the day that my husband came home early to take care of the kids." Debbie calmly separated her sons, who were wrestling on the floor of the examining room, without missing a beat in her story. "When I got home, my husband very seriously told me he felt that all the children needed therapy. When I asked him why, he described their typical evening behavior. It wasn't easy to convince him that their behavior was normal."

Many families had similar stories. The results of my poll were almost unanimous. Two trying times of day were cited. Bedtime was difficult for many families, but the most difficult time, the time that almost everyone dreaded, was the late-afternoon/early-evening "witching hour"—that time when children turned into animals just as their parents' reserve of patience was ebbing. The time when dinner still had to be made and the bath and bed and homework scramble was still ahead.

Like me, the parents I talked to took little solace in the fact that this was happening in almost everyone's home. They wanted answers . . . a solution . . . something concrete they could do to make this time of day easier.

Using my family as guinea pigs I tried different strategies. Would taking them outside work—attempting to exhaust them with physical activity? What about television? Bribery? Ignoring them? None of this worked. In fact some of it made the problem worse. But I didn't give up.

One day I came home to a particularly chaotic house. It had been an exhausting day, and I wanted nothing more than peace and quiet. "You, you, you, and you," I yelled over the din pointing to my two children, wife, and dog. "Come with me." They surprised me by following me up the stairs to our bedroom. I took off my shoes and lay down on the bed. "Gordon, please go and get a book you would like to hear." Once again, to my amazement, I was blindly obeyed.

Within a few minutes we were all sprawled comfortably on our bed and the only sound in the house was my voice reading *The House at Pooh Corner.* Twenty minutes later we had finished our story, but the calm that had settled over the house remained. I was helping Gordon with his spelling, and Susan was preparing dinner with Lisa by her side, happily drawing.

Would this work every time? Sorry, but unfortunately there is nothing that will work every time. It's a question of trial and error and a lot of creativity. While story time worked that day for us, Play-Doh was a soothing activity for some other preschoolers, while water play in the kitchen sink worked for many other children. In nice weather a walk or playing outside also can do the trick. Having older children help with dinner can work, but nothing works 365 days a year.

The Bucholz family lucked into what I call "the fresh horses" approach. Trisha worked a regular nine-to-five schedule, while Ned, a police officer, worked the late-night shift. Ned took care of the children during the day and prepared dinner. When Trisha came home from work, shortly after five, dinner would be on the table. The family would eat dinner together, then Ned would immediately go to bed, while Trisha would clean up the kitchen and take care of story, bath, and bedtime. This didn't totally preclude the witching hour but it did allow the parent who was most burnt out at that moment to do what most parents want to do at that point—go to bed!

The next time the Cooneys came in I shared the results of the poll with Sally, and I gave her some ideas to try with her brood. "The thing to remember," I told her, "is that they will all, eventually, be school-age, and then the problem will be driving them around to all their various activities every afternoon. In the meantime, I suggest that each and every night you look in on them when they're finally asleep, and after you get your fill of them—silent and still—tell yourself that tomorrow will be a better day and try to believe it."

Yet another source of stress for me was the system in place at the Norwalk Hospital for dealing with sick or premature newborns. The hospital didn't have the house staff that could take care of premature or critically ill infants. These babies had to be transported to Yale/New Haven Children's Hospital, which was thirty minutes away. The baby had to be stabilized while waiting for the Yale/New Haven team to come for the transfer, then the infant had to make it through the trip itself, and it was always touch and go.

I realized that this was a situation I could do something about and it was clear that I wasn't the only doctor who wanted a change. Six of us got together and formed a neonatal newborn group. Our initial mission was to establish a set of protocols, a format that would always be followed, to ensure that the babies would be stabilized before going to Yale. The six of us went on a rotation so that one of us would always be on call. This way, we hoped, we were giving these infants the best possible chance of survival.

It soon became clear that we could handle a number of things that we had been sending the babies to Yale for, right at home. We decided to care for the not-quite-critical babies ourselves rather than transport them.

Then Dr. Jack McNamara, a member of our neonatal group, took over as head of pediatrics in the hospital. Now Jack was in the hospital full-time and the members of our group were quickly developing the expertise needed to care for ill and premature babies through our various appointments at Yale and Columbia as clinical professors. This allowed us to keep up with the tremendous leaps that were being made in this area, and the group continued to grow in expertise and experience with much success.

* * *

We would soon celebrate our first anniversary of living in Norwalk. It was time to look for a new house, this time a house we would own. We were advised to look for a "starter" house in Norwalk with an eye toward moving to a "better" community as the children got into middle school.

This was advice we had no intention of taking. We purposely decided to remain in Norwalk because of its diversity. What we loved about Norwalk was that it was a multiracial, multiethnic, multifaceted community of eighty thousand. Norwalk had the diversity of a city but with the warm feeling of a small town. It had a good school system, and it was on Long Island Sound. We were happy here and had no plans to move out.

The task of finding our dream house fell to Susan. She would go around with various real estate people looking at what seemed to be every available house in Norwalk. Occasionally, she would find one that she liked. Then I would be called in. It seemed that we couldn't find that perfect house. Susan kept looking, though, because although we liked the house we were renting on Homer Street, we were anxious to be home owners and settled for good.

One of our agents was Patricia Lightfoot, the consummate real estate woman. Everything about Patricia was big, from the high heels and layers of flowing clothes that she wore to her blonder-than-blond hair piled precariously on top of her head. When she walked into an entryway and waved her hand to demonstrate the "flow" of a house, she seemed to fill the whole room.

"I know exactly what you want," she told us often as we were leaving yet another house that was not, in the least, exactly what we wanted. She did, however, know a builder who was selling his custom-built house. "It's exactly what you want," Patricia Lightfoot said. "It's exactly where you want to live," she said. Susan and I exchanged doubtful looks.

But this time she was right. It was a modern house, surrounded by handsome trees, sitting on two acres of land, with a pool in the large backyard. The house was just four minutes from both the office and the hospital. To our delight it was obvious that the neighborhood was full of children. The yards had swing sets and the driveways were littered with bikes and skateboards. A group of kids was congregating in front of one of the houses. We immediately felt at home. Patricia Lightfoot had come through for us, and we quickly put a deposit down on the house.

On a glorious July day we proudly and joyfully moved into the new house on Inwood Road. I cleaned the pool so the kids could go for a swim and Susan began unpacking. Monty, even more wild than usual because of the move and the new surroundings, was tearing wildly through the yard, barking loudly with no sign of letting up.

I thought that I had better set up his line run before he got away and caused any trouble. I ran a thick cable from the house to a tree by the pool. This would give Monty fifty or sixty feet of running room and plenty of shady trees to lie under. I attached his leash to the cable and, as he had done on Homer Street, he ran the full length of his leash over and over, getting snapped back each time.

"You'd think one of these days he'd learn," I said to Susan as we watched Monty go through this routine several times. Susan just shook her head.

The next day as I was pulling into the driveway I saw little Chad Porter, an eight-year-old neighbor and a patient of mine, knocking on our door. Before I had even stopped the car Monty came racing around the house, obviously off his line, and in a mighty leap, knocked Chad to the ground, knocking the wind right out of him.

Susan opened the door to find a bloodied Chad, who had quickly regained his voice, screaming, Monty barking, and me racing out of the car toward Chad. I scooped him up and took him into the house. Susan grabbed Monty and dragged him to the backyard.

I took Chad into the bathroom to clean him up. He was still

sobbing both from fear and pain. I gently cleaned the blood off his arm and knee, talking to him the whole time. "Boy, Chad, what should I do with that crazy dog? Do you think he got hurt at all?" Chad's sobs slowly turned into sniffles.

Susan joined us in the bathroom. She dampened a washcloth and wiped off Chad's tear- and dirt-stained face. She smoothed his blond hair out of his eyes. "You're certainly a brave boy," Susan told him. He managed a weak smile.

I could see that Chad needed stitches, but I didn't want him to know that just yet. "Susan, why don't you call Chad's mom and have her meet us at the office. I think I want to take another look at him there." Susan nodded knowingly and went off to call Mrs. Porter.

I put a light dressing on Chad's knee and arm. "That will do until we get to the office," I told Chad. Chad's knee was pretty cut up from the fall, and his right arm had been clawed by Monty. "Come on Chad," I said, picking him up, "you get a special trip to the office."

Mrs. Porter arrived at the office, worried and flustered. Chad started to tear up again when he saw his mother. "Chad, tell Mom how brave you were when I cleaned you up."

"I stopped crying almost right away, Mom," he said in a shaky voice.

"We're going to go into this room." I led Chad and Mrs. Porter into the room where we performed minor surgeries and suturing. I lifted Chad onto the table and took off the already blood-soaked bandages. Mrs. Porter grimaced at Chad's injuries.

"Well Chad, I'm going to have to stitch some of this up so that it heals properly."

"No!" he replied.

"Here's what I'm going to do." I spoke in as calm and quiet a voice as possible. "I'm going to give you a local anesthetic. That's something that will make it so that you don't feel the stitches going in. Then I'll stitch you up. Then I'll put a bandage over the stitches so that it stays clean and dry. I'm going to tell you each thing I do before I do it, so that there won't be any more surprises today. Okay?" Chad nodded. "I'm going to start now."

Chad was a trouper. We quietly talked the whole time. Once, he looked down at what I was doing, and the color drained from his face. I paused. He took a deep breath, and I continued.

I bandaged him, and he sat up on the table. "Now you can brag to all your friends that you were my bravest patient, who's had thirty-two stitches."

Chad went to the bathroom, and I turned my attention to his mother. "My wife told you what happened?"

"Oh, yes," she replied.

"I can't tell you how sorry we are. I don't know how Monty got off his line. I just . . . we're both so, so sorry."

"I know these things happen, and I want you to know that I appreciate you taking care of Chad the way that you did."

Chad didn't seem to have any lasting effects from his meeting with Monty. His arm and knee healed nicely and he remained the outgoing, friendly kid who would still visit—but he would always approach our house somewhat warily.

On the other hand Monty couldn't shake the reputation he earned that day as the killer dog of Inwood Road.

I was sitting at my office desk, feet up, coffee in hand, staring at the starched white lab coat that was hanging on the back of my door. I hated that coat and I didn't want to put it on. In training and in the service I had had to wear one. After all it was the universal symbol of doctors everywhere. However, I was beginning to realize that it scared many of my young patients and kept others at a distance. I imagined all the doctors in private practice arriving at their offices in their suit jackets and immediately replacing them with their white lab coats; authoritative, sterile, impersonal, and forbidding. It brought to mind the famous Norman Rockwell painting of a doctor preparing a shot as a small boy, rear exposed, fearfully looks on. It represented everything that I did not want to be. I thought about how relaxed Chad had been, despite his injuries, when I was treating him without wearing the lab coat, and I wondered if there might be a connection. I went to see my first patient—leaving the lab coat hanging on the door.

I remembered shortly after arriving in Norwalk, while making rounds at the hospital, I ran into Dr. Thayer Willis. He wasn't wearing a white lab coat. He was decked out in bright plaid Bermuda shorts, white socks and shirt, penny loafers, and a natty little striped bow tie that almost matched the Bermudas. I pretended to shield my eyes from the glare of his outfit.

"Summer fool, be cool," he explained, as he meandered down the corridor.

If Dr. Willis could get away with an outfit like *that*, then certainly I could make my own modest, but unique, sartorial statement. After all I was in private practice now. There was no hospital dress code or military uniform. Perhaps just being myself would relax my patients—maybe even intrigue them.

Cowboy boots would have to be part of my uniform. I started wearing them when we first arrived in Montana and, even with becoming a born-again Easterner, I couldn't see giving them up. Kids, in general, love cowboys. So the boots seemed the perfect choice.

With cowboy boots you need jeans and a Western-style shirt, but Western shirts were an endangered species in Connecticut. So I settled for the East Coast equivalent—a blue oxford cloth button down, and finished the outfit off with a colorful tie.

Size fifteen and a half feet in cowboy boots are fairly conspicuous, so I shouldn't have been too surprised when one of the first patients to see me wearing them—four-year-old Catherine Miller—couldn't take her eyes off my feet.

When I walked into the room, her eyes grew wide looking at my boots. I strolled across the room. Her eyes followed my every step. I did a little tap dance on the linoleum. Her eyes moved in time with my dance. Finally, I hopped up on the table next to her. She still couldn't take her eyes off my boots. "So, how you doing, Catherine?" I asked. I waited for her response but she just kept staring at my feet.

"Catherine, Dr. Weinberger asked you a question," Mrs. Miller said.

"That's all right," I said. "Catherine, what's so fascinating about my boots?"

Without taking her eyes off my feet she said, "With feet that big you must have a very, very, very big horse."

While the kids were enjoying my cowboy look, I noticed that many of them had an aversion to my stethoscope. They didn't want to be touched by it. But unlike the white lab coat this was not something that I could just discard.

One day I spotted a tiny koala bear in a gift shop. It had flexible little legs that could grasp around objects. I tried mounting him on my stethoscope. Sure enough, children focused on the fuzzy bear rather than the cold stethoscope, and before long, with all the attention and handling it received, the koala bear was worn out. So I replaced it with other bears and then a raccoon, elephant, frog, and before long the stethoscope animals seemed to be multiplying on their own. A corner of my office became Noah's mini-Ark.

I decided to make yet another change. If a casual outfit could make the kids more relaxed, then imagine what speaking directly to the child, instead of the parent, could do for patient relations: allowing them to answer and ask any questions—and explaining everything to them in a way they could understand.

Five-year-old Denny Delfrio, the human H-bomb, was in the examining room. He had always been a difficult kid to examine. It was nearly impossible to get him to stop running around, much less sit still for an exam.

Sure enough Denny was hopping wildly about the room on one foot. He was literally bouncing off the furniture and walls. His mother, Ella, was trying, unsuccessfully, to get him to sit down.

"Denny Delfrio! You're looking mighty sickly today. What's your story?" I said, somewhat sarcastically, directly to Denny. He stopped in mid-hop.

"He has an earache," Mrs. Delfrio answered. I found that this was usually the case; you ask the child a question and invariably the parent answered.

I continued to talk to Denny. "Did you hear something?" I said, looking sharply around the room. "Where did that come from? I didn't see your lips move." Denny giggled. Ella got the message and she sat quietly back in her chair, with a smile, and waited for Denny to answer.

"So, did you come in just to get your free stickers? What's the problem?"

"My ear hurts," Denny responded, cupping his hand over his right ear. He climbed up on the table without me having to ask.

"How long has it been hurting?" I said, sitting down next to him.

"Since last night."

"Does it hurt real bad?"

"It hurt real bad last night. I even cried," he admitted seriously. "It's not so bad now."

"I'm going to look into your ears." I showed him my otoscope. I pretended that I couldn't turn it on. "This thing never works when I really need it. Hey! You don't happen to be magic do you?" Denny shrugged his shoulders. "Do me a favor and blow on this for me, will you?"

Denny blew on the otoscope and, of course, it came on.

"Cool," he said.

"Great. Help me out. Which ear hurts?"

"This one," he said, holding his ear.

"Could you cover the other ear so that the light won't go through? Now, I'll look through the other side. You're really good at this. You must have been practicing."

I peered into his ears. "Whoa, what are you growing in there?"

"Why, what's in there?"

"Take a look," I said.

He rolled his eyes toward his right ear, as if he could see inside it. "I can't see in there," he said, just realizing you can't see inside your own ears.

"Well, it looks like my vegetable garden," I responded. "Now hold on to the other ear."

I completed the rest of the examination. "Denny, you have a good old-fashioned ear infection. I bet you've been doing a lot of swimming this summer."

"Every day," he responded proudly.

"I'm going to give you a prescription for some medicine. You and Mom make sure that you put four drops in that ear— that's the ear and not the mouth—four times a day for five days. Now, do you want the good news first, or the bad news?"

Denny thought seriously and long. "The good news first," he finally decided.

"The good news is that your ear should feel better by tonight. The bad news is I want you to stay out of the water for a couple of days. Okay?"

"Yeah! I don't have to take a bath!" Denny clapped his hands.

"Wrong! You know I mean no swimming."

"Nuts!" he responded. I wrote out the prescription and handed it to him. "One more thing, make an appointment to come back and see me in ten days so I know for sure that you've weeded that vegetable garden." I gently touched his ear.

He jumped down from the table. "Come on, Mom."

"That's it?" Ella asked, looking relieved.

"That's it. His ear should clear right up." Denny shook my hand wildly up and down and then shot, Denny Delfrio style, down the hall to make his next appointment.

I knew I was on the right track with this new style of child-centered practice when the patient of another doctor came in for a visit. Jay Patel came in with his father. He was a thin four-year-old, with a very serious expression. He had been ill for some time with a severe case of strep that had been slow to respond to oral antibiotics. At the last visit he had just begun to show signs of improvement.

When I walked in, he was sitting on the examining table, swinging his legs. He stopped immediately when he saw me in the doorway. He started to open his mouth as if I had asked him to open up and say "ahh." I walked over to him, put my thumb gently under his chin, and shut his mouth. I held out my hand.

"Hi, I'm Dr. Weinberger. Slap me five!" He very softly slapped my outstretched hand. "And you are . . ." I looked at the chart. "Priscilla Popcorn? No, that can't be right."

A slow grin spread over Jay's pinched little face and opened it right up. "I'm Jay."

"Well that makes a whole lot more sense. How come you came to see me today?"

"Well, I had strep throat for a long time. Nothing made it feel better and I couldn't go to school. I had a fever and got to eat ice cream. Then I got a big shot in my butt and now I feel better."

"So sorry about your butt, but I'm glad that you're feeling better. Do you mind if I have a listen to your heart? You can have a listen too."

We both listened to his heart, then I looked into his throat. "Jay, you certainly are getting better. I wish you could see how handsome your throat looks! Listen, I need to take a throat culture. So open up and see if you can sing like an opera singer. AHHHHH!" I quickly touched the back of his throat with the cotton swab and handed it to my nurse to be cultured. He gagged slightly. "Boy, Jay, you really can sing, but a little flat. Do it again for me. This time concentrate on making a perfect sound, and try it without the cotton swab."

"AHHHHH," he sang.

"Jeez, Jay, that was perfect."

Jay looked at his dad, who was standing in the corner of the examining room, hands in his pockets, smile on his face. "Did you hear that, Dad? Dr. Weinberger thinks that I sing good," and he let out another long high note, his version of an aria.

"Bravo, Jay!" I said, applauding. Jay giggled.

Mr. Patel walked over to me and shook my hand. "I'm Frank Patel, Dr. Weinberger. I appreciate you treating my son with such respect. His doctor talks only to me or my wife. He treats him like a doll. It makes us very uncomfortable. He has been Jay's doctor since he was an infant and he still treats him like he can't understand or explain for himself. In fact, we've been talking about switching doctors." Sure enough, shortly thereafter Jay Patel became my patient.

Four-year-old Lisa Buck perched uncomfortably and unhappily on the examining table. I stood in the doorway of the examining room, hands on my hips, looking disapprovingly at her. "No, no, no, Lisa! Get off my table. That's where I take my naps. Go sit on Mom's lap." I helped her down and she scurried into her mother's lap.

I initially had the lap idea for babies. It was clear that they were more comfortable and relaxed when I examined them on their mother's lap than on the examining table, and the mothers seemed to like it better too. Then I realized that many of the toddlers and even some of the three- and four-year-olds were uncomfortable or even scared on the examining table. Of course, it was high for them and covered in scratchy paper. It was always easy to spot the kids who would be more comfortable on their mother's or father's lap. Eventually on their own, these children would choose the examining table when they were ready. Then most of them would master the table by climbing up and jumping down repeatedly while their parents said, "That's enough now." But they loved showing me that they had conquered that big, intimidating table.

Of course there were patients who were still scared, even in their mother's laps. Lisa Buck was one of those kids. She was one of my most fearful patients. Her visits were always fraught with high drama and great discomfort for her, her parents, and me.

As I approached her she wrapped herself around her mother like a boa constrictor. "How are you feeling, Lisa!" I said happily. She buried her head deeper in her mother's neck. I pulled my stool over to her and kept talking, more quietly now. "We're going to do something different today," I said hopefully. "Now usually *I* examine *you* but I'm getting kind of bored with that. So, today *you're* going to examine *me.*"

That got a reaction. She removed her face from her mother's neck long enough to shoot me a very suspicious look, and then dipped her head back down so her long blond hair hid her face from me. This kid was a tough sell.

"Here's your stethoscope," I said, pushing it under her cloak of hair, holding it out to her. She had to let go of her mother and raise her head to take the stethoscope and put it on. She turned slowly on her mother's lap until she was facing me, her blue eyes big and round. "Okay. How does my heart sound? Am I in good shape?"

She looked back at her mother as if to say, "Is this guy serious?"

Her mother said, "Go on, honey. Listen to Dr. Weinberger's heart." She turned back to me with trepidation and I helped her put the stethoscope in her ears and find my heart. She listened intently. A smile slowly broke out over her face. "Mommy, I can hear his heart." She was still treating me like I wasn't there.

I gently pulled the stethoscope out of one of her ears. "How do I sound?" I asked.

"You're very healthy," she said in a small, serious voice, not yet looking me in the eye.

"Thanks. What a relief!" I put my hand over her hand and moved the stethoscope to her chest. "Now you want to listen to your own heart?" She nodded and delightedly listened to the workings of her own body. "Maybe Mom wants to hear," I said and she let her mom listen. "I feel kind of left out. Can I have a listen?"

This time she looked right at me and handed me the stethoscope with a smile. And so we progressed. She examined her mother and me and finally herself, and then let me examine her. Slowly she became relaxed and even happy. So it took a little longer than the average exam. It was sure worth it. She came in next time feeling a little more comfortable, and we continued our games even long after she was sure of herself and relaxed at our office.

The Steele family, however, did not like my rootin'-tootin' child-centered approach. Mr. and Mrs. Steele had been trying a long time to have a child when they finally had a son. So I wasn't surprised when they turned out to be overly concerned—bordering on overly protective—about Eric. He was a small, frail-looking boy, with close-cropped brown hair, and huge, almost black eyes.

He was a very bright child—verbal but withdrawn. This made him extremely difficult to examine. He would cling to his mother and no matter what I did or said, nothing worked. A two-and-a-half- to three-year-old who is clingy and hard to examine is not uncommon, but most older children are easily assuaged if you just take your time and talk and joke with them a little. This simply was not the case with Eric. Even at five years old, he was clearly not going to be one of my buddies.

When he was in for his five-year-old exam, I came into the room with a big welcoming smile. "Eric, how are you doing?" He buried his face in his mother's neck.

His mother looked daggers at me. "You frightened him. You're always so loud," she scolded.

I was surprised and a little hurt, but I decided next time I would be different with Eric. I would try a quieter, softer approach with him. However, I didn't have a chance because that was the last time I saw him. The Steeles switched to my partner and I felt a very personal, deep hurt that I had not been able to say the right words or find the right way to relate to Eric.

*　　*　　*

Along with being doctor, cowboy, and magician I was slowly learning most of what I said carried tremendous weight with my families. Barbara Zuckes, a longtime friend and patient, came in with her second child, Jonathan, for his six-month checkup. Something about Barbara wasn't right. I was immediately concerned. Normally an attractive, well-dressed woman, today she was wearing no makeup, her hair was hurriedly pulled back, and she was dressed in sloppy jeans and a baggy gray sweatshirt.

I sat down next to her. "How are you doing, Barbara?"

"Fine, thanks," she answered perfunctorily.

"Don't give me any of that 'fine, thanks,' " I said. "I asked you how you were doing because I really want to know."

There was a pause. She looked down at the baby in her arms, then she looked back at me. I thought she might cry. "God, Norman. I'm so depressed. Look at me. I can't even get myself together."

"Why can't you get yourself together?"

"No, the question is why *should* I get myself together when there's absolutely no reason to. All I do is drive Matthew around, and go to the grocery store, and take care of the baby, and do the washing and the cooking—what's the point?"

"The point is you always enjoyed being a put-together, well-dressed woman who enjoyed that aspect of life. You still are that person, and that part of your life *is* still important to you. Having kids doesn't mean you have to give up what you want. When you were teaching, didn't you always make it a point to be elegant and immaculate?" She nodded. "Do you still have those clothes?"

She smiled for the first time that visit. "Of course."

"So," I continued, "every morning get up and take the time to get yourself together the way that makes *you* happy and comfortable, even if you're only going to the grocery store or driving to music lessons. You'll feel better. Trust me on this one."

Several months later she came in looking great—hair combed, nice outfit, and a smile on her face.

"You look like your old self again," I said.

"You bet. I couldn't stop thinking about the advice you gave me last time we were in. So I finally took it. I have to get up earlier in the morning just to put myself together but it's worth it. I can't believe how much better I feel. I'm me again!"

"I'm so glad," I said. "You fell into a common trap for stay-at-home moms. They tend to give up important, vital parts of themselves when they get wrapped up in their children. It's much better for everyone when they take care of themselves and their needs. Then they feel good about themselves. In turn they have so much more to give their children."

Of course being a role model and authority figure can sometimes backfire. Shortly after joining the Norwalk practice and before my consciousness was raised, I began calling all the little girls "Princess." I thought that this was pretty cute until one mother reported an altercation of major proportions that took place in the local supermarket—and it was all my fault.

Four-year-old Dana was shopping with her mother, Mrs. Pappas, when they ran into five-year-old Sara and her mother, Mrs. Barone. The mothers stopped to chat and the conversation turned to the girls and their various illnesses and the mothers eventually realized that I was their common pediatrician. As soon as little Dana heard my name she walked over to Mrs. Barone and proudly informed her, "Dr. Weinberger calls me Princess."

"Hey," Sara spoke up loudly and angrily, *"I'm* Dr. Weinberger's Princess."

"No, Mommy you tell her, *I'm* Dr. Weinberger's Princess." And back and forth the girls went, getting louder and louder, causing a commotion in the cereal aisle of the supermarket, each insisting they were my only Princess. Meanwhile, the mothers tried, unsuccessfully, to explain that Dr. Weinberger could have lots of Princesses and probably did. There were no injuries, and after hearing the story I promptly broke the "Princess" habit and called each patient by his or her name, which, I readily admit, I should have done in the first place.

3

Busy, Busy, Busy

"You remind me of those jugglers on the old Ed Sullivan show. I see you juggling four balls. One of those balls is Scotty. One is your job. Then there's Mike, and the fourth ball is your personal life."

Susan was going back to work. When she was a student at Carnegie Mellon she had studied languages and after she graduated she taught Spanish at a suburban high school until Gordon's birth. Now she was excited to be returning to teaching, this time in the bilingual program at the school where Gordon would be attending second grade and Lisa would be starting kindergarten.

This would involve just a small adjustment, we reassured ourselves. After all, Susan had always been busy with many community and charity activities. She was never one to sit at home waiting for the children. The difference was that now she would get paid for her time. So, we figured, after a couple of weeks of getting used to the new situation everything would return to normal.

Just one week into the school year we received a note from Gordon's teacher expressing concern. "Gordon seems a little down and unable to concentrate. Could there be a problem?" Come to think of it, Gordon did seem to be in a bit of a funk. He used to get up in the morning, happy as a clam, and run out to meet the school bus, but now he refused to get out of bed, complaining of stomachaches or other ailments.

"Gordon, is everything okay?" I asked him that night as I was putting him to bed.

"Uh-huh," he answered in his usual seven-year-old-boy, noncommunicative way.

"Are you sure? Is everything going well at school and with your friends?"

"Uh-huh."

"He says everything's fine," I reported back to Susan. But it wasn't. Gordon's moodiness continued.

"He likes his new teacher. He's not having a difficult time academically. He's in a class with most of his friends. Norman, there's only one other thing that has changed in Gordon's life that could be making him this miserable."

"If you mean you're going to work, it doesn't make a whole lot of sense. You're at the same school with him and you're still home in the afternoons and evenings."

"I still think my working is the problem. What else could it be?"

That night at dinner Susan casually said to Gordon, "Gordon, what would happen if things went back to the way they were before I started teaching?"

A huge smile broke out over Gordon's face. It was the first genuine smile that I had seen from him in some time.

"Yeah! I want that back!" Gordon said enthusiastically.

"Why do you want that back?" Susan asked.

"I just want you to be home again," Gordon said quietly, pushing his food around his plate.

"Why? Isn't it nice that I'm at school with you?"

"No! I want you safe at home where you belong." Like many children, Gordon had just assumed that Susan had spent her days at home waiting for him.

But I had to admit I knew just how Gordon felt. I missed coming home for lunch with Susan. It had been the high point of my day. Now it felt like there was a hole in the middle of each day.

"Well, Gordon. I'm safe at school. I'm just down the hall and around the corner from you."

Gordon didn't answer.

"Gordon, would you like to visit me in my classroom?"

Gordon brightened up again. "Do you think that Mrs. Harper would let me?"

"I'll talk to her tomorrow. Okay?"

Gordon nodded.

"But whatever happens and wherever I work, you know that I'll always be safe and I'll always be your mom. Right?"

"I know that," Gordon responded with that "why-are-parents-so-dumb" look.

After two weeks of Gordon visiting Susan's classroom he became more comfortable with the fact that she was working and not at home. He felt that his mother was safe and he perked up again, happily going off to school with Susan in the morning and becoming a productive and content member of his class again.

The rest of life did not prove that easy. Things did not return to "normal" in a couple of weeks as we had foolishly imagined. "Normal," in fact, became a whole new reality. Shortly after she started teaching, Susan decided to go back to school to pursue a graduate degree. This meant that she would be going to school two nights a week and studying whenever she could make the time.

I would now be chief parent, chauffeur, and cook on those nights. This was more difficult than it sounded since on Wednesdays, my day off from the office, I spent the day teaching and being taught by the pediatric residents at Yale University. I had to budget my time to be home for the kids when they arrived from school. But I took these responsibilities very seriously and especially looked forward to my job as chef.

I prepared for my first evening meal as if it was a state dinner. I read cookbooks like novels. I cut out the "Wednesday

Food Section" from the newspaper in search of healthy and appetizing meals. There would be no grilling hot dogs or TV dinners for my children. Not while I was in charge.

I called the kids down to dinner and proudly sat down with them, hardly able to wait for their response to the beautiful dinner I had prepared.

"What's this stuff?" Gordon said, suspiciously poking his salmon with his finger.

"It's salmon and it's delicious," I said cheerily.

"There's green stuff on it," Lisa added. "Mom says I'm allergic to this."

"It's just spices and you're not allergic to anything." I was starting to get angry. "Pick up your forks and eat your dinner." "Ungrateful animals," I thought, but didn't say.

"Mom only makes us eat one bite of vegetables," Gordon said, spreading his broccoli out on his plate. "This is way too much broccoli."

"Nice try, Gordon, but who do you think sits across from you every night? I know that you know you're supposed to eat your vegetables."

Lisa took a microscopic bite of salmon and dramatically coughed, gagged, choked, and spat it out onto her plate. "The green stuff is not just spices. I think it's poison. And everyone's allergic to poison, right Gordon?"

Uh-oh, they had united against me. Now I was really in trouble.

"She's right. Dad is trying to poison us. Dad is trying to poison us," Gordon chanted, although he had not taken a single bite.

"Dad's trying to poison us!" Lisa chimed in. They continued for several minutes as I proceeded to eat my salmon, the whole time fighting the impulse to grab my throat, roll my eyes back in my head, and fall to the ground.

"Actually I was going to wait until next week to poison you," I said quietly when they tired of their chant.

"Very funny, Dad." Now Gordon tried a new tack. "Can I

please have a peanut butter and jelly sandwich?" he asked in his most polite voice.

"If Gordon gets a peanut butter sandwich then so do I-I-I," Lisa whined. "I" now had three syllables.

"What's the matter with you two? This is a great dinner."

"I want mine with the crusts off and just a little grape jelly. And smooth, not chunky peanut butter," Gordon ordered, as I got up to make their sandwiches.

"Daddy, remember that the jelly belongs on the bottom and I want it in four triangles," Lisa ordered.

They happily ate their gourmet peanut butter and jelly sandwiches and carrot sticks while I reassessed what I would serve for dinner in the future, all the while enjoying my salmon, broccoli, and roasted potatoes.

I had learned my lesson. My dinners would have to be appetizing. Not adult appetizing but kid appetizing. That meant hamburger or chicken served with very little garnish. That meant ketchup and lots of it. Ketchup was the nectar of the gods in our house. Food would have to be lightly seasoned. The less taste the better. I would save my salmon recipe for a night when it was just Susan and me, if ever such a night would occur. For the kids it would be chicken and hamburgers, spaghetti, lamb chops, and meat loaf.

Hazel's Meatloaf Surprise
(in honor of my mother, Hazel Weinberger)

1 tablespoon olive oil

2 pounds lean ground beef

1/2 cup seasoned bread crumbs

1 1/2 tablespoons Italian parsley, finely chopped

2 eggs, one hard-boiled and shelled, one raw

1 small onion, finely chopped

salt and pepper to taste

1/2-3/4 cup barbecue sauce

Preheat oven to 450° F. Brush a 10-inch loaf pan with the olive oil. Mix beef, bread crumbs, parsley, raw egg, onion, salt, and pepper together. Cover bottom of loaf pan with half of the meat mixture. Place hard-boiled egg, with care, in center of meat mixture. Cover with one quarter of the barbecue sauce. Place rest of the meat mixture on top and press edges together. Spread the rest of the barbecue sauce on top. Refrigerate for at least one-half hour. Cook for 25-30 minutes.

The surprise comes when you cut into the center of the meatloaf and the egg looks like a big yellow eye. Kids love this. For a less dramatic surprise, try putting crushed pineapple, or a mixture of ricotta cheese and parsley in the middle.

Dinner turned out to be the least of our problems. Between Susan's schedule and mine, not to mention the ever growing schedules of Gordon and Lisa, we needed a dispatcher to keep track of who should be where and when. We were always on the go, always covering for each other. The only way to survive in any sort of normal fashion was to keep a large and detailed calender of all four of our schedules. This needed to be constantly updated and responsibilities shared and assigned.

Yes our "normal" had changed and it wasn't that our new reality was better or worse, it was just different, different from what we had planned and nothing like what I had expected. What a strange and startling realization: that I would not be raising my children the way that I had been raised.

While our family was growing through this difficult transition from at-home-mom to working-and-student-mom I was amazed by how many of the families in my practice were going through similar adjustments.

There was the Weiss family. Four-year-old Melissa had been brought in three times in one month with various illnesses. She had always been a very healthy child. I had seen very little of her other than for her regular yearly checkups.

On her third visit of the winter, I noticed that her mother, Joan, a well-dressed businesswoman, kept checking her watch.

Melissa sat very quietly and still on the examining table. She had dark circles under her eyes, a nose that wouldn't stop running, and long, curly blond hair hanging wild and uncombed around and in her face. She was wearing a short-sleeved T-shirt even though we were in the middle of a very cold winter.

"Melissa, my darling, you have a viral infection, and I'm afraid there's not much we can do about that but make you as comfortable as possible. I want you to get lots of rest and drink plenty of juice and water and if you have a temperature Mom or Dad can give you some acetaminophen to make you more comfortable. Okay?" I patted her on the back. She had been so quiet and unresponsive. Not at all the usual chatterbox that came in healthy and active once a year.

She nodded. "Now I want you to go out into the waiting room and play with some of the toys out there and I'm going to go over some things with your mother." Melissa slid off the table and, without a word to me or her mother, left the room.

"Let's go sit in the consultation room where we can be more comfortable."

"Will this take long? I have a meeting in thirty minutes," Joan said as she followed me out of the examining room, dragging her coat, large purse, and overstuffed briefcase.

"No, this will just take a few minutes." We settled into our seats. "So, Joan, what's going on?"

"What do you mean? Nothing's going on."

"Certainly there have been some changes in your family. I can see it reflected in Melissa's health and behavior."

"Well, Mitchell's starting his own business. So he has to work fifteen or sixteen hours a day and I got a promotion at work which I felt I had to take since things would be tight for a while. It's a lot more work, so life has been very hectic."

"How has all this affected Melissa?" I asked, even though it was obvious.

"Well for one thing she's in a day-care center now because our sitter couldn't give us as many hours as we needed. I think that's why Melissa is getting sick so often. She's never been with so many children. And they keep the place so hot. That's why she's just wearing a T-shirt. At first I was making her wear a sweater or sweatshirt over it, but she lost so many of them that now I just send her in a shirt. She does enjoy it when she's feeling well and it's a very well-run place, but even though they're supposed to nap, she doesn't seem to get enough rest."

"How many hours a day is she there?"

"Well," Joan hesitated. I could tell that she was embarrassed to answer the question. "I usually drop her off between seven-thirty and eight and pick her up at six when they close."

"You know, that's quite a long day for Melissa."

Joan nodded, looked down at her watch, then back at me. "For now we don't have a lot of choices."

"What's she like when you get her home?"

"Well most days we don't go straight home. I'm trying to lose weight and get in shape, so we go to the athletic club. She goes into the children's program there for an hour. Then we pick something up for dinner on the way home."

"Joan, this has to stop. Melissa is exhausted. For her health, both emotional and physical, cut back somewhere and let her have some restful downtime. It wouldn't hurt you to cut back either, for your own health."

"I know, I know. This is just temporary, I keep telling myself, but I can see what it's doing to her."

"So, tell me, if you have this important meeting now, then what are you going to do with Melissa?"

"She's going back to the day-care center."

"No. They won't allow her in with a fever . . . feeling like that?"

"Actually they've had me come and get her several times. But I can only take so much time off from work and Mitchell has no time. My company won't let me use my sick days to stay home with Melissa. I wish I had an alternative."

I was angry at Joan but I could also hear her desperation, and it was clear she felt there was no other way.

"What about grandparents or aunts and uncles?" I asked.

"None of them live in the area. We're pretty much on our own here." I shook my head. Like our family, this was more and more the case. The extended family was becoming a thing of the past just when it was most needed.

"You tell me what to do, because I don't have a clue." Joan was starting to sound defensive and angry.

"I'm not judging you, Joan. I'm just trying to do my best for Melissa. After all, that's my job. I know how difficult it is. My wife is working and going to school but I'm one of the lucky ones. When Gordon or Lisa gets sick I can just pick them up from school and set them up right on this sofa until it's quitting time. But you and Mitchell have to give something up, or Melissa is going to get seriously ill and then you'll be forced off this merry-go-round schedule."

"Well I suppose I could give up the jogging . . ."

"Think bigger," I suggested. "Think creative. I know there's got to be another solution that would work better for your whole family."

"We could look into finding a new sitter or a smaller day-care setup. Maybe home day-care? I just hate to keep moving Melissa around. She really does like this center. And these things take so much time."

"You'll have plenty of time when you're sitting home or in the hospital with a seriously ill child."

"All right. I get the message. But I do have to go now." She hurried out, dragging Melissa behind her, juggling her briefcase and purse so she could check her watch one more time.

About three months later Melissa came in holding the hand of a young woman I had never seen before.

I introduced myself. "Hi, I'm Dr. Weinberger."

"I'm Melissa's sitter, Mary Beth Connelly."

Melissa looked brand-new. The bags under her eyes were gone. She was well-rested. Her hair was combed and put up in pigtails.

"Nice hairstyle, Melissa," I said, giving one of her pigtails a tug.

"Thank you. Mary Beth did it. She does my hair differently every day." Melissa spun, model style, so that I would get the full effect of her new do. Then she looked at Mary Beth with pure hero worship in her eyes. "She taught me how to do Barbie's hair too."

"Do you miss day-care?" I asked her as she climbed up onto the examining table.

"You mean school? I still go to school, of course. Everybody has to go to school," Melissa replied, speaking to me as if I were the child.

"I pick her up there at one. I'm in college so I have classes in the morning and evening."

"Mary Beth is going to be a teacher for little kids like me. So I'm good practice for her," Melissa volunteered.

"You seem pretty happy with this, Melissa."

"Mary Beth's fun."

When I spoke with Joan I learned that they had been pretty creative in finding this solution. Mitchell had the idea of calling one of the local junior colleges that had a strong early education program to see if any students might be looking for part-time employment. After one false start—a sitter who didn't turn out to be reliable—they found Mary Beth and life started to be easier, especially for little Melissa.

With more and more mothers working outside the home there were more and more families dealing with the same issues as the Weiss family. These issues were universal: child care, the need for downtime, private time with your spouse, and enough time with your children—in general how to find the right balance to allow for your spouse, yourself, and your children to grow and flourish.

There aren't any simple solutions to these problems because, despite the myth, you really can't have it all. Somehow each family must decide what their priorities are in the balance of family and career.

The only way to make all this work is to be vigilant. Watch for signs that something isn't working—that the balance is out of whack, and then address that problem. And, like the Weiss family, be creative in finding a solution.

The Taylors were another family who were feeling overwhelmed with their busy schedule. Lonnie brought one-year-old Scott in for his checkup.

"Is Scotty still going to the sitters?" I asked.

"He's still with Mrs. McCrea." Scott had been in a small home day-care situation since he was three months old. The Taylors had been happy with this setup. They felt he was getting plenty of attention and stimulation in a warm and cozy environment. He enjoyed being with the other children, but wasn't overwhelmed as he might have been in a bigger, more sterile day-care center.

"What's his schedule like?" I asked.

"We get him up at seven, give him breakfast. Then we get him dressed and I usually drop him off at Mrs. McCrea's before eight. Mrs. McCrea serves a snack at ten and lunch at one. Then it's nap time. Either Mike or I try to pick him up between five and five-thirty. On the way home I usually have to make a stop or two—you know—dry cleaners, grocery, that sort of thing. We usually get dinner on the table by seven. By the time we're done with dinner and bath and story time, it's around nine when we put him to bed."

"Wow! I'm exhausted just listening to your day."

"That's *his* day. After we put him to bed, I usually have some work to do or bills, laundry, or calls to make. I find I can't get to bed until midnight or one."

"When do you have time for yourself and for you and Mike to have some private time?"

"It's catch-as-catch-can. We always say we're going to take a night out, but we never do, and I can't remember the last time I went out with a girlfriend or went window shopping or played tennis. I guess I just can't figure out how to fit that into our schedule."

"You remind me of those jugglers on the old Ed Sullivan show. I see you juggling four balls. One of those balls is

Scotty. One is your job. Then there's Mike, and the fourth ball is your personal life. You only have two hands so you can only be holding two balls at any given moment. Because of your priorities, you're mostly holding on to the Scotty ball and the job ball. So your personal life and your spouse are always in the air. They're the things that are neglected."

"That sounds about right. But what can I do about it?"

"From time to time you have to throw the Scott and career balls up and embrace the ball of *your* life and your relationship with your husband."

"Yes . . . and how am I supposed to do that?" She picked up Scotty who was playing happily on the floor, as if to say, "How can I let go of this ball, even for a moment?"

"You stop and look at what you're doing. You try to s-l-o-w d-o-w-n your pace a little. Then you arrange for a sitter or have grandma or Aunt Sally take Scotty so you and Mike can get out. You don't just talk about doing it or just think about doing it. You actually do it. Then occasionally you have Mike take Scott on a Saturday afternoon and you play hooky from paying bills or catching up on your work. You call a friend and go to a movie or shopping. Then you return the favor for Mike so he can do his thing. And you make these things as high a priority as work and Scotty are."

"You make it sound so easy."

"I know it's not easy, but it's necessary. You don't want your life to run you. You want to run your life. The work will wait and so will Scotty. Actually he'll enjoy having each of you to himself."

"A night out with Mike does sound like heaven."

"So?"

"We don't have a grandma or an Aunt Sally any closer than Michigan. It's always a hassle to get a sitter."

"Do you have any friends with a kid about Scotty's age?"

"Sure."

"You give them a call and tell them that you want to arrange a baby swap. You offer to take their kid so they can go out.

Then they take Scott so you can go out. I know families that do this every Saturday night and that way each couple is assured of two nights out each month without having to pay a sitter."

"That's a great idea. I wish I had thought of it." Scotty squirmed off her lap, crawled over to a chair, and pulled himself upright on it, then gave his mother a huge smile. She got up to leave. "I could definitely see this working," she said happily as she left.

Diane Strauss left a message for me. She wanted me to call her. She had a question about what constituted child abuse. The words "child abuse" tend to make me hit my panic button, so I returned her call as soon as I could. She wasn't in her office or at her home. I left messages at both places. I continued to try to reach her. I finally tracked her down, two days later, at her office. I thought it very odd that she had not tried to reach me since leaving the first message.

"I got a message that you had a concern about child abuse?"

"Yes. We were very concerned about the way our nanny, Mrs. Williams, is treating Jason." Jason was an adorable and very typical two-and-a-half-year-old—full of energy and eager to control and conquer his world.

"Why? How is she treating him?"

"She orders him around and expects him to always sit very still. When he doesn't, she yells at him. She makes him stay in the crib for four hours at a time. She claims he needs a quiet time. She won't let him have a bottle and I've seen her rip his pacifier right out of his mouth."

"How is Jason responding to all of this?"

"Well, that's why I called. Mrs. Williams has been with us for almost two years and we've always been concerned about her strictness . . . in fact, behind her back we've always called her 'The Commandant.' Jason always seemed okay, but now he's dragging one of my shirts around like Linus with his blanket. It's very disturbing."

"If you were concerned about this nanny, and she wasn't taking care of Jason the way you wanted, why would you keep her on for two years?" I asked, trying to keep the amazement and anger out of my voice.

"Well, it's very, very difficult to find a nanny, but anyway, it's all over now. We have a new nanny coming on Monday and we're letting Mrs. Williams go this evening. That's why I didn't call you back. We realized whatever you told us, we still would want to let her go."

"Well, I'm glad to hear that. I do think that a gentler approach is much more appropriate, but I also wonder why Jason is still getting a bottle. At his age he should be on a cup."

"Well, he really loves his bottle and I hate to take it away from him. He's so little and I'm gone all day long. It's very hard on him. I think he can really use the comfort and security of the bottle, at least for a little longer."

It was clear that Diane was identifying with Jason in his missing her during the day. *She* needed to allow him to keep his bottle and this was her way of being maternal when she couldn't be with him. This was something I saw a lot in families where both parents were working outside the home.

"I understand," I said, "but start thinking about getting him off the bottle and pacifier."

"I know. I'll try," she said with a touch of sadness in her voice.

"Were there any other concerns?"

"No. Not really."

"Well, I wish you good luck with the new nanny, but if she's doing anything that causes concern, please don't wait to take action."

"We won't. We learned our lesson with Mrs. Williams. Thanks. Bye."

It was several months before I saw Jason Strauss. He came in with his new nanny. She was warm and gentle with him. I was sure that Diane Strauss was not calling *her* "The Commandant."

When I hear a story like Diane Strauss's I wish there was a hard and true formula to finding a nanny—that there was some magical list of questions, or a special test you could give prospective nannies to find out if they would be *the* Mary Poppins for that family. But of course, there is no such test.

It helps tremendously if the parents can look at the nanny's role as that of an extra pair of hands, much like a grandmother or aunt would have been in the days of the extended family. With that in mind, the nanny should be someone who is responsible and reliable. She should be someone who can love your child, not as you would love them, but as a teacher or clergyman or pediatrician loves children—someone who has a general affection for kids and can transmit that in the most nurturing way, a way that helps children flourish.

Parents who hire a nanny must be mature enough to know that the nanny's style of child care won't be exactly like their own. She will certainly have a different style in the way that husbands and wives and grandparents all have different styles. However, the nanny should understand the parents' basic philosophy so that she can make the appropriate adjustments to her own style.

Tanya Rittenberg came in complaining about her nanny. "She feeds Sally way too many cookies. All Sally has to do is point to the cookie jar and Anna is doling out the cookies." One-year-old Sally looked up expectantly at the word "cookie." "No, you're not getting a cookie," her mother told her. "See what Anna's done? She just won't listen to me when I tell her I don't want Sally having a lot of sweets."

"What are you going to do about it?" I asked.

"I'm quitting my job and firing her."

"That seems a little drastic, doesn't it? Couldn't you just stop buying cookies?" I said.

Tanya laughed. "I'm not quitting because of the cookies. I'm quitting because I realized when Sally turned one I had missed almost her whole first year. I felt so guilty and I had to ask myself, 'Why did I have this child? Was it so someone else could raise her?' No—I had this child so I could raise her. So I could give her my love and values and watch her grow. I've cheated not only Sally by not being around much in her first year but myself."

"How does your husband feel about this?" I asked.

"We've spent a lot of time talking about this. We're going to have to cut back a lot, and I might have to do some part-time work to supplement some, but he agrees that this is the right thing for us to do. It might not be right for everyone, but it's the only way for us."

"I give you a lot of credit then, because you're talking about a major lifestyle change—and I'm not talking about the money. I'm talking about the difference between getting all dressed up and going into an office and dealing with adults every day as opposed to playing with a toddler on the floor in your jeans all day. It's quite a shock for many women."

"Oh, I've thought about that and let me tell you, I can't wait."

"Then all I can say is congratulations and good luck!"

I saw the Rittenbergs three months later and it was delightful seeing how much Tanya was reveling in being with Sally. "I've never been happier," she told me. "If there was any doubt that we were making the right decision before, there's no doubt now. We're all much happier and life is so much more relaxed."

The moment I walked into the examining room Ronnie Cummins announced that she was quitting her job.

"Really?" I asked.

"Yes, really. I've had enough juggling sitters, day-care, and nannies. I'm going to stay home." In the eighteen months since she'd had her son, Christopher, she had run the gamut of child care situations.

"I thought the part-time job was working out fine for you," I said, remembering a few months ago when she seemed happy with her work situation.

"At first it did. But then the more I was at work the more I was worrying about Christopher. When I was with him, I always worried about getting my work done. I couldn't stand feeling so torn all the time. So we decided to cut back on expenses—to tell you the truth with working only part-time my salary was not a whole lot more than the child care expenses—and we're going to try it this way for a while."

"And you're happy with this?"

"Yes, I am—at least for now. I know that I'm not staying home forever. There will come a time when I can comfortably return to my career, but right now, we feel it's better for everyone if I stay home with Christopher."

Ronnie Cummins realized a fact that many women don't when they make their child care decisions—*you can change your mind.* It's important to be able to assess the situation you're in, and take into account how you *feel* about what you're doing. This decision—to stay home, or not to stay home—is not cast in iron. It benefits the entire family to stay flexible, and to realize that a new choice is always yours to make.

Jamie Marshall brought nine-month-old Rebecca in for a checkup.

"How are things going?" I asked.

"For a while there, not so good—but it's better now," she replied.

"What was wrong?"

"You know I always planned to stay home with Rebecca, but shortly after she was born there were certain periods of the day when I was feeling pretty miserable. I just wished I was doing something else. At first I thought it was postpartum blues and not being used to staying at home. But then I realized that wasn't it.

"I felt so guilty for wanting to be doing something other than being home with Rebecca. I know so many women who have to work but want to be home with their babies, and here I really didn't need to work, and I was itching to get back to teaching."

"So what are you going to do?"

"I already did it—I got a part-time job teaching at a private school," she said with a tentative smile. "The best part is that they have a day-care center right on the premises. I can stop in and see Rebecca between classes."

"And do you still feel guilty?" I asked, sensing she wasn't one hundred percent comfortable with her decision.

"Well . . ." she sighed.

"A little—huh?"

"It's hard not to—especially when I always planned to stay home. Sometimes I just wonder if something's not a little wrong with me. Other times I just think I must be a terrible mother to have this wonderful opportunity to stay home and not take advantage of it."

"I know my telling you not to feel guilty won't stop you, but your doing this in no way, shape, or form makes you a bad mother. You've managed to put together a near perfect situation for yourself and Rebecca. You should be congratulating yourself—patting yourself on the back for recognizing that you were unhappy and doing something about it."

"Really?" she asked with a worried expression.

"Really. But you don't need to take my word for it. You watch Rebecca and see if she seems to suffer at all from this change. My guess is that she'll be just fine. She'll have a mother who is thrilled to be with her, but also feels happy and fulfilled. She'll also have the input of the people at the day-care center. I predict she'll be fine and so will you."

The stay-at-home versus return-to-work dilemma was an ongoing one for many mothers. It is partly a case of the grass-is-always-greener-on-the-other-side and partly a case of feeling split in two. My role in all of this was to be as nonjudgmental and as supportive as possible. Whatever the decision was—whether it be to return to work, to stay at home, or to work part-time—I wanted to be there to help each family achieve their goals and feel good about what they were doing along the way.

* * *

"I don't know if there's room for me in here," I joked as I joined Elizabeth Campbell, two-year-old Erin, five-year-old Mark, and their nanny, Emma, in the examining room.

"You can sit on my lap," Mark said and then laughed hysterically at his own joke. These kids were always happy and giggling.

When Mark was born, the Campbells hired a Polish nanny but she returned to Poland to get married shortly after Erin was born. Emma had been with them ever since. Sometimes Emma brought the kids in. Sometimes, Elizabeth, but most often they both brought the children in. There were a lot of families in the practice that utilized nannies and sitters and the Campbells had always done this very smoothly and successfully.

The children were happy, healthy, and well taken care of. The parents appeared happy and balanced, and the nannies always seemed content with their jobs and were loving and involved with the children. I decided this was the perfect time to find out what their secret was to this relationship working so well.

"Well, part of it is luck," Elizabeth said. "We loved our first nanny and when she left we didn't think we would ever find anyone so wonderful again, but then we found Emma. So lightning did strike twice for us."

"It has to be more than luck," I said.

"It is," Emma put in. "I've worked for a lot of families, but I've never worked for anyone like the Campbells. They're very clear about how they want the children raised, and they told me these views when they first interviewed me."

"So if your ideas about child rearing were very different, would you have declined the job?"

"Probably," Emma continued. "But that's not the only thing that makes working for the Campbells different. You see they treat me with respect. I feel like we're all working together raising these kids. From the beginning they encouraged the kids to love and respect me, instead of being jealous when the kids showed me love, like a lot of the other people I worked for."

"Aww, Emma. You're making me blush," Elizabeth said, giving her a hug.

"That's quite a report card."

"Well, Emma fit right into the family and that's what we wanted. After all, she's with the kids more hours a day than we are. Of course we wanted them to love and respect each other."

There was no doubt that the special chemistry between Emma and Elizabeth made this an extraordinary working relationship, but the openness and respect with which the Campbells welcomed Emma would have started any nanny off on the right foot. The fact that Emma saw them as working *with* her had kept the lines of communication constantly open. Everyone knew what everyone else expected and they all were working hard to meet those expectations. The result was evident in the happy and well-adjusted children.

It's a rare dual-career family that doesn't go through some succession of caregivers. It's important for parents to understand and acknowledge the depth of the attachment and love of the child to the caregiver, whether it be nanny, baby-sitter, day-care worker, or even teacher. Even though these separations will certainly be sad times, they also give parents a chance to help their children see that there can be many people in their lives who will love and care for them.

It's difficult when a caregiver who has been involved with the family for a long time is leaving. When it happens it's important to let the children know early on that their caregiver is leaving, so they have time to discuss their feelings openly. They might feel abandoned, afraid, or even angry. They should be encouraged to talk about any of these feelings, and reassured they will always be well taken care of. And it's always nice if the caregiver writes letters to the child after she's left so the relationship doesn't feel so suddenly severed.

*   *   *

The Websters, patient family and dear friends, had a different solution to their child care problems. Bill Webster had been a very involved and committed father. Bill always claimed that their two children, David and Dara, were his priority and that was, in fact, how he lived his life.

Maida was enjoying a slowly but surely growing family therapy practice when Bill was offered a wonderful new job. On the first day, the boss took Bill aside and said, "This is how we do things here; everyone comes in at 8:00 A.M. and stays until the job is done, whether it's six, eight, ten, or midnight."

Bill replied, "I'm willing to come in at five or six in the morning but I have two kids and a wife and I intend to be out of here at five every afternoon so I can be home with my family. My wife works a couple of evenings a week as well, and it's my responsibility to be home with the children so that she can be on time for her clients."

Bill convinced his new boss that he could get his job done well working within his own schedule, and not long thereafter he was offered another, more lucrative job. He turned it down because it involved a lot of travel and he felt it was more important to be home with his family, not only because he enjoyed them but also to support Maida in her career. Bill did this knowing full well that this would alter his career path.

This was the Bill that we loved and respected and of course we assumed that he had always been that way, but Maida confessed that things had not always been so. There had been a time, at least once, when Bill's commitment wavered.

We were all sitting together at dinner when Maida told the story. "I was working for Children and Family Services when we had Dara. After my maternity leave I was looking somewhat forward to getting back to work, but I was also a little nervous. Of course there would be an important meeting scheduled for my first morning back, and I had reminded Bill several times that he needed to stay home from work that morning so I could be at the meeting. After all, he had encouraged me to go back and had said he would do anything he could to make that happen."

Bill smiled guiltily at us and took Maida's hand. "You know that I would do anything for you."

"Sure honey, any day but that one," Maida said sarcastically. "When I reminded him again on Sunday night that he was staying with the kids in the morning, he looked at me like I was nuts. 'I can't stay with the kids tomorrow. I have an important appointment at work,' he said as if I had never mentioned this to him. 'But Bill, this was set weeks ago.' 'I guess I forgot. I'm sorry but there's nothing I can do about it now,' he told me.

"I could have killed him, I was so angry. But not as angry as I was the next morning when he left for work without feeling sorry or guilty or anything other than self-righteous."

"What can I say? I was a jerk," Bill said. "I left with Maida at the door yelling, 'You son of a bitch, you lied! You said that this would be a fair and equitable marriage and now look at you . . .' But I made it up to you, didn't I?"

"By the time he got home that evening he was feeling pretty bad. So he arrives with flowers and champagne. He sits me down with a glass of chilled champagne and says, 'Maida, you're right. I knew deep down I should have been here, that the children are as much my responsibility as they are yours, if not more. So I'm going to quit my job and stay home to take care of the kids.'"

"Really, he said that?" asked Susan, in shock.

"No, of course not. But he did bring flowers and he apologized profusely and he never let it happen again," Maida said. "I know he's one in a million when it comes to the amount of time he gives our kids." She took Bill's hand and suddenly looked quite serious. "I know how lucky I am," she said almost in a whisper.

And she was right. The more I saw of dual-career families the more I knew how unique the Websters really were. There were far more families like the Bruces.

Robert and Shirley Bruce had, from the outside, what many would consider the perfect family. They had three sons within four years, now ten, eight, and six, all healthy, hardy, nice kids. Robert was a successful advertising executive, commuting daily into Manhattan, and Shirley was a hardworking stay-at-home mom. But she was one of those moms who made it seem easy. The kids were always immaculate and well-behaved. She was very put together and they all were constantly on the go, on their way to skating or Little League or rushing home to bake brownies.

She was the kind of woman who always hung a different homemade wreath on her door to celebrate whatever holiday was coming up. I imagined Robert Bruce coming home around eight o'clock each night to a house that was neat and clean and tidy, children who were tucked cozily into bed, and a gourmet, candlelit dinner.

Then Shirley had enough. Or maybe what she had was not enough—not enough mental stimulation, not enough doing for herself, not enough of a challenge—and she decided to change things. Shirley went back to work. Bravely, I thought, she picked up her career where she left off when she had her first son. She went out and got a position in a small local law firm, practicing personal injury law.

"How's the law?" I asked her the next time she brought the kids in.

"The law is a piece of cake," she said, barely looking up from buttoning up her son Charlie's shirt. "It's the rest of life that's tough."

"So tell me," I said.

"Robert was not thrilled when we discussed my going back to work. He didn't want anything to change and didn't understand why in the world I would want to complicate life by working. He said he didn't like the idea but he would support me if that was truly what I wanted."

"So, what's the problem?"

"I thought by support he meant that he would help a little.

You know, with the kids and around the house. But apparently what he meant by support was that he wouldn't try to forbid me from doing it."

"So now you have all the responsibilities you had before, that more than filled your days, plus a full-time job. And you're doing it all by yourself."

"Well, I do have some help. A sitter comes in the afternoon but she doesn't cook or clean, or do the wash or the grocery shopping."

"Which of those things did you think Robert would help with?" I said with a smile, knowing the answer.

"You know I can't imagine him doing any of those things. But it hardly seems right that he gets to pursue a career and I don't. Don't get me wrong. I love these guys and it's wonderful being their mom, but they're, all three, in school all day now and they're going to want me around less and less."

Six-year-old Charlie looked up from his coloring book. "I want you around, Mommy," he said in a sweet voice and climbed into Shirley's lap.

"I know you do, honey." She stroked his hair absently. "What am I supposed to do? Just bury any hopes I had for a law career? Just waste my degree? Or worse, try to get back into it twelve years from now when Charlie finally goes to college?" Charlie smiled at the thought of going to college. "That would be some trick, wouldn't it, not having practiced law in twenty-two years and trying to get back into it when I'm fifty?"

"Not only would it be tough, but it's not what you want. Is it?" I asked her.

"No, I'm really enjoying practicing law. And the boys like their sitter. There're just not enough hours in the day to do everything I have to do."

"I know, but knowing Robert, is it realistic to think that he's going to help with the household chores?"

"No, I guess not. I don't see any chance of changing him."

"That's right. So you have to change some of what you're doing."

"What can I change? Dinner has to be made. Groceries have to be bought. Clothes have to be washed," Shirley said, pulling an Etch-A-Sketch out of her big canvas bag and handing it to her middle son, Sam, just as he was about to grab the coloring book out of Charlie's hands.

"You change your attitude about who has to do everything and how well it needs to be done."

"Like what?" she said, sounding more than a little defensive.

"Like the vacuuming doesn't have to be done every day and your sitter can surely throw a couple of loads of laundry in the machine or do the grocery shopping. You've got to be a little more flexible and a lot less of a perfectionist or you're going to run yourself into the ground. You can have it all, but you can't have it all at once, or all perfect."

There were a few moments of silence and then Shirley looked at me, a smile slowly spreading over her face, and said, "How could you possibly know that I vacuum every day?"

4

The Terrible Teens

I see a lot of parents who don't want to deal with their kids once they get into adolescence ... but this is the time when they need all that structure more than ever.

"Mrs. Stender is on line two," Edith said, barely slowing down as she passed the open door of my office.

"Lois Stender! What's up?" I asked.

"Hi, Dr. Weinberger. I don't know if this warrants a visit, but Sara has been acting very strange lately."

"How so?" I asked. Lois Stender was a reasonable, not overly protective mother of two. Jeremy was six and Sara was nine and a half.

"Well, for the last month or so, she's been really difficult and defiant. She's always been a little bit of a wild woman, but now she's impossible."

I had a feeling I knew what was going on, but I wanted to be sure. "Give me some examples."

"Well, if we tell her it's bedtime, she'll just look at us very matter-of-factly and say, 'No!' And she means it. Star charts don't work, threats don't work, punishments don't work. She just says 'I don't care' to everything. But I know she does care if her television privileges are taken away, or if she misses out on someone's birthday party." As Lois told her story her voice was getting higher. I could tell how anxious she was over her daughter's changed behavior.

"Go on . . ." I encouraged.

"Mornings are the worst. She was never a morning person, but now I really dread getting her up. It takes forever to get her out of bed, and as for deciding what she's going to wear, or what she wants for breakfast, forget it. She can't make a simple decision. After school she comes in, slams her books down, goes to her room, slams the door shut, and that's the last I see of her until dinner. She used to be a real chatterbox, but now she just grunts. God forbid we do start a conversation, because we end up yelling at each other. The worst part is, I think she's doing all this just to drive me crazy—and it's working."

"Okay, calm down. I think I know what's going on. Now let's see, Sara is nine, closing in on ten, right?"

"Right," she said.

"I don't think you need to come for a visit," I told her.

"No?" she said. I could hear relief in her voice. "Then what do you think is going on?"

"Believe it or not, I think Sara is starting adolescence."

"Adolescence!" Lois shouted in my ear. "That's not supposed to happen for another two or three years." I love parents' initial reaction to their children entering puberty.

"Well, apparently Sara has other plans. All the things you described are signs of adolescence."

"Isn't nine awfully early for puberty?" she asked, sounding anxious all over again.

"Most people assume puberty hits at twelve or thirteen, but the fact is the onset usually starts at nine or ten."

"My God, Sara an adolescent. That's hard to take. How am I going to tell Ted? He still thinks of her as his baby."

"That's not uncommon. You can tell him she needs him now more than ever. I see a lot of parents who don't want to deal with their kids once they get into adolescence. They think the rules and structure and hands-on parenting is over, but this is the time when they need all that structure more than ever. You thought the terrible twos were bad, just wait. This is when it really gets tough. She's going to test, and test, and test to see how far she can go, and you've got to stick to your guns."

"You're scaring me, Dr. Weinberger." I could tell she was only half-kidding.

"Well, this is a scary time for Sara," I said. "Everything is changing: her body, how she thinks, what she thinks, how she feels, and how contradictory those feelings are. Don't you be afraid. Just keep the lines of communication open for her. Let her know you're there when she is ready to talk, and then talk, don't lecture. You don't have to agree with her, but listen to her side. And be very clear about what the rules are. Keep it simple, not a whole lot of rules. Start letting her take more responsibility for herself."

"Like what?"

"You know the trouble you're having in the mornings? Well, that's not your problem. You need to define the problem and then assign it to the appropriate person. The problem here is Sara needs to be up, dressed, fed, and at the bus stop at seven-forty-five. You have agreed to wake her up. The rest is up to her. Let her know what the consequences are if she is not at the bus stop on time, and I would advise it not be you driving her to school."

"I don't understand why this would work when nothing else has."

"The methods you used before—the ones that don't work anymore, like star charts—were geared to her desire to please you. She's not as interested in that at this age. Now she wants to be more independent. This way you're giving her the space to have some of that independence."

"I guess that makes sense. I still can't believe I have an adolescent—but at least she's not going nuts like I thought she was."

"No, it will just be you who goes nuts. Oh and one more suggestion—from here on in, remember this quote: 'hide all the matches and knives.' "

"Oh my God!" she mumbled, and hung up the phone.

Lois Stender's response to her daughter's entering puberty wasn't too surprising. Adolescence can be a scary time. In some basic ways adolescence now is the same as it has been through all time. The adolescent is dealing with physical and emotional changes that are often overwhelming and difficult to understand. They're walking a thin line between trying to become more independent from their parents, while at the same time knowing they still rely heavily on the support of their families. This can be a trying time for parents as well, as they try to judge from moment to moment if their child wants and needs to be treated as a teen or a child.

In this day and age the challenging time of adolescence is made even more difficult by the constant bombardment by the media. Through television, movies, and music, children and young teens are introduced to sex and violence at an early age. Through advertising they are being urged, not only to be tremendous consumers, but to look and act older and more mature than is appropriate.

The societal structure and rules of generations ago, which helped guide adolescents, are all but gone. It is so accepted that our children will be introduced to drugs and alcohol in the middle school, or even earlier, that drug abstinence programs are taught in many grade schools.

Yes, today's adolescents have a tough road to navigate, but parents can make it easier by staying involved in their children's lives, keeping the lines of communication open, and offering some of the structure and guidance that is now a thing of the past in our general society.

Madeline Martell brought in her twelve-year-old daughter, Tracey, whose allergies were acting up. After I examined Tracey and gave her a prescription, Madeline asked if she could speak to me alone. We went to the consultation room.

"What's up?" I asked her.

"I'm at the end of my rope with Tracey. I don't know how to

say this nicely, so I guess I'll just say it—Tracey has become a pig. Her room always looks like a tornado hit it, and there's nothing I can do to get her to clean it up. I've tried promises, bribes, threats, punishments. Nothing works. I end up having to straighten it myself, and two minutes later it's a pigsty again."

"The last thing you should be doing is straightening her room. It's her room and if she can't or won't keep it clean, then just shut the door and pretend it's not even there."

"Uhhh. I can't do that. It just turns my stomach knowing it's like that," she said.

"Then I don't know what to tell you, except as long as she knows you'll clean the room she's certainly not going to do it herself."

"Well, thanks anyway," she said, sounding defeated.

"If it makes you feel any better, this pig stage is fairly normal."

"A little better, I guess," she said as she left.

Two days later I got a call from Madeline. "I just wanted you to know that Tracey, the pig girl, cleaned her room and did a darn good job of it."

"How did you manage that?"

"Yesterday, when I got home, Tracey was sitting in front of the TV with her room upstairs worse than ever, and I really lost it. I slammed the TV off and said, 'You go upstairs this minute and clean that room.'

"She looked up at me and said in this incredibly annoying voice, 'Well, Mother, I'm just not comfortable with that.'

"I looked at the smug expression on her face and something in me just snapped. I said, 'You better get comfortable with that, because you're not eating another bite of food in this house until that room is straightened and cleaned.' I wasn't yelling or screaming or out of control; in fact, my voice was almost a whisper.

" 'You wouldn't do that,' she said.

" 'You want to find out?' I asked her. I realized at that moment I absolutely meant what I had said.

"She must have realized it too because all of a sudden her

whole expression changed. Her mouth dropped open. She thought for a moment, and then she said, 'Oh God, you're serious.'

"I just nodded and she got up, went upstairs without a word, and didn't come down until her room was perfect. Can you believe that?"

"Sure I can. She was testing you and the limits you set. It sounded like you'd been a little wishy-washy with the room issue before. Particularly when you started straightening Tracey's room for her, she must have felt too much power was in her hands. Kids Tracey's age will tell you they want total freedom and to be left alone, but they still really need and want the structure and limits that give them a sense of security. When you got tough and meant what you said, she felt it, and responded, because she felt the structure was in place again. Of course if you asked her why she finally cleaned her room she'll tell you it was because she didn't want to miss out on the spaghetti you were cooking that night."

"That's exactly what she said, only it was tacos."

"So all in all, are you feeling you're back in control?"

"You know, I feel like I won the battle, but the war's not even close to being over." She gave a huge sigh.

And that, I thought, was a pretty apt description of life with an adolescent. There was the constant obstinance and defiance to deal with, plus the sudden mood swings and emotional outbursts, something I was treated to, firsthand, in the office one day.

Eleven-year-old Tyler Freeman came in with his mother, Kathy. He had been suffering with a sore throat and general fatigue for over a week. It turned out that Tyler had mononucleosis.

"Let's talk about what you need to do to ensure a complete recovery. First I want you to stay home until you feel better—that should be a week or so. Once you feel better and return to school, you will still need to take it easy. For about six weeks I want you to cut back on the sports and—"

"Hey, wait a minute. What about skiing?" Tyler said, looking panicked.

"Skiing? Tyler, you have mono. You won't be able to ski for six weeks," I said.

It was like a bomb had dropped in the examining room. "What do you mean I can't ski?" Tyler yelled. "You can't tell me I can't ski. What kind of a doctor are you anyway?" His face contorted, his eyes becoming little slits. "You're just wrong." He jumped off the table and grabbed his coat. "I'm not going to listen to this crap. I'm getting the hell out of here and finding a decent doctor who knows what he's talking about."

Meanwhile his mother was struck speechless, her face getting redder by the minute. All she could say was, "Tyler!"

Tyler, ignoring her, stomped out of the room, leaving his mother and me stunned, staring at the door he had slammed on his way out.

Finally I spoke. "I take it Tyler's into skiing?"

"Well, yes. We have a place in Vermont. All winter we go up there every weekend so he can compete in the Vermont State Ski Champion Series. He does very well in it and he's absolutely dedicated to it. But, Doctor, I'm so sorry . . . I don't know what to say about his behavior. Sometimes he just has these emotional outbursts. I'm so embarrassed that this one was aimed at you."

"Well, this outburst can be explained by three things. The first is that he's an adolescent and this is what adolescents do. The second is because of the mono, he's simply not feeling well. And the third is he's really angry he can't do what he loves to do and he has a right to be angry. I understand how he feels."

"Thank you for understanding, but I still feel he had no right to take it out on you."

"It's just a case of killing the messenger. I think you're in for a rough winter though, because it's very important you don't allow him to ski. If he skis he runs a serious risk of rupturing his spleen."

"I promise—if I have to tie him down, he won't ski."

I didn't see Tyler until late March, when he came in for a strep test.

"Tyler was able to ski in the final championship meet," his mother proudly told me.

"Really. How'd you do?" I asked him, bracing myself for another outburst, in case he hadn't done well and it was, once again, all my fault.

"I came in eighth in my age division," Tyler said proudly.

"That's great," I said.

"Think of how high I would have placed if I could have skied the whole season," he remarked.

I stepped back to the door and put my hand on the knob. "You didn't bring a gun or anything, did you?" I said, feigning fear.

Tyler laughed. "Nah, you know I wasn't really mad at you about the skiing."

"Oh yeah sure," I said, thinking, "typical adolescent, typical to get so very angry when things didn't go his way." It was typical to have to find someone to take the blame when it was truly a blameless situation and typical to later on refuse to admit he was ever angry in the first place, after everything had blown over.

Shortly after my visit from Tyler, I walked by the waiting room. There was sixteen-year-old, six-foot, two-inch Jerry Reiss, who was packed into one of the kiddie chairs, his long blue-jeaned legs stretched out in front of him creating a hazard for the toddlers playing around him.

We need to do things differently, I thought to myself. We have the adolescents thrown in with the babies, toddlers, and children, and they really need their own time and space—a place they can be comfortable. Their needs have to be addressed in a special way.

Bert and I devised a new plan. We would have late-afternoon/early-evening "adolescent hours." We told the parents we were making a new contract, directly with their children, one based on confidentiality. This confidentiality did not extend to violence either to themselves or anyone else. The patients could make their own appointments or just drop in. And they could assume responsibility for their own bill. We scheduled longer appointments with them and conducted the examination and interview to allow them to learn more about their health and themselves. Younger patients could still come in with their parents, who stayed in the waiting room or came into the examining room, depending on what the patient wanted.

After their physical exam we sat down with them in the consultation room, as we had done with their parents previously, to go over the findings of the exam, and answer any questions they had. We would also discuss how they were doing in school, with their peers, and their families.

As they got older we talked about drugs, alcohol, smoking, peer pressure, and sexuality, and offered to provide additional information if they needed it. If a subject came up they wanted kept confidential we would do that, as promised, but we always encouraged them to keep the lines of communication open with their parents, even if it meant that we were needed to mediate.

Our new system had been up and running for almost a year when fifteen-year-old Jeffrey Zar came in for a checkup for his summer soccer camp program. The physical exam went well. He was a normal, healthy teen, in exceptionally good physical shape. He was a good student with a quick sense of humor and a great sense of drama. He followed me into the consultation room.

"Hey, Doc! You've got to help me. I have to do something about this nose," he blurted out before we even had a chance to sit down.

Jeffrey did have a really big nose. I remembered hoping, when he was younger, that he would grow into it, but it grew right along with him. "What exactly did you have in mind?" I didn't want to mention rhinoplasty (better known as a nose job) until I was sure that that was what Jeffrey was thinking.

"I want a nose job because this thing is ruining my life." He roughly tried to push his nose in.

I gently removed his hand from his face. "Come on, that's not true. You're a good kid, you're a soccer star by your own admission, and I'm sure that you're a popular guy."

"No, I'm not. The girls don't like me and the boys make fun of me—all because of my nose."

"Why don't you take some time and really think about it? It's a big step and a big change." It wasn't unusual for adolescents to become fixated on a single aspect of their appearance or detail of their lives, and blow it—no pun intended—out of proportion. If I could stall Jeffrey in his decision to have a nose job, then he might become comfortable with his appearance. But at the same time I could understand Jeffrey's point. His nose *was* really big.

"Take time to think about it? That's all I think about. Don't you understand what it's like to be called 'The Honker' or 'Hawk' every day of your life?" I was surprised to see tears fill his eyes.

"They're really giving you a hard time?" Knowing teens, I didn't think Jeffrey was exaggerating the abuse he was experiencing at school.

"It's been going on since fifth grade, and I'm sick of it. One of the girls in my class had a nose job and it really made a big difference in how she looked and acted and everything."

"What do your parents say about this?"

"I've mentioned it to them but they don't think I mean it. They don't get how important this is to me."

"You know that pediatricians don't perform nose jobs. The best I can do is give you the name of a plastic surgeon, but he won't do anything without your parents' involvement."

"I know. I was thinking maybe you could talk to my dad and tell him how important this is. Maybe he'll listen to you."

"Sure, I could do that."

"Great! My dad is in the waiting room. I'll go get him."

"Now? You want me to talk to him now?" I said, but Jeffrey was already out the door.

Mr. Zar walked in. All I could see was his nose. The exact same nose that Jeffrey so desperately wanted altered, filled his father's face. Oh no, we're dead before we even got started, I thought.

"Everything was normal? Jeffrey's healthy?" Mr. Zar and his nose gave me a look of concern.

"He's a very healthy young man. But there *is* an area of concern."

"What's that?"

I waited for Jeffrey to speak, but he was nervously picking at his shoelace. "Come on, kid, ask for your nose job," I silently urged but he just sat there.

I took a deep breath and continued, "Jeffrey is not very happy with his nose. He feels, and may I add that these are his own words, it'sruininghislifeandhe'dlikeanosejob." I couldn't look Mr. Zar in the face—nose—when I said it.

"What!" Mr. Zar looked at Jeffrey, wounded. "You want to have your nose changed? This nose has been in the family for generations."

"Dad, I told you that the kids make fun of me. They call me names. I told you before I wanted a nose job."

"I didn't think you were serious. I'm sorry you're having a hard time, but that's the nose God gave you. I suggest you accept it because there's no way you're changing it."

I attempted to intervene, although I felt the battle was lost. "Mr. Zar, Jeffrey's self-esteem is really taking a hit over this. Perhaps you could consider it from his point of view."

"His grandfather did fine with this nose. I did fine with this nose. Jeffrey will be fine too. End of discussion."

"I gave it my best shot, Jeffrey. I'm sorry."

"Thanks anyway, Doc," he said sadly, dragging slowly out of the consultation room after his father.

I patted him on the back. "Chin up. It will be all right," I told him, but there was no comforting him.

Late that night, I was awakened out of a deep sleep by the phone. "Dr. Weinberger."

"This is the emergency room. We've just admitted Jeffrey Zar. He tried to commit suicide—"

I hung up the phone without another word and was at the hospital in a matter of minutes.

"Dr. Weinberger!" It was the resident on duty, the same one who had called me. "You hung up before I could finish. I wanted to tell you there was no need to come in."

"What do you mean, no need?"

"He cut his nose. He claimed he was trying to cut it off, but the only damage is a small flesh wound. When his mom walked in on him, he told her he was trying to kill himself. You can imagine her reaction. She called the police and they brought him in. Everyone was in hysterics by the time they got here."

"Where is he?" I asked.

"He's in examining room three. I put the parents in the lounge. They were upsetting him."

I knocked on the door of the examining room and walked in as Jeffrey said, "Come in."

He was lying on the examining table, his arm slung across his face. Other than the butterfly bandage across his nose and a general look of exhaustion, he seemed to be in good shape. "Scoot over," I said, pushing his legs off the examining table and sitting next to him. "What's happening?"

"Doc, I swear to God, next time I really will cut it off."

I knew there was no way he would really do it, but I could also tell how important this nose job was to him. "Jeffrey, you're right. This is a medical emergency. We're going to admit you, tonight, to the psychiatric ward, and I'm going to tell your parents what a serious situation this is."

Jeffrey looked at me in disbelief. "Really, Doc?"

"We're going to handle this for you."

I left him, relieved, swinging his legs in the examining room, and went to find his parents.

They were sitting nervously in the lounge, untouched cups

of coffee on the table in front of them. Jeffrey's mother, a small energetic woman, was still wearing her coat, her eyes were puffy and she looked terrified. I shook their hands. "Mr. and Mrs. Zar, I just spoke with Jeffrey. His nose is patched up and there won't be any permanent damage but, as I'm sure you know, anytime there's a suicide attempt we have to take it seriously."

"Oh my God. Oh my God! What can we do? What will we do? He's all we have." Mrs. Zar started to cry.

"We'll have to admit Jeffrey to the psychiatric unit and have a full evaluation done."

"Do anything you need to do," Mr. Zar said.

"Can we see him now?" Mrs. Zar asked through her tears.

"I think it's best if you wait until the morning. It's been a tough night. You could all use some rest."

First thing the next morning I called Dr. Peter King, the top plastic surgeon in the area. "Peter, can you do me a favor and consult on this kid who wants a nose job?"

"Sure, have him call my office to set up an appointment."

"I can't. He's on the psych unit."

"Sorry, but I'm not going to see someone on the psych unit."

I told him the whole story of Jeffrey Zar and his nose from the beginning to the latest chapter, and he responded, "No problem! I'll see him today."

Later that morning Dr. King and I met Mr. and Mrs. Zar at the hospital. They had been there all night. They were clearly exhausted and extremely distraught. "Dr. Weinberger, when will Jeffrey meet with the psychiatrist?" asked Mr. Zar.

"Well, I think I might have another way to deal with his problem. I believe his self-esteem will be tremendously improved if he has a nose job," I told them.

Before Mr. Zar could speak Mrs. Zar spoke up. "Of course, anything."

"Well, then I'd like to introduce you to Dr. Peter King. He's a top-notch surgeon."

So, Jeffrey had his nose job, and sure enough, his life did

change. He radiated a new confidence and self-assurance. He felt confident enough, in fact, to question me about my own somewhat prominent, but undeniably handsome, nose on his next visit. "Hey, Doc, can I ask you kind of a personal question?"

"Sure—I think."

"About your nose . . ."

"What about my nose?" I knew what was coming.

"How come you never got that thing fixed?"

"Why? What's wrong with my nose?"

"Ahh, nothing, I was just, umm, uhh . . ." he stuttered, suddenly looking panicked.

"Just kidding, I know my nose is um . . . generous. But it never bothered me. No, for me it was my feet I was self-conscious about. I remember when I was in seventh grade I made the junior high basketball team. The coach was asking everyone what shoe size they wore so he could order team shoes. When I told him I wore a size fifteen he laughed and said he would just give me the shoe boxes to wear. All the kids laughed. I was devastated.

"You can get a nose job but you can't get a foot job. I decided that since I couldn't hide them, I'd beautify them—I'd show them off. So while everyone else was scuffing up their white bucks, I always kept mine bright white. I thought it showed my individuality."

"You're still showing your individuality," Jeffrey said, kicking my cowboy boot with his toe. "But I felt like *my* individuality couldn't get out through my old nose."

"Well," I said, as I walked him to the door, "we all have to find what works best for us."

It's often hard for teens to find what's best for them because of the intense desire to fit in, blend in, and all but disappear into the crowd. Self-esteem is important for all of us, but it is an enormous issue for teens because of the physical changes they're going through, and the sudden self-consciousness about their appearance. Because of this they want to look just like everyone else. Things like a large nose, being overweight, or not having the right clothes or haircut can make a teen feel not only self-conscious but out of it and socially unacceptable.

It's very important for parents, teachers, and any other adults dealing with adolescents to give them a pat on the back, let them know how well they're doing, and how much you approve of them, so they can feel how highly they're valued for just being who they are.

It's also important to keep the lines of communication open—to talk to them in a nonjudgmental, noncondescending, and nonpreaching way. It's even more important to listen, not just to the words they say, but to try and empathize with the emotions they're feeling as well. Adolescents must be respected as growing, changing individuals who will often need time to themselves to think their own problems and issues through.

However, if a child is suddenly spending a large amount of time alone, becomes extremely uncommunicative, or is isolating him or herself from both family and friends, then it is time to be concerned and intervene to find out what's going on.

Jack Markham was a kid who was bound and determined to find out what worked best for him. In ninth grade Jack was one of the smaller and thinner boys in his class and this, understandably, bothered him tremendously. He was also not much of an athlete, but he was certainly willing to give anything and everything a try. He felt that he needed to prove himself. Each time I saw him he had tried another sport or two. He tried soccer and baseball and basketball and rowing, but he wasn't very good at any of them. Jack continued to search, in a most methodical and diligent manner, for a place where he could excel.

Toward the middle of his sophomore year he came in all bubbly and excited. "I've found it, Dr. Weinberger. I've found my sport and you won't believe what it is."

"Well, how long are you going to keep me in suspense?"

"I'm a bodybuilder," he said proudly.

"Really, that's wonderful. But you know it can be dangerous if you don't know what you're doing."

"Oh I know that. My mom and dad took me to the Y and set me up with a trainer. I go every day. It's really cool."

From then on every time he came into the office he would have questions about his diet and nutrition. He showed me articles from his weight lifting magazines and wanted my opinion on whether he should take this supplement or that, and whether the vitamins they sold through the magazine really worked. I assured him that as long as he had a proper diet and stayed away from anabolic steroids, he'd be fine.

One day he came in complaining of acute diarrhea.

"Have you had any changes in your diet?" I asked him, knowing he was constantly revising his diet for bodybuilding purposes.

"Well, yeah. I found that if I drink two gallons of milk a day I can get the perfect combination of all the nutrients I need."

"You also get a perfect case of diarrhea. Instead of drinking two gallons, which is really excessive, why don't you take eight ounces of milk and mix it with a packet of Carnation Instant Breakfast. That should give you the extra nutrition without the runs. Another thing you can do is carry around a bag of granola or raisins or dry cereal, and nibble on that through the day."

"Well, I thought the milk was working great, but I'll try the other stuff if you think it will work."

"Nothing that makes you sick, works. Remember, too much of any one thing is never a good idea."

Over the next two years I watched Jack bulk up, and finally asked him what he planned to do with his avocation.

"I don't plan to do anything with it really. It's just my thing. You know, something I can do really well—something that always makes me feel good."

"You spend so much time with it. Doesn't it interfere with your other responsibilities?"

"No, not at all. You know, I get good grades and I have everything scheduled out. That way I can keep up with everything. See." He pulled a tattered piece of paper out of his book bag. It was a detailed daily schedule. I had never seen anything quite like it from a high school boy.

He pointed to the schedule. "See, here's my study time, eating time, class hours, weight lifting, running, and here's my free time." It was all color-coded on his schedule.

"This schedule is really something," I said.

"Well, I got used to working from a schedule with the weight lifting and the running. I plan everything out ahead of time. It worked so well for me that I thought I could do the same with the rest of my life."

"You know you're one in a million, don't you?" I told him.

"Aw go on," he replied. But he was. He was a kid who knew he needed to find something he could do that would make him feel good about himself, and with the support of his parents he found it and stuck with it and excelled. Instead of letting it interfere with his responsibilities he carried the discipline it gave him into the rest of his life. He truly was one in a million.

One of the trickiest times for adolescents is the second part of their senior year of high school and the following summer, the summer before they start college. The anxiety of waiting for college acceptances, choosing a college, and then anticipating being on their own, many for the first time, is an extremely stressful time for many teenagers. This is also a very tough time for the families. Parents are seeing their child strike out on their own—probably for the first time, and siblings can feel sadness and stress over the "loss" of their brother or sister and the overall change in the family structure.

Janine Sommers, in her senior year of high school, was an honor student, all-around athlete, and class leader. She was also spending a good part of the late winter and early spring in my office. "Still not feeling yourself?" I asked as I joined her in the examining room, for the third time in a couple of months.

"I'm still having some stomachaches and headaches, but mostly I just feel tired all the time."

I looked at her file. "Let's see. We tested you for strep and mono. Those both came back negative. You haven't had a fever. Let me take a look at you.

"So what's new? You heard from any schools yet?" Janine had applied to almost all Ivy League schools. She shook her head as I examined her throat.

"Well, your throat looks fine. Lie down for a minute so I can check your stomach. Tell me if this hurts or causes discomfort. Say you get in everywhere you applied, where would you go?"

"Brown. It has to be Brown. But I don't think that I'll hear until April. It's horrible waiting. I wish that I had applied early decision. I have two friends who have known where they're going since January."

"It must be tough waiting—not knowing."

"I hate it. I call my mother every day from school to see if anything came in the mail. But I've only heard from my back-up school and I don't want to go there."

"Where's there?"

"Tufts University."

"What's wrong with Tufts? It's an excellent school."

"It's okay, but it's not Brown."

"It seems to me you're putting a lot of pressure on yourself."

"Not me. It's this horrible system. They make you wait and wait. Most of my friends are going crazy too."

"So, how's this affecting your schoolwork?"

"What schoolwork? I'm a second semester senior. I can goof off as much as I want. I'm having a blast, but at the same time there's something really sad about it."

"How so?" I asked, continuing my examination as we talked.

"I've been with these friends so long, some of them since kindergarten, and in just a few months we'll all be going our own way."

"It's a big change, all right. I'm not surprised that you're having stomachaches and feeling run-down. You're under a tremendous amount of stress."

"Stress? I'm having fun this year. Last year was a hundred times more stressful."

"Well, in the short conversation we just had, you told me that the only college for you in the whole world is Brown, but you don't yet know if you can go there. If that weren't stressful enough, in a matter of months you will be leaving all your friends, the people you've been close to since you were five. I'd have a stomachache if I were you."

"Yeah?"

I nodded my head. "We see a lot of kids going through the same thing you're going through."

"So what do I do to feel better?"

"First of all, take it easy on yourself. I hear how much you want to go to Brown, but all the schools you applied to have excellent reputations. Don't make it the end of the world if you don't get into Brown. You're starting to anticipate leaving your friends and family and, of course, you're feeling sad. That's perfectly normal. It's a huge step you're taking and you should treat it as such. If you want to talk to a counselor, I can help with that. You have an exciting but stressful year ahead of you. You need to recognize that and be good to yourself."

"That's it?" she asked.

"I don't know what else to tell you. If you weren't feeling this way I would be worried about you. You're responding normally to the situation you're in. You just haven't recognized it as stress. Now that you know what's going on and that you're A-OK physically, you might start feeling better. But it will be the talking about it and being good to yourself that will really help. If you still have these symptoms call me and we'll see what else we can do for you."

I heard from Janine twice more before her graduation. The first was an appointment. Her physical symptoms had improved but were still present. The second call came in mid-April. She had gotten into Brown and, miraculously, all of her physical symptoms disappeared, helped along, I believe, by the fact that not only was she going to her first-choice school, but one of her best friends would be attending Brown along with her.

For the vast majority of teens, going off to college is their first big separation from their parents and families. This can be a very frightening and challenging time. It's important for parents to try to understand what their almost-but-not-quite-grown children are going through and be supportive without being intrusive.

It's critical to let the child/young adult know their home is still there for them. With this in mind, I would caution parents to fight the natural urge to clear out their collegian's newly vacated room and turn it into a den, sewing room, or office. Doing this will, no doubt, make your child feel somewhat unwelcome.

As their offspring go off to college, many parents feel like they're losing their child, that their job as a parent is done. The truth is if they have fulfilled their responsibilities—nurtured and imparted a sense of the workings of the world so the child can now become independent and evolve into an adult—then they are, indeed, almost done—at least with this phase of being a parent. And as it's a bittersweet time for me when my patients outgrow me (which some don't do until they're practically ready to have their own kids), I'm sure for most parents it's also a time of ambivalence—joy and pride, tinged with a sense of sadness and loss.

5

If You Could See What I See

All parents have a set picture of what and who their child is and it's often devastating to have that image challenged. It takes a lot of courage to be realistic about recognizing problems and addressing them.

Lena Kalkoff was always concerned about her eighteen-month-old son, Alexander's, eating habits, or lack thereof. "He never eats anything," she would moan to me at every visit. "I don't know how he survives." Then I would show her how he was in the fiftieth percentile in weight, which was perfect for his height, and she would exclaim again, "But he never eats!"

Then I would say to her, "Take the bottle away from him. He doesn't eat because he's getting all his calories from milk. He's too full of milk to have an appetite for food."

"But he loves his bottle," she would say. This was certainly true. I had been taking care of Alexander since his birth. I had even circumcised him at his bris, and I couldn't recall ever seeing him without a bottle hanging out of his mouth. So Lena and I would play out this tired scene at every visit. And at every visit Alexander would show up with the bottle planted firmly in his mouth.

I had my own concerns about Alexander. There was something not quite right about his development. He wasn't making eye contact. He never smiled. And he didn't seem to be forming a strong bond with his mother. At every visit I would attempt to discuss this with Lena. She would brush me off. "Dr. Weinberger, Alexander is just fine. He's only like this when we're here. You wait until next time."

When Lena brought Alexander in for his eighteen-month examination I knew that my intervention could no longer wait until the next time, but I also knew that I would have to move slowly.

Alexander was a very busy boy, wandering around the room, his almost white hair sticking out wildly from his head, but he would not talk, nor make eye contact with anyone. He would touch everything as he hurried around, but he was unable to engage himself with anything or anybody, including his own mother.

I was also concerned that he had no words yet. However, he did seem to understand everything that his mother and I said to him. "Lena, I am very concerned about Alexander. If he doesn't start speaking a few words in the next couple of months I'll need to see him," I told Lena, "and if you don't call me, I'm going to call you. This is very important. Do you understand?" Without taking her eyes off her son, she nodded.

Three months later I got a call from Lena. "You said that you wanted to see Alexander if he still wasn't speaking and . . ." She paused.

"He's still not speaking?" I offered.

"No," she replied, beginning to sound alarmed.

"No words at all?" I asked.

"None," she said.

"What about when he's playing with other kids?"

"He doesn't play with other kids. He just goes off on his own."

"Bring him in," I told her. "We'll check him out."

Alexander didn't acknowledge me in any way when I walked into the examining room. He was wandering aimlessly around, touching everything in his path.

"Alexander, come on over here. I have some questions to ask you."

He didn't respond. He looked toward—but not directly at—his mother, then pointed at a little plastic car that was left on the desk, and let out an animal-like whine. His mother immediately went to get it for him. "Is that the only way he has of asking for what he wants?" I asked her.

"That's right. The only time he tries to communicate is when he wants something," Lena replied, as she got the car off the desk for him. He looked at it for a split second, then let it drop to the floor as he went on to something else.

I kneeled in front of Alexander and tried to look into his deep blue eyes, but he wouldn't allow me to make eye contact. I held him gently by the shoulders. He looked all around me but never eye-to-eye. "Alexander, where's your nose?" There was no response. "Hey, pal, can you point to your nose for me?" Still no response.

"Does he know any of the parts of the body?" I asked his mother.

"I don't know. I don't think so. Should he know the body parts?" she said, her voice tight. I nodded.

"Alexander, what's this?" I asked, pointing to his nose. No response. "Come on, Alexander, I've got one too," I said, pointing to my nose. Again there was no response.

"Where's your tummy?" I tried again. Alexander had already lost interest. I let him squirm away from me.

"What does he respond to?" I asked his mother.

"Well . . ." Lena had to think hard to come up with something that interested Alexander. "He loves to listen to music—particularly country and western music. He even dances when it comes on the radio."

"Really?" I said.

I picked the toy car up off the floor where Alexander had dropped it and tried to hand it to him. "Alexander, would you please give this car to Mommy?" Alexander took the car, but made no move to give it to his mother.

"Alexander, give Mommy the car," Lena said in a strained voice. She was getting very anxious.

Again Alexander simply dropped the car on the floor and went to examine the stool I had just vacated.

"I guess he really doesn't follow directions yet," Lena reluctantly admitted.

I just nodded. With each task I tried to get Alexander to perform I became more and more concerned. These were all things that Alexander should have been mastering. He should have been speaking and following simple directions. He should have been able to identify parts of the body. He should have been able to better communicate his needs and focus on a myriad of activities. Something was very wrong with Alexander's development, something that couldn't be fixed by simply getting rid of a baby bottle.

There is no easy way to tell parents that there might be something wrong with their child. I don't know any other way than straight out. I wasn't about to guess what might be stifling Alexander's development. So all I could do was tell Lena what the next step would be in finding out, then help her get that assistance, answer her questions, and reassure her as best I could.

I sat down again, across from her, and looked into her troubled eyes. I took a deep breath and spoke as slowly and calmly as possibly. "Developmentally, Alexander is not in the range where he should be. I'm concerned because of his lack of speech and his inability to relate socially." I watched Lena's face go into a deep frown, but she remained silent. "I'm going to set up an appointment for a hearing test and speech evaluation, and I strongly recommend that Alexander have a complete evaluation so we can pinpoint exactly what might be slowing his development. Then we can get some recommendations for ways to help him. I'd like to set you up with a pediatric neurologist. He'll be able to coordinate the tests, interpret and explain the results, and help coordinate whatever help we need."

I paused for a moment to let it all sink in. Despite my trying to prepare her, I knew what a blow this must be. I looked at her and waited to see if she had anything to say. She just sat there, looking distraught and stunned. I continued. "I can't answer every question that you might have at this point, but I'd like to try."

Lena took a deep breath and looked across the room at Alexander, who was still flitting around the room, bottle hanging out of his mouth, not the least bit interested in what we were doing. "I don't even know what to ask. I know you thought there was a problem but I just didn't believe you, and now you're talking neurologists. I don't know what to ask. I don't even know what to think."

"Well, I'm sure many questions will come to you and your husband as you discuss this and talk to the neurologist, and I'm here to help you pull it all together. So please don't hesitate to call."

"Do you think Alexander will be well, you know . . . normal?"

"I think we should wait and see what the tests tell us. Whatever is going on, we will do everything we can to help Alexander, and to help you and your husband deal with all this."

Shortly after Alexander had the tests, both Lena and Mr. Kalkoff met with me to discuss the neurologist's report.

"I can't really say that there are any surprises in the report. It says that Alexander is developing atypically. We knew that much. Now we have a name for it. The neurologist calls it autism. The good news is that he feels with early intervention—with speech and language and occupational therapy—Alexander can be helped."

"Why does he have this—autism?" Mr. Kalkoff asked.

"We don't really know why. I wish I could give you an answer."

"I've given this a lot of thought, Dr. Weinberger, and I think Alexander is just a little behind. I think if we just give him a chance, maybe he'll catch up on his own." Lena sounded scared and angry at the same time.

"I wish I could agree with you, but I think that Alexander's problems are more serious than that. He will need a special preschool and therapy: occupational and speech and language."

"Do you really think that Alexander needs all that?" Mr. Kalkoff asked, looking stunned. He took off his glasses and rubbed his eyes. "I remember my mother saying that I was a slow baby. Maybe Alexander just inherited that from me."

"Yes, he is developing slowly, but so slowly that he will need this extra support. I know it's hard to accept. But I feel that Alexander definitely needs all these extras and the neurologist feels that way too."

There was a long moment of silence, and then Lena asked slowly and carefully, "Will Alexander ever catch up? Will he ever be a normal child?"

"I certainly hope so. Because of your concern and early intervention, I think he should do well, but ultimately we'll just have to wait and see how Alexander does when he gets the help he needs."

We talked for two hours and in the end the Kalkoffs agreed to look into specialized preschools that could benefit Alexander.

Alexander's new school reported he was making slow but steady progress. They too were concerned with his overall developmental delays but they felt that they could continue to help him.

Three months later, Lena came in for a consultation. "Dr. Weinberger, I have wonderful news. Alexander is making eye contact. I think he's on his way now. I want to take him out of that school. I want to put him in a regular school."

"It's wonderful that Alexander is making eye contact but I feel that, if anything, it's an indicator that he should stick with the program. He still has a ways to go and, as you can see by the fact that he is making the eye contact, the school *is* helping him."

Lena became very upset. I suddenly felt like I was facing a bear protecting her cub. "I don't like Alexander going to that school. Everyone, including Alexander himself, will think that he's not normal."

It was so clear to me what Alexander needed, but so hard for Lena to be objective about her own son. I didn't want to be harsh, but I had to speak for Alexander. I had to be his advocate. "I understand how you feel. This must be very hard for you and your husband, but you must do what's right for Alexander. He needs this program." She hesitantly agreed.

Two months later Lena was back for another consultation. "Alexander is speaking now," she announced proudly. I could sense what was coming.

"Really? That's a breakthrough. How many words?"

"Just a couple," she replied, "but he uses them correctly." She paused. "I'm withdrawing him from the school." She couldn't look me in the eye.

"It's really wonderful that he's talking. He's starting to make progress but he needs to stay where he is and get further help."

"Yes, yes, yes . . ." she assured me, waving at the air like I was some annoying bug.

We talked for a while longer, mostly about Alexander not being, what she called normal, and then she went on her way.

I was surprised and saddened the next day when Lena called to have Alexander's records transferred to another pediatrician. I could only hope that he would stand up for Alexander and what he needed, and encourage the Kalkoffs to keep Alexander in the programs that would help him continue to progress.

Maybe I had been too hard on Lena. But as a pediatrician there is hardly anything more difficult than trying to get parents to look at their child objectively. All parents have a set picture of what and who their child is and it's often devastating to have that image challenged. It takes a lot of courage to be realistic about recognizing problems and addressing them. It's truly one of the hardest jobs of parenting. I hoped that in time Lena Kalkoff and her husband would be able to do that for the benefit of Alexander.

"What's up with Ian Edwards?" I asked Bert. Everyone in the general vicinity of the office always knew when Ian came in. He was a twelve-year-old whose severe mental retardation caused him to behave with the abundant, exuberant energy of a three-year-old.

"I suspect that he might be hyperthyroid. We're running tests to find out for sure."

"Really?" I responded.

"Yep, he's lost a lot of weight in a short amount of time and he's occasionally soiling himself. You know I give the Edwards family a lot of credit for calling about this. It would have been very easy for them to blame at least the soiling on Ian's mental state. But they're really on the ball when it comes to any changes in his habits or health."

The Edwardses were right to bring in Ian, and Bert's theory proved correct. The tests did show that Ian was suffering from hyperthyroid disease—an overfunctioning thyroid. Bert prescribed the appropriate treatment course and kept a close eye on Ian. It didn't take long for Ian's weight to return to normal and for the soiling to stop completely.

With Bert's help the Edwardses continued to both meet Ian's special needs and appropriately challenge him, as they had always done. Bert had helped them get Ian into special classes and Ian took a tremendous amount of pride in eventually receiving a "diploma" for finishing twelve years of schooling.

Ian developed a passion for electronics—radio-powered cars and trucks and anything with lots of buttons, whistles, and bells. So when he was in his late teens his parents helped him get a job in a small neighborhood electronics store where he cleaned and did an occasional odd job, and—most importantly—was treated with kindness and respect by the owners and other employees.

Bert continued to see Ian into young adulthood and was always a source of information, support, and help for the Edwardses as they helped Ian reach his full potential.

"Hello, Dr. Weinberger? This is Stephen Rawlins—Jenny and Peter Timmons's stepfather."

"What can I do for you, Mr. Rawlins?" I asked, thinking how odd it was that Mr. Rawlins would be calling. In the five years I had taken care of Jenny and Peter I had never met this man.

"I know you probably think it's strange that I'm calling, but I didn't know what else to do. Jenny came home from a summer trip about a week ago with something very wrong with her."

"What do you mean?" I asked.

"She's not herself. Even Peter commented that it's like someone else is living in Jenny's body. I know Jenny has fooled around with drugs, and I think that might have something to do with this, but I don't know—she's just so quiet and withdrawn.

"Peter said they went out for lunch, and Jenny couldn't even decide what to order. Peter finally had to order for her." That was alarming. Jenny was sixteen and Peter fourteen, and as long as I had known them she had always been the leader.

"What does Pat think?" I asked, wondering why his wife, Pat, hadn't been the one to call.

"Pat insists that Jenny's just going through a phase. She won't believe anything's wrong. It's like she's blind to Jenny. But . . . could she be right? Is that possible? I have to admit I'm not really all that close to the kids. So maybe I'm the one who's way off base."

"No, I think you're right—something's going on, especially if she's been fooling around with drugs. Do you think you can get her to come in this morning?"

"I think so. I'll have to convince Pat though. Peter could help with that. He's very alarmed too. He was in tears after their lunch."

I was surprised to find Peter in the examining room with Jenny. It had been years since they had stayed in the room during each other's exams.

"Hi, Jenny. I'm glad you came in today," I said. "Your dad was very concerned about you."

"Stepdad," Jenny and Peter said in unison.

"Stepdad," I repeated. "Well, he's very worried about you."

Jenny nodded slightly. She looked down at her hands, folded in her lap, her long blond hair hiding her face. Peter nervously twisted a button.

"Peter, why don't you go on out to the waiting room so I can have some time with Jenny," I suggested.

"I want him to stay," Jenny said quietly from under the veil of her hair.

"You sure you want him in here for your examination?" I asked gently.

"I thought we were just going to talk today. Stephen said we were just going to talk," she said in a shaky voice—near tears.

"He promised her no exam," Peter added, looking very concerned for his sister.

"Okay, no exam today," I assured her. "But we need to find out what's going on with you. Can you tell me how you feel?" I didn't want to push her too much in her obviously fragile state.

"I just feel tired—very, very tired," she said quietly.

"Do you have any appetite?" I asked.

She answered with a shrug.

"She hasn't eaten much since she got back from her trip," Peter responded for her.

"How about sleep? Are you sleeping all right?"

Again Jenny just shrugged.

"She sleeps all the time," Peter responded again.

She didn't need Peter there just for support. This normally talkative, outgoing, funny kid was in such a depression that she couldn't seem to answer even the simplest question for herself.

But I kept trying. "Jenny, have you been using any drugs or alcohol?" I found that sometimes patients were very candid with me about this.

Another shrug.

I looked at Peter. He was scowling down at his shoe, clearly not knowing what to say. He shot a look up at me, frowned, and looked back down at his shoe. I didn't want to press him or Jenny. I could tell from Peter's demeanor what the answer was.

"Jenny, I'm going to give your stepdad the name of a doctor who can help you. It's really important that you try to talk to this woman. Okay?"

This time I didn't even get a shrug.

"Jenny will talk to her. Right, Jen?" Peter said, standing up and going to her.

She looked at him, smiled faintly, and nodded.

I walked the two of them out to the waiting room, where their stepfather was nervously flipping through a magazine. He stood up when he saw us coming.

"Mr. Rawlins," I held out my hand. "Norman Weinberger." We shook hands. "Can I speak with you a moment?" He followed me to the consultation office. "You were right about Jenny. She definitely needs help. She appears to be in a deep depression. I don't know what part drugs and alcohol play in this, but from Peter's reaction when I asked, I'm sure there's some involvement."

"So, what do I do now?" he asked.

"I'm going to give you the name of a psychiatrist. I think she'll be a good match for Jennifer. She does a lot of work with drug rehab patients and adolescents in general." I wrote down the name and number for him. "What about Pat? Is she any more open to accepting Jenny's condition?"

"After a lot of discussion she finally agreed to listen to whatever you had to say. I think she figured you'd give Jenny a clean bill of health. She's that much in denial."

We talked for a while longer.

"If you need me to speak with Pat, I will. If not, please just keep me informed about what's happening with Jenny. Don't hesitate to call if there's anything else I can do for any of you."

About a week later I got a call from Pat Rawlins.

"Dr. Weinberger, Stephen said he promised to keep you updated on Jenny. I wanted to be the one to call so I could thank you. You must have thought it was strange to get that call from Stephen.

"I don't know what was wrong with me, but I just couldn't see how troubled Jenny was. I just couldn't admit that something could really be wrong with her. She's sixteen, but she's still my baby. And now she's hospitalized for depression and drug dependency. The psychiatrist said that she was suicidal. If Stephen hadn't intervened she might have killed herself. I just can't believe I couldn't see it. How could I have missed all the signs?" She sounded like she was struggling not to cry.

"Please don't beat yourself up over this," I tried to comfort her. "The important thing is that she's in a place where she'll get the help she needs. I find it's not unusual for parents to miss the signs their children give when they're in trouble. Sometimes it takes someone with more objectivity, more distance—a teacher, or aunt or stepparent—to catch the signs. In this case we were all lucky your husband and Peter could see there was a problem, and take the action to help Jenny."

"The doctor suggested that we all go for family counseling. She said when a child is using drugs and alcohol to the extent Jenny was, it's a sign of much deeper problems. She said this could be a lengthy process, but we're prepared to do anything to help Jenny."

It did turn out to be a lengthy process for the Timmons-Rawlins family. Jenny spent three months in a psychiatric hospital going through rehab and intensive therapy. After her release from the hospital she continued with therapy and the twelve-step program that she had begun in the hospital. The entire family saw a family therapist once a week, at first to get the support they needed to help Jenny, and later on to work on the many issues that had led to Jenny's problems.

Two years later, almost to the day, Jenny came in for a pre-college checkup. Now she certainly didn't need Peter to speak for her. She had, once again, become the happy, funny, outgoing girl I knew.

Ten-year-old Natalie Genger had been my patient since she was two. Natalie had spent the last three years watching her parents go through one of the most bitter divorces I had ever witnessed. Donald Genger, a high-powered executive with a major insurance company, and Gerri Genger, a boutique owner, couldn't even decide who would have custody of Natalie. In fact it seemed to me that instead of fighting over who would get custody, they were fighting over who wouldn't have to have custody. Between the divorce wars and their careers, they seemed to have little time for Natalie.

I rarely saw Natalie and when she did come in, she was usually with one of a parade of live-in sitters who hadn't bothered bringing her in until the ear infection was draining or the strep throat was raging.

It had been almost two years since I had seen Natalie. But on this day, Gerri was with Natalie. She had brought her on a Saturday morning for a school checkup, the school having finally threatened to bar Natalie from class until they received updated health records and inoculations.

Natalie was alone in the examining room—in a ten-year-old fit of modesty, she had banished her mother from the examining room. I was surprised when I saw her. She was a beautiful child, but now her green-gray eyes were almost lost in her bloated face. Her red hair was disheveled and dirty, her nails were bitten down to the quick, and she was wearing a very worn-out T-shirt and sweatpants. She had put on twenty pounds.

I hid my surprise and greeted her. "Hi, Natalie. Long time no see. How're you doing?"

"I'm not sick or anything. I just have to have my checkup for school."

"I know. That's what your mom said when she made the

appointment. So," I said, sitting in front of her, on the stool, "how're you doing in school?"

"Not great, I guess. Fifth grade is kind of hard."

"Do you have a lot of homework?"

"Too much for me to do."

"Does Mom help you?" Mom currently had custody.

"No, she's out most nights. Sometimes Vivian tries to help me but she doesn't speak English very well." Natalie spoke in a quiet monotone.

"Is Vivian your sitter?"

"Uh-huh." I started to examine her, talking to her the whole time.

"What other activities do you do?"

"Nothing much."

"Well, what do you do after school?"

"Watch TV."

"TV hmm? Who's your best friend?"

"No one. Well, it used to be Jessica Freund, but now she's best friends with Stephanie and Christine Cooper. They're twins."

"No new best friend, then?"

"No," she responded sadly. I continued to examine her.

"What TV shows do you like?"

"I like just about everything, except the news."

"How many hours a day do you think you watch TV?" I had the feeling that Natalie was doing little else when she wasn't in school.

"I watch all the time, I guess. I don't know how many hours."

"What about books or friends or playing outside, or piano lessons, or swim lessons?" I asked her. She looked at me blankly and shrugged her shoulders.

"Will I have to have a shot?" she asked, changing the subject.

I looked at her chart. "Looks that way, kiddo. We'll get it over with quickly. Then you can wait for your mom in the waiting room. I want to talk to her for a minute."

Natalie rolled up her sleeve and took the shot without

much upset. Apparently she had outgrown the ear-splitting tantrums I remembered from her earlier days.

I walked her out into the waiting room. Her mother immediately started to put on her coat. "Excuse me, Mrs. Genger. Do you have a minute? I'd like to speak with you in the conference room." She looked questioningly at Natalie, then followed me into the room. "Have a seat," I offered. She sat down, coat still on.

"Is there a problem? Natalie seems perfectly healthy."

"Her health is fine. How does Natalie seem to you otherwise?" I asked.

"Well, now that things have settled down I think she's never been happier. She's not a great student, if that's what you're getting at, but it doesn't seem to bother her. In fact I wish it would bother her more."

"What about friends and activities?"

"What about them?" I could feel her getting defensive.

"Natalie tells me she doesn't have a best friend and she spends most of her time watching television. Does Natalie play with other kids very often?"

"I'm not around after school during the week," Mrs. Genger said. She thought a moment. "Whenever I call the house—I do call every afternoon—Natalie is always home but she never has company. On the weekend when I am with her, it's always just the two of us. Now next month we're planning to have a birthday party for her, but she hasn't told me yet who she wants to invite."

"When was the last time she was invited to a birthday party?" I tried to ask gently.

"I honestly can't remember," Mrs. Genger answered, looking embarrassed. "Maybe she's just going through a phase. Kids go through phases like this all the time, right?"

"I don't think it's a phase," I told her. "Has Natalie ever had any professional counseling? You know, with the divorce and the custody changes, it's a lot for a child to handle."

"No!" she replied, obviously insulted. "Natalie hasn't needed any counseling. She's a happy child. She always has a smile on her face."

"It seems to me to be a nervous smile, not a happy one. I'm concerned about Natalie. You see there are several signs Natalie is displaying of depression and isolation."

"Don't be ridiculous. She's ten years old."

"Believe me, ten-year-olds get depressed. Her weight gain for instance is an indicator that something's not right. That alone wouldn't concern me, but she admittedly has no friends. She spends almost all of her nonschool time in front of the television. The clothes she has on are totally worn out—"

"Those are the only clothes she'll wear," Mrs. Genger said defensively.

"What do you mean?"

"For more than six months she's worn that T-shirt and those sweats every day. Our housekeeper washes them each night when she takes them off, and Natalie puts them back on in the morning."

"Why would you allow that?"

"It started when she was living with her father. Vivian, the housekeeper, says it's easier than arguing with her. Natalie can be very stubborn."

"Well, the clothes are certainly another sign there's a problem."

"So, you're saying my kid needs a shrink?"

"I'm saying that Natalie is doing everything she can to tell you that she needs help. I can give you the name of a couple of good therapists who specialize in working with children."

"I'm sure Natalie is just in a stage and all of this will work itself out soon now that everything is settled. If it doesn't, I'll give you a call and get the referrals." She stood up to leave.

"Mrs. Genger, I think Natalie is showing signs of being at risk. Why don't we do something now, rather than wait until she's more depressed and isolated."

"Because I'm her mother, and that's how I want it," she replied in a nasty voice and walked out.

"Damn," I thought to myself, "I should have been less direct, and moved more slowly." But would it have made a difference? Here was a woman who thought her daughter was happier than she had ever been, when she was clearly depressed, clearly isolated and alone, and she didn't want to see any of this. Was there anything I could have done or said that would have made Mrs. Genger see her daughter objectively and get her the help she needed?

My question was answered three weeks later. I had a message to call Mrs. Genger with some referrals of child psychologists. I immediately called her back.

"Mrs. Genger, I have three names for you. I think that any of them will be able to help Natalie."

"Thank you. I appreciate the referrals. I also apologize for the way that I spoke to you. You were right. Natalie does need help. I got a call from her school yesterday and had to go in for a conference. They also recommended that she get help. Aside from simply not doing any of her work, she's been stealing things from the other children and acting very immature. I don't know how I could have missed all of this.

"When I went into her room last night there were all these little things on her desk—plastic bracelets and a necklace and a ten-color pen—all things that her teacher told me had been missing from her classmates. When I asked Natalie where she got them she told me that her father had given them to her. I knew he hadn't. I can't believe my daughter has been stealing from her classmates."

"Did you tell her that you know where they came from?" I asked.

"Yes. And she went into a rage. She wanted to know why I hadn't noticed the things before. She said they'd been sitting on her desk for weeks. You were right. She was trying to let me know that she was hurting."

"Well, now she'll get the help she needs."

"I know. But how could I have thought she was so happy when she was clearly miserable?"

"This isn't unusual, Mrs. Genger. Parents all want and expect their children to be happy. Sometimes we just see what we want to see. You know it's very difficult for all of us to see our children objectively. And even when we do see a problem, it's hard to turn to a professional for help. We feel like we've failed when we send our kids to a psychologist, but that's not failure. On the contrary, we're doing our best and most conscientious parenting when we follow through and get our children the help they need."

Little did I know that soon those words would come to mean even more to me.

There's something about sitting in an almost empty classroom, folded into a too-small desk, and waiting to talk to the teacher—any teacher—that makes you sweat. Even if it doesn't bring back every single memory of being asked to wait behind when your class is dismissed, or being sent down to the principal's office, it certainly evokes that feeling of "Uh-oh I'm going to get it now."

On this particular occasion, Susan and I were sitting in Gordon's fifth-grade classroom waiting for his teacher, Miss Lynch. Here it was, only one week until school let out and we were called in for a conference.

"There's no reason to be nervous," I told myself. "Gordon's only eleven. What could he possibly have done. They probably just want to discuss his placement for next year."

Miss Lynch rushed into the room, apologized for being late, and sat across from us at her huge teacher desk. I shifted in my seat, pushing my legs and feet out from under the desk, into the aisle.

"Well, let's see how our boy Gordon is doing," she said in her teacher voice and opened a thick folder. "Gordon gets along with the other children. He never disrupts the class. He's really a joy, but I think there is a problem," she said, looking extremely uncomfortable.

Suddenly I got that strange feeling in my stomach. It was the same as the feeling you get when you see flashing police lights in your rearview mirror. Susan looked over at me. She looked how I felt. I managed a weak smile at her.

"A problem?" I asked.

"In general, schoolwork is a problem for Gordon. I'm sure you've noticed this."

"Well, yes," I admitted. "His homework is taking an awfully long time for him to complete. It's very frustrating for him. And the rest of the family as well," I said, thinking of the scene we had almost every night as we struggled with Gordon, struggling with his work.

"That's what we're seeing here too. In the last month or so, as the work has become more demanding and he's been expected to work more independently, he's fallen behind. I decided to take a look at his file. I thought that his test scores from the last few years might hold the key to his problem." She paused and looked at us for a moment with a strange expression on her face. "Well, there were no test scores. It seems that with the random testing method we've used here, Gordon has fallen between the cracks."

"Random testing? You mean not all the students are tested every year?" I asked.

"That's right," Susan said. "Only one third of each class is tested each year. But Gordon should have been tested two or three times by now."

"You mean he's never had any standardized testing at all? How could that happen? Don't they keep track?" I asked, shocked.

"Of course they're supposed to. I'm sorry . . . I don't know what happened," Miss Lynch said apologetically. "But I feel that Gordon should have a more comprehensive battery of tests than we give at school, anyway. He's obviously an intelligent boy, but there is something going on, and we have to find out what it is so that we can give Gordon the appropriate help." She ended with a little sigh. It was clear how difficult this was for her, sharing her assessment of Gordon with us, and I was reminded how difficult it was for me to share this kind of news with parents.

She continued. "I don't think we should wait on this. Middle school is even more demanding than fifth grade."

Middle school! It was a major effort to get Gordon through his fifth-grade homework each night. The thought of middle school homework terrified me.

"I want to show you some of his work." She pulled several papers out of the file. I immediately recognized Gordon's distinct messy handwriting. She laid two papers out in front of us, both covered with red marks. "This one is from October and this one is from last month. You can see he's having a great deal more difficulty with the recent assignment."

Susan and I stared down at the mess that was our son's schoolwork. Did I feel surprise? Only that the school had, for five years, overlooked the fact that Gordon hadn't been tested. But there was no surprise that he had fallen behind and that he needed help. There was concern and worry and sadness, but I had to admit—no surprise.

As we left school I tried to put aside my anger at the school for their testing blunder and focus on Gordon and how we could best help him. "What do you think?" I asked Susan, trying to look at her and the road at the same time.

"I'm wondering why we didn't do something about Gordon's schoolwork before now. You and I both knew that something wasn't right."

"That's pretty much what I was thinking," I replied sadly.

With this dilemma haunting us we went off to vacation in Rhode Island for the first few weeks of summer. While the children dug for clams and collected seashells, Susan and I discussed Gordon and his problems, and what we needed to do to help him.

"Maybe we're wrong. Maybe he just needs a little time to come into his own," I suggested hopefully.

Susan shook her head. We sat in silence for some time.

Finally she spoke in a quiet voice. "Norman, what would you do if this was one of your patients?"

"That's easy. If this was one of my patient families, I know exactly what I would advise."

"And what would that be?"

"I would refer them to a psychologist, someone who specializes in learning difficulties."

"Oh!" Susan said. She sounded as if she had been punched.

I felt it too. Sending Gordon to a psychologist felt like such a black mark against our parenting. It felt like we had failed. Then I remembered what I had told Mrs. Genger and I knew that it was the right thing to do, that it was the best possible parenting we could do. Now I better understood what many of my families went through. It was so hard to look at your children objectively and give them what they needed.

"How will we explain this to Gordon?" Susan asked, watching him happily play in the waves.

"I think that we'll just have to put this in the category of it's-for-your-own-good."

As soon as we returned, Susan, through her connections at the university, found a highly recommended psychologist, Dr. Jerome Schiller, an expert in education.

We carefully planned how to explain Dr. Schiller to Gordon. We sat Gordon down in the family room and I said, "Gordon, we have an appointment on Thursday with a very special doctor. He's a doctor who helps kids who are having some trouble with their schoolwork. Mom and I felt that he might be able to help you." I waited for the explosion.

"Okay," he said.

"Okay. That's it?" Susan said, a smile slowly spreading across her face.

"Yeah. Okay. I think I need help too."

Of course, Gordon would know better than anybody that he needed help.

So, off we went to Dr. Schiller loaded with all of Gordon's records, which Susan had liberated from the school. After going over the records and talking to all of us, we agreed that Gordon would be tested.

To no one's surprise the tests indicated that Gordon was behind in several areas, but the area that he seemed to be having the biggest problem with was organizational skills. Simply put, Gordon was having trouble getting himself together—so much so that he was constantly stressed and worried, trying to deal with his responsibilities.

Gordon spent sixth grade going to an educational psychologist, Dr. Margaret Deignan. Together they spent two hours a week going over Gordon's schoolwork, with the doctor teaching Gordon how to organize his schoolwork and time. The results were immediate and gratifying and by the last quarter of sixth grade, a very proud Gordon made the honor roll.

While Gordon had learned to organize himself, Susan and I had learned to trust our instincts about our children and we pledged to try to continue to be objective about our kids. I learned what it felt like to be on the parent end of recognizing problems and seeking help, and that, in turn, helped me be more understanding of the difficulties my patients' parents had in acknowledging problems and seeking help.

6

A Day in the Life

"When did this happen?" I thought to myself. The wait-
ing room was jam-packed, the phones ringing, and all
the examining rooms were full. How long had it been
that every single moment of my day was filled?

By 7:00 A.M. Friday, I was at the hospital making my rounds.
I examined Jonah Frietag. Jonah was two days old, and doing
quite well. His birth had been, medically speaking, uneventful.
Although I'm sure it was viewed as quite an event by his family. I weighed him. He was back up to his birth weight
already—obviously feeding well. I went down the hall to see
his mother, Phyllis. She was sitting up comfortably in bed,
watching television.

"I've got some good news for you. Jonah's doing great.
How'd you like to take him home?" I said cheerily, waiting for
the usual happy response this announcement brings.

"Well, I talked to Dr. Grossman yesterday, and he said there
was really no rush," she said.

"That's right. No rush. You can take him home tonight, or
you can wait till tomorrow morning. It's up to you."

"Then next Wednesday would be most convenient for us,"
she said casually. I looked at her closely. Unbelievably, she was
serious. At this point in time a three-day stay in the hospital
was the average following a normal birth, assuming both

mother and baby were fine and healthy. This gave the mother a chance to recuperate from giving birth and be instructed in the care and feeding of her newborn. After three days, most mothers were anxious to return home to begin adjusting to and enjoying their new offspring.

"Well, that's not at all convenient for us. There's absolutely no reason to keep a healthy, thriving baby in the hospital. And there's no way your insurance company would ever allow it," I said, wanting to add, "Hey this isn't the Ritz, take your kid and go home!"

"Oh yes. We called the insurance company and they said it would be fine to stay."

"I've never heard of an insurance company doing that," I said, thinking, "Let me take you upstairs for a full psychological exam since you're obviously delusional." "Look," I said, "I can understand if you're not organized for today, but you and the baby really need to go home by tomorrow evening."

"I don't know. Let me talk to my husband. Why don't you give me a call around—"

I interrupted her. "No, you call me. I'll be at the office all day." I quickly left, happy to get out of there before I blew up at this incredibly trying woman.

I finished my rounds and hurried to the office, knowing my first patients were already waiting for me.

I opened the door of the examining room. Two-year-old Carrie Rosen was playing on the floor. She had come in for her two-year checkup.

"Good morning, Carrie," I said enthusiastically.

She looked up at me from the floor. Her eyes turned into huge saucers, and she let out a tremendous howl. "Noooo, Mamamamama, noooooo!" she sobbed. Her mother picked her up and Carrie clung to her.

"I don't know what's going on," her mother shouted over Carrie's head and the din. "She's never reacted like this. I'm sorry."

"It's no problem," I yelled back. "We'll get her calmed down.

"Carrie, hey Carrie. Have you seen my new bear?" I said, holding out my stethoscope with the teddy bear on it.

"Nooooo, Mamamamamama." I could see her fingers digging sharply into her mother's shoulders.

"Carrie, you want to listen to Mama's heart with my stethoscope? I only let my special patients do that," I coaxed.

She took a deep breath, and I thought for a split second that she might be settling down, but it was more like she was loading a cannon. "AHHHHHHHHHHH," she screamed.

I tried a few more of my tricks, but it quickly became clear that nothing was going to work with Carrie.

"Maybe we should try this another time?" her mother shouted, above her cries.

"No, let's just get it over with as quickly as possible," I said. "Hold on to her and I'll do what's necessary."

I quickly examined her while she moaned, cried, and screamed. I wondered if there was still anyone left in our waiting room. If I had been outside the door, I would have been certain someone was being tortured and fled.

I finished and stepped back from Carrie. "Hey, Carrie, that's it. We're all done. Now you can go home."

She immediately stopped crying. "Done?" she said, sniffling, as if the idea of it was too good to be true.

"Yes, all done," her mother assured her.

Slowly a sad little smile lit up her face. She looked up at me. "Kiss you goodbye?" she said, as if that would make up for the yelling and screaming and carrying on. And it would.

"A kiss goodbye from you, Carrie, would make my day," I said. I leaned over and she planted a big wet one on my cheek.

She slid off her mother's lap and went to the door, totally calm and happy. "Goo-bye," she waved, opened the door, and left.

"What was that all about?" her mother asked, getting ready to follow her out.

"Welcome to the wonderful world of a two-year-old," I said to her.

"No! She's not going to be like that?"

"Not always. But let's just say you shouldn't be surprised by any off-the-wall behavior for the next six months to a year. I would say she's right on schedule." I followed her out of the examining room. Down the hall, Carrie was attempting to leave the office. "You might want to hurry. You're being left behind."

"Sorry about the hysterics. Gotta go," and off she ran to keep up with her daughter.

Up front in the waiting room I spotted Megan Waters, a happy, active, adorable eighteen-month-old, admittedly one of my favorites. Looking at the schedule, I saw she was next, so instead of the nurse, I went to get her. "Megan Waters, my sweet, it's time for your exam."

"AHHHHHHHHHH," she screamed and flew into her mother's arms.

"Not this again," I thought.

Her mother, Eve, looked up at me, shocked.

"What's wrong with me today? Did I turn into some sort of monster during the night?" I asked Eve as we walked down to the examining room, a screaming Megan glued to her mother.

Eve sat down, Megan still clinging to her. She finally got Megan turned around. Megan looked like Niagara Falls—tears flowing, nose running, saliva dripping. The front of Eve's shirt was drenched.

I tried all my tricks all over again, and again there was no calming this child. She continued to drip and scream all over the place. I continued to speak gently to her, trying to calm her. Again the only solution was to get the exam over with as quickly as possible.

Finally it was over. Megan sat on her mother's lap, hiccuping and sniffling. I sat on my stool across the room, out of flood's danger. I was soaked. I held up my tie, pretending to wring it out. It was a bold colorful tie with a huge fish on it.

Megan, tears still streaming, nose at full flow, pointed to the tie, and said, "Glub glub." She made a face like a fish and then continued, "Glub, glub, glub, glub." Eve and I looked at each other and laughed.

I left Eve and Megan in the examining room with a box of tissues. As I went to my next patient I thought, "Today can only get better."

My next patient was little Alice Broderick. She was in for her two-week exam. In setting up the appointment, I suggested to Mrs. Broderick she bring her three-year-old son, Andrew, along. I had found that if I involve the older brother or sister in the exam, it alleviates some of their anxiety. My alliance with the older sibling seems to help them see the baby not only as nonthreatening, but in a dependent position that allows them to feel more in control.

Andrew came to my office well-prepared. "Dr. Weinberger," he said, hopping up and down with excitement, "I'm going to help you examine my sister." He held up his little Fisher-Price doctor bag as proof he was prepared for the job ahead.

"You certainly are. You stand on this stool, right next to the baby table, and help me examine your little sister." Andrew climbed up onto the stool and opened his bag to ready his instruments for whatever important procedures he would need to perform.

He pulled out a toy stethoscope and held it up proudly for my approval. "I've got a stethoscope just like you," he said, pronouncing stethoscope correctly, something I couldn't do until my early twenties.

He continued to pull out his bright yellow and blue plastic instruments, naming each instrument as he showed them to me. "This is my ophthalmoscope. This is my blood pressure cuff. This is a tongue depressor," he said holding up an unidentifiable piece of plastic.

"No," I told him, opening my storage drawer, pulling out a handful of tongue depressors and depositing them into his bag, "these are tongue depressors. These are Band-Aids . . ." I added a handful of Band-Aids to his bag, "and cotton balls, and gauze pads. You'll need those."

I went on adding things to Andrew's bag as he watched delightedly. "Thanks, oh thanks, Dr. Weinberger."

In the drawer, I finally came to a box of finger cots. Finger cots are little rubber covers that you place over your finger when applying rectal medication. I pulled out a couple and held them out to him. "These are special," I told him. "Your daddy will explain what they're for," I told him, knowing his dad was a psychiatrist and would get a kick out of it.

"Oh, he won't have to," Andrew insisted. "I already know what they are. Those are condominiums!"

I was right. The morning was improving.

My next patient was twelve-year-old Joree Bensinger. She was a very dramatic young lady who often came to visit me when there really wasn't much of anything wrong. "Hey, Joree, what's going on?" I said as I joined her in the examining room.

"Oh, Dr. Weinberger. I don't feel well at all. I'm real tired and I have a horrible sore throat . . ." Then she began to list her ailments in the organized way she always did. She even used headings. "*Pain*—back pain, headache, sore throat. *Food*—I ate a little breakfast this morning, but it made me feel yucky. Yesterday I couldn't even eat a whole strawberry. *Fever*—when I woke up this morning it was 98.2, but when I took it again before I came to see you it was 100.6."

"Well, Joree, it sounds like you might have strep throat. So we're going to take a culture." I took the culture, and while waiting for the result, felt a bunch of swollen glands on Joree's neck. The strep test turned out to be negative.

"You know, Joree, you don't have strep, but I think you might have mononucleosis."

"Oh God! I don't want to have mono!"

"I don't think you get to choose," I teased her. "Let's just do the test and find out what's going on."

Sure enough it came back positive. "Believe it or not, Joree, your symptoms are all real this time. It all fits—the fatigue and nausea and lack of appetite. Your aches and pains and sore throat—they're all symptoms of mono. Looks like you're going to have to stay home for a while."

She threw her arms around me. "YES!" she shouted happily.

"I'll want to see you at the end of next week, and then if everything is okay you can go back to school the following week, but you won't be able to take gym for six weeks."

She threw her arms around me again. "YES! Oh Yes! Thank you, Dr. Weinberger!"

"Well, I can't say I've ever seen anyone so happy about being sick, but I guess whatever floats your boat. Don't forget to make an appointment for next Thursday or Friday, and enjoy your week off."

"Don't worry, Dr. Weinberger, I will," she said happily.

Rushing through the narrow hall, knowing I was already behind schedule, I almost knocked Edith over. She didn't seem to notice. "Mrs. King and Danny are in room one. Danny has a fever of 101. She's panicking," Edith reported.

"Hi, Mrs. King. I hear Danny's a little under the weather."

"Oh, Dr. Weinberger. I'm so scared. Danny woke up with a fever of 103. Now it's 101 but he's burning up."

"Let's see. Danny's not quite two. Right?"

"That's right. He's twenty-two months."

"Is anything else going on with him? Has he vomited? Does he have diarrhea or a rash? Has he been pulling his ears or crying?"

"No," she replied, sounding a little more calm, "he's not doing any of those things."

Danny looked a little lethargic, but perfectly happy and comfortable sitting in his mother's lap.

I examined Danny thoroughly. "He doesn't seem to be in any distress, does he?" I asked.

"No, I guess not. But he has a fever."

"I know, fevers can be a scary thing for parents, but in a child Danny's age it's really nothing to worry about. Everyone's temperature goes up and down throughout the day, well or sick. There's really no need to worry. Fever is just the body's mechanism for fighting infection, and if there are no other symptoms, and your child has a somewhat normal activity level, then you can just give him some acetaminophen and observe him for other symptoms. Now if Danny were still an infant, say six months or younger, then I'd want to see him for a fever, but when they get to be big boys like Danny, unless there are symptoms accompanying the fever, you can take care of it at home."

She looked suspicious. She shook her head. She wasn't buying any of this.

"Really, Mrs. King, everything looks quite good. There are no other signs that would indicate a bacterial infection. I believe it's just a virus. Why don't you give him acetaminophen and fluids. Keep him comfortably undressed. Since there's no medication for viruses, we'll just have to let it run its course. But you should call me if there are any changes."

"No medicine!" Mrs. King responded incredulously. This appeared to be all she heard. "What do you mean no medicine? He's sick. There must be something you can give him other than the acetaminophen."

In my head I flashed back two years ago when Mrs. King and her husband came in for their prenatal consultation. Mr. and Mrs. King asked all the usual questions: "What medical school did you attend?" "Where were you trained?" "How do you feel about breast-feeding?" "How long have you been practicing?" etc., but then they asked, "What is your philosophy of medication?"

"I'm not sure what you mean," I responded. I had never been asked that one before.

"What are your feelings about using medications on babies and children. We wouldn't want to go to a pediatrician who uses too much medication."

I replied, "Oh, we wouldn't think of using too much medication. We use just enough."

And now she was all but begging me to medicate her son. This from the woman who wanted to make sure I wouldn't needlessly prescribe medication or overmedicate her child. I wanted to remind her of my "philosophy of medication," but I refrained. Still, in cases like this it's best to prescribe something.

"Listen, Mrs. King, I have just the thing," I told her. I took out my prescription pad and explained as I wrote:

Dr. Norman Weinberger's Famous Two-Chicken Chicken Soup

Take a large pot and fill it with about four quarts of water. Now you need your chicken. If you can, I prefer that you find pullets because they make a much better soup, but pullets are hard to find so you might have to settle for oven roasters. So, take the two roasters (or pullets if you can find them) and put them, giblets, neck, and all (make sure you take those out of the plastic bag), in the water along with a large onion, carrots, preferably two, two stalks of celery, and some parsley. Bring this to a boil and when a foam forms on top, skim it right off.

Now put the pot on a simmer, a slow simmer, a slight simmer—small bubbles—and cover with a vented lid. Open the vent halfway and cook the soup at this gentle rolling simmer, with small bubbles, for exactly four hours.

Now you need some egg noodles. I recommend Mother's wide egg noodles. Add those to your soup. Noodles are very important for the health content of the soup. Now you have the most magnificent chicken noodle soup and it will cure all ills.

"Chicken soup," Mrs. King said. "Chicken soup?"

"It's perfect for what ails Danny and for what ails you too. You won't have time to worry if you're busy cooking."

"Okay, I get the message," she said, finally smiling.

"Have some chicken soup and, I promise, you'll both feel better."

Perhaps more important than chicken soup curing all ills is

the fact that in times of stress we all need something to do to keep busy, even when there's nothing to do. My philosophy is the something you do might just as well taste good. Therefore, I've used this recipe in many situations such as:

• When Mrs. Ritchie called me one morning, dangling from the very end of her rope. Jocelyn, the second of her four children, was, as of that morning, in full chicken pox bloom. Teddy, the oldest, hadn't yet crusted over. (Crusted over? That's the wonderful sign that the pox are over and you can once again send your children outside.) Her third child, Michael, was running a low fever—the very first sign of the onslaught of chicken pox, and, being a pro, she knew that it was just a matter of time before the youngest, Matthew, would be showing her a red bump on his tummy or in his armpit. There was nothing I could do for her, other than give her the chicken soup recipe.

• When Mrs. Davis called, apologetic because she felt she was bothering me since I had just seen Emily, who only had a mild cold. But her mother-in-law was visiting from out of town and had badgered her into calling. I told Mrs. Davis, "I have the perfect thing for your mother-in-law to do. It can't hurt, and it will keep her out of your hair for a while." I prescribed the soup, but in this case I also added the recipe for matzo balls.

Dr. Norman Weinberger's Light-as-Air (And Slightly Nouvelle) Matzo Balls

You'll need:

2 tablespoons chicken schmaltz (chicken schmaltz is rendered chicken fat that no one eats anymore; if they did it would automatically clog their arteries)

So instead use: 2 tablespoons safflower oil

2 large eggs, slightly beaten

1/2 cup matzo meal

1 teaspoon salt (if you dare)

2 tablespoons chicken soup

Dr. Norman Weinberger's Famous Two-Chicken Chicken Soup

Blend oil and eggs together. Add matzo meal and salt and blend well. Add 2 tablespoons of the chicken soup and mix until uniform. Cover bowl and place in refrigerator for fifteen minutes. (My mother never bothered with this step. Consequently, instead of light, fluffy morsels, she produced what we affectionately called Hazel's Howitzer Shells. Moral of the story: don't omit this important step.) Bring chicken soup to light boil. Form balls of matzo mixture approximately one inch in diameter and drop into lightly boiling soup. Cover and cook for thirty minutes. Serve HOT. Makes about eight to ten matzo balls.

Mrs. King left, recipe/prescription in hand, and I carried on with my day, moving quickly from room to room, feeling more overwhelmed as the day went on. "When did this happen?" I thought to myself. The waiting room was jam-packed, the phones ringing, and all the examining rooms were full. How long had it been that every single moment of my day was filled? There were no breaks, no breathers between patients. I rushed past Bert in the hall. "Hey, Bert, we need to do something about this," I said with a sweep of my hands.

"I know, but when are we going to find time to discuss it?" he replied.

"Today, before we go home—definitely today," I said as he disappeared into one room and I into another.

Four-year-old Brittany Hunt was in with her mother. Her checkup went well. "Are there any questions or concerns?" I asked her mother.

"Well, I did want to ask you about nutrition. I'm really concerned because Brittany won't eat any meat. Is that normal and healthy for a four-year-old?"

"What does she eat?" I asked.

"She loves breads and pasta and cheese and, of course, cookies and candy and pizza." I nodded. "And she loves fruit and vegetables. In fact when I asked her what she wanted to bring to preschool for her birthday treat, she told me she wanted to bring a salad with oil and vinegar dressing."

I laughed. "No! You didn't ask for that really, did you?" I asked Brittany.

"I sure did," she replied proudly.

"Now, that's not normal," I said to her mother. "Most kids like fruits, but a lot of parents have trouble getting them to eat the vegetables. So be very grateful for that. Since she won't eat meat, the question is, does she get enough protein?"

"She does eat peanut butter and an occasional egg and I mentioned cheese."

"That sounds fine. You do want to watch the fat intake, but I think she's doing great. You know, during well checkups, nutrition is the number one thing I'm asked about, and the truth of the matter is if you offer your child a healthy assortment of all different foods, they'll choose exactly what they need to grow and be healthy."

"Really? I never heard that. You're sure I shouldn't try to force the meats."

"Don't try to force anything. Meal times should be happy, social times—not battles. You've got a very healthy kid here who's making healthy choices. Meat is an acquired taste and she might never acquire it. My advice to you is, if it ain't broken—don't fix it. Brittany is doing great."

"Thank you, Doctor." She got up to leave.

"Wait, I have a question," I said, following her out.

"Yes."

"Did you actually bring salad to preschool for her birthday treat?"

She laughed. "No. I thought the other kids might enjoy cupcakes more, but we did have a nice big salad at her birthday dinner that night."

On to the next appointment. Seven-year-old Ethan Mayer needed to have some sutures removed from his chin. Ethan and his mother were no strangers to sutures, casts, and crutches. Ethan was one of those kids who was known personally in the emergency room. When he was five, he was sure he could parachute off the roof of the carport by jumping off it with a knapsack containing a blanket strapped to his back. That time he broke his arm. Another day he tried skateboarding down the stairs and sprained his ankle. He was lucky that time.

His chin had been sewn up following a sudden midair decision not to jump into the pool. He had jumped, changed his mind about swimming, turned and made a grab for the side. Unfortunately his chin hit first.

Both Ethan and his mother were very calm and chatty while I went about removing the sutures. "This really doesn't ruffle you at all, does it?" I asked.

"Not really. It didn't even get to me when he cut his chin. I just grabbed his clothes because I knew we had a family thing to get to, and he was just in his bathing suit and towel. Then we high-tailed it to the emergency room. It was no big deal. Right, Ethan?"

"No big deal," Ethan confirmed through closed lips since I was working on his chin.

"You know there are plenty of families, thousands of families, who would have taken him home and put him to bed and babied him for a week."

"Not us—just sew and go—that's our motto," she said with a smile.

"It was true," I thought to myself. Not just with accidents, but with any sort of illnesses, some families just sort of fold, shut down and come to a dead halt, while there are others, like the Mayers, where illness and mishaps and accidents are just part of life and you take them in stride and keep going. Was one way wrong and the other right? No, I thought. It was just a matter of personal style and habit.

I finished removing the sutures. "I don't think you'll even have a scar," I told Ethan.

"Darn. I wanted to look like a hockey player," he replied.

"Something tells me you still might," I told him. "Try to stay in one piece for a while. Okay?"

"That wouldn't be any fun, would it, Ethan?" his mother said as they left the room.

"Naw, that wouldn't be fun."

He went down the hall, literally bouncing off the walls.

Helene Jeffries brought in six-month-old Spencer. His nose had been running, he had been cranky and pulling on his ear.

"I think he must have gotten the ear infection from teething," she told me.

"I don't think so," I told her. "It's really an old wives' tale that babies get ear infections or fevers or convulsions from teething. The only thing they get from teething is some discomfort and, eventually, teeth."

"Well, he's teething and he's clearly in pain because of it," she said.

"He's in pain from the ear infection. But that's just coincidental. I'm going to give you a prescription for that. He'll feel better in no time."

"But his gums will still bother him. They did before. He cries and whimpers."

"Well, I have the cure for that. After you go to the drugstore to get this prescription filled, stop at the liquor store and get a bottle of one hundred proof vodka. You take it home and put it in the freezer till it's ice-cold. Then you take two shot glasses and fill them both with the vodka. You dip your finger into one shot glass and rub the vodka on Spencer's upper gum. Your husband dips his finger into the other shot glass and rubs the vodka on Spencer's lower gum. Then you each down the shots. You can repeat the second part every ten minutes until you no longer hear him crying."

"Sounds good," she laughed.

"Or you can give him a frozen bagel to chew on."

"I guess that makes more sense," she admitted.

"Either way I want to see Spencer in two weeks to make sure the ear infection cleared up."

Eighteen-month-old John McKay was toddling around the examining room making a strange deep noise in his throat,

"MMMMMMM MMMMMMM." The first time I heard him make this noise was at his one-year exam. Even then his mother said it had become a strange little habit, like the way some people talk or sing to themselves when doing busywork. Although I had never heard a sound quite like it, I saw no reason to be concerned. He was developing normally in every way and this was in no way a form of communication for him. He was starting to build a perfectly age-appropriate vocabulary.

I finished the exam and asked if there were any questions.

"No questions, but I have a story you'll get a kick out of," his mother said. "I took John to Boston to see my sister. She hadn't seen him since he was six months old. So she hadn't heard the MMMMMMM yet. When he did start MMMMMMMing my sister got the strangest look on her face and insisted that she had heard that exact sound before. She went to her record collection. She's a professor of music at a small college in Boston so she has this really huge and bizarre record collection. She put on a record and there it was, MMMMMM, the same exact sound that John makes. When he heard it he went bonkers, jumping up and down and MMMMMMing for all he's worth."

"What was the record?" I asked, enthralled.

"It was—get this—Mongolian throat singing. We decided on the spot John was a Mongolian throat singer in a previous life."

"That's as good an explanation as any I could come up with," I told her.

"Oh, there's one more story I have to tell you. You know the ice cream parlor across from the library? The ice cream there's terrific, by the way. You have to try it. Anyhow, it's so good everyone goes in, even though the owner is this mean crotchety old coot. He never smiles or gives anyone the time of day. So I take John in there the other day. As usual the old guy is kind of nasty and rude, but John is his usual happy self, MMMMMMing away. The owner looks around. It's clear he's trying to figure out where this strange sound is coming from. Finally I hear him say, 'Damn, it's those freezers again. I'll have to call the repairman.' "

"Did you tell him it was John?" I asked.

She smiled at me with a real twinkle in her eye. "Nope. We just took our cones and went on our way."

Four-year-old Lily Strohl had a severe headache. A headache is fairly uncommon in a four-year-old, but certainly not unheard of. Yet Lily's mother, Polly, seemed inordinately anxious.

I examined Lily. "Lily, I think you have something called a sinus infection. In fact I think you have a really major sinus infection. So we're going to give you some medicine that will help you feel better."

"Are you sure it's a sinus infection?" Polly asked.

"As sure as I can be, based on the equipment I have here. The only way to be positive would be a CAT scan, but I'm sure she'll respond to the antibiotics I'm prescribing."

"I want her to have the CAT scan," Polly said forcefully.

"Why? She'd have to go to the hospital. If she doesn't respond to the antibiotics I could see having the CAT scan, but until we try this, that seems extreme."

"Lily. I want you to go play in the waiting room. Go look at Dr. Weinberger's fish, okay?" Polly said to her daughter.

Lily obediently left the examining room.

"What's up? You're really worried about something," I said, pulling my stool closer to Polly's chair.

"I want her to have the CAT scan because I think she has a brain tumor," she blurted out.

"A brain tumor? Why in the world do you think Lily has a brain tumor?" I asked, not being able to imagine what could be going on in Polly's head.

"Because Lily eats hot dogs."

"Excuse me?"

"She eats hot dogs all the time and I just read in one of the magazines if you eat more than one hot dog a week you have an increased risk of developing a brain tumor. Well, Lily's been eating hot dogs two or three times a week. Hot dogs are one of her favorite foods. You're a doctor, don't you know about this hot dog thing?"

"I know hot dogs aren't exactly the healthiest food in the world, but I never heard of them causing brain tumors. I wouldn't get all excited about this. Stuff like this is always in the media. Lily doesn't have a brain tumor. She has a sinus infection."

"Are you one hundred percent certain?" she asked.

"I can't be one hundred percent certain without a CAT scan, no. Are you going to drive yourself crazy until I agree to a CAT scan?"

"Probably," she answered honestly.

"Then I want Lily to have the CAT scan. But I want it not because I think she has a tumor, but because I don't want you making yourself or her crazy, okay?"

"Okay, thank you. I know it's not rational, but I read that stuff and then Lily got these terrible headaches. It just seemed to fit."

"After the CAT scan, will you be able to let this go?" I asked her.

"Well, I'm not letting her eat any more hot dogs, ever, period."

What could I do but sigh. If the media wasn't scaring parents out of using a product, they were manipulating parents into using a product.

"You know the trick to this is really moderation. You don't give her hot dogs every day, but you don't make it so she can't have a hot dog at a birthday party or the ball game. You know what I mean?"

"I guess so."

"We'll schedule the CAT scan and you'll feel better," I reassured her.

"Okay. But let's do it as soon as possible," she said as she left.

I looked at my watch. It was 5:15. I had just a couple of more patients to see.

Graham Frick was waiting for his five-year-old checkup. Graham was a very gregarious little guy, who loved to chat. "Guess what I got for my birthday last week, Dr. Weinberger?" he chirped, before I even began the exam.

"A new car?"

"No," he giggled, "guess again."

"A diamond watch." I started examining him as he kept talking.

"You're not even close. You want me to tell you?"

"Yeah. Tell me."

"I got a brand-new bunk bed," he said, proud as can be.

I stepped back and looked at him in mock awe. "No! You didn't. That's a present for a big grown-up boy."

"I'm a big grown-up boy now. That's why my dad put up the bunk bed. You know what?" This time he wasn't going to waste time waiting for me to guess. "It's really, really high."

"Do you sleep up on the top?"

"No. My daddy said when I get older he'll put a ladder on the bed, but for now I sleep on the bottom. It's like being in a little fort."

"You like it a lot, I guess."

"Oh yes. Going to bed is my favorite time of day. I pull my comfy covers up under my chin and I say AHHHH and go right to sleep." He snored for an extra added effect.

"You know, Graham, I'm in one hundred percent agreement with you. Going to bed is my best time of the day too. And you know, I would be happy as can be to do that right now."

And I wasn't kidding. It had been another long day at the end of a long week. At last I saw my final patient and tracked Bert down . . . he was also just finishing up.

We settled in the consultation room. After discussing several options we came up with the idea of having an early-morning sick bay. We would trade off taking the early shift starting at 8:00 A.M. Parents could just bring in their sick kids without an appointment. Not only would this cut down on the last-minute appointments during the day, but it would also cut down on the phone traffic. The added bonus would be a tremendous help to our dual-career families as well.

I was just getting ready to leave when the phone rang. "Dr. Weinberger."

"Hi. Dr. Weinberger. It's Mrs. Frietag." My jaw immediately tightened, my teeth started to grind.

"Mrs. Frietag. Hello."

"My husband's here now and we just talked to Dr. Danoff." Dr. Danoff was the head of the newborn unit. "He says the insurance company won't pay for this. He wants us to go home this evening. I told him you told me we could stay until Sunday."

"Now, wait a minute. I never said you could stay until Sunday. I said you had two choices. You can go home today. You can go home tomorrow. That's it. That's all. Those are your only choices," I said firmly.

"What if I can't feed the baby?" she asked. Now, there are babies who are difficult to feed at first, and the mothers understandably get anxious about this. But Phyllis Frietag had been easily and successfully feeding Jonah for the last two days.

"You've been feeding the baby just fine. Your husband can feed the baby. Your mother-in-law can feed the baby. The way Jonah eats I'm sure your cat could feed the baby."

"I'm worried about so many things," she said.

I suddenly realized that Mrs. Frietag, like so many new moms, was terribly frightened of being responsible for this living human being who was totally dependent upon someone else for its survival. What a terrible responsibility this is, and as with many parents, she felt ill prepared. The hospital and its staff provided a support base from which this family was verbalizing what many families felt—don't cut the cord.

We needed to provide a way of making the transition from hospital to home supportive and accessible. "Okay, Mrs. Frietag, I'll call you in the morning to make sure things are going okay and answer any questions you have. We will make an appointment to have you come in to the office in two days to weigh and check the baby and make sure you are comfortable. I'm on call tonight, so if you have any problems, just call."

As I hung up the phone, I realized that having your first baby is the most significant life cycle event in a couple's experience and we, as pediatricians, have to be aware of the positive role we must play in making the transition from couple to family.

7

Lovies, Pacifiers, and Other Ways to a Stress-Free Life

Parents tend to forget that kids experience stress as much as adults. . . . But as the everyday events of an adult's life can create tension and stress, so can the events of a child's life.

As I walked by the waiting room a familiar red head popped up from the crowded, toy-strewn waiting room smiling and waving madly at me. "Dr. Weinberger, hi, Dr. Weinberger. Hey, Dr. Weinberger, I came to see you." It was three-year-old David Webster, son of our friend Maida Webster and the spitting image of Howdy Dowdy.

Even after David and his mother had been settled in the examining room he would poke his orange-topped head out the door every time he heard me in the hallway as I hustled between exams. "I gotta talk to you, Dr. Weinberger." "This is a really long wait today, Dr. Weinberger." "Is it my turn now, Dr. Weinberger?"

"David, come sit down," Maida's slightly exasperated voice came from inside the examining room. He waved again, grinned, and disappeared into the examining room.

Finally, it was David's turn. I walked into the examining room singing, "It's David Webster time!" David, who had been at his post right by the door, scurried to the examining table and declined help in climbing up. I sat down next to him on the table.

"What's up, David? You seem sort of anxious to talk to me."

"He wants to get to you before I do," Maida said from the corner of the small examining room where she was sitting under a pile of coats, mittens, hats, and gloves. Maida is the only person I know who speaks faster and longer than her son, David.

"Yes, I have to talk to you about my Binky," David jumped right in, giving a worried look at his mother. David's Binky (aka his pacifier) was an ongoing source of discord between David and his mother. David took a deep breath, leaned back, and crossed his legs, looking very grown up. "I knew I was coming in to see you and I knew my mother was going to talk to you about my Binky, *again.*" He shot his mother as dirty a look as I've ever seen a three-year-old give anyone.

David continued, sounding like a cross between Perry and Jackie Mason. "I was determined to break the habit so when Mommy told you about my Binky, I could say, 'Well, I don't use a Binky anymore,' and everyone would be surprised and proud of me."

I struggled to keep a straight face and professional demeanor as David rambled on, barely pausing to take a breath.

"So, several nights ago I decided I would put my Binky into the drawer of my nightstand and I did. But you know what?" He didn't wait for a response to his question but forged on. "I couldn't sleep at all because, you see, I just couldn't relax. I just became more and more tense, and the tension became huge. Finally, last night, I just couldn't stand it anymore, and I jumped out of bed and I grabbed my Binky from the night-stand drawer, and I put it right in my mouth, and I jumped back into bed and got right under my covers, and I felt better right away, and I fell right to sleep." David paused and sighed, as if remembering how wonderful it felt to have his Binky back in his mouth, where it belonged.

"So, Dr. Weinberger," he now sounded like a very small attorney making his closing argument, "as you can see, I really, really need to have my Binky." He stopped talking and grinned hopefully up at me, big Howdy Dowdy eyes shining, waiting to see if I would give his Binky my stamp of approval.

"Well, David," I said in my most professional doctor voice, "as far as I'm concerned, you can take your Binky to college with you, and I have a feeling that college might very well be Harvard."

Maida was not happy that I had given my stamp of approval to David's Binky. She was not alone in the ongoing struggle between what children need to have for comfort and what their parents find unacceptable. On an almost daily basis I talk to parents who are concerned, worried, and sometimes angry that their child needs a pacifier, blanket, or stuffed animal to ease their tension and stress and feel comfortable, relaxed, and secure.

Often this discussion takes place after a particularly distressing episode. The blanket gets lost and the child is inconsolable. Grandma makes a disparaging remark such as, "*My children never needed a pacifier.*" Or, like Maida, the parent simply thinks the child should have outgrown the need for the comfort object or "Lovey," as I like to call it.

The McGrath family had been coming to me for many years, ever since the birth of their oldest child, Scott. Then came Jennifer, Julia, and Laura.

The day school resumed following Easter vacation, I received a call from their mother, Jean. "Dr. Weinberger, I need a foolproof method of getting Laura off the pacifier."

"Why?" I asked her. Jean McGrath, a petite blond dynamo, had never expressed concern over any of the older children's pacifier or blanket habits. She had always been the kind of mother who took those things in stride.

"Laura is way too dependent on that pacifier. It almost ruined our vacation."

"The pacifier almost ruined your vacation?" I knew I was in for a good story. There's nothing like an eighteen-month-old with a mission.

"We drove down to Florida for Easter break. We stayed with

my in-laws in Tampa and everything was going fine. Then we headed to Orlando to go to Disney World for a couple of days. We had the grandparents with us, all the kids, Ted and myself. You know how organized I am. I had everybody together, backpacks, fanny packs, the diaper bag. I thought we had everything we could possibly need."

It was true. Jean ran a tight ship. I pictured the four tow-headed children following her like ducklings through the mobs of Disney World.

"Everyone was having a great time when suddenly Laura started crying for her pacifier. I looked through the stroller. I looked through the backpack and the fanny packs and the diaper bag. I knew she had her pacifier when we started out that morning. I couldn't believe the one thing I forgot was extra pacifiers. Laura continued to cry. She was getting louder and louder. You would think in an amusement park full of children, no one would notice one screaming baby, but she was really turning heads.

"The other children were whining to go on the rides. Ted's parents were giving me the most horrible looks, and Laura showed no signs of letting up.

"Ted went back to the car, but the pacifier wasn't there. We retraced our steps, going back to the rides we'd been on, but there was no sign of the pacifier. So we started looking in the stores. We finally found pacifiers in one of the shops, but it wasn't the kind Laura was used to. She just kept hollering and spitting it out. At this point, Laura was in such a state I figured she would either throw up or pass out.

"Then Jennifer came running through the store yelling, 'I found one, I found a pacifier just like Laura's.' She was, indeed, carrying a pacifier. However, hanging from the pacifier was a huge, stuffed baby Minnie Mouse doll.

"I showed it to the salesperson and explained the situation over the din of Laura's screams. 'I'm sorry,' she shouted back at me, 'but you'll have to buy the whole mouse.'

"So I bought what turned out to be a twenty-five-dollar

pacifier and ripped it out of Baby Minnie's little hand or paw or whatever you'd call it, and Laura sniffled for a while and finally calmed down. I won't go through that again," she finished.

"Has she formed an attachment to the Baby Minnie doll yet?" I asked.

"Very funny," Jean replied. "Now, how do I get her off that pacifier?"

"Well, that's a tough one, although I do know one family that convinced their three-year-old that the Easter Bunny comes around and picks up used pacifiers to bring to new babies. Their child packed all of her pacifiers into a little basket to be carried off Easter morning. Of course, you'd have to wait a whole year before you could try that."

Jean laughed. "Okay. Now seriously, how do I get her off it?"

"There's always the cold turkey method, but before you do that let me ask you, do you think after that experience you'll ever forget to bring extra pacifiers with you again?"

"Never!" she said. She waited for me to continue but I was silent. "That's your answer?" she finally said.

"Uh-huh. She'll give it up when she's ready. I haven't had a patient yet who went to college with a pacifier in their mouth."

"I can't tell you how comforting that is."

"Okay, here's something you can do. Starting today you tell her the pacifier can only be used in her room. Let her know she can go to her room and use it whenever she wants. She can sleep with it, nap with it, but she may not take it out of her room. At first she'll put up a fuss, and she'll probably keep returning to her room, but she's a very social child, and I'm sure she'd rather be where the action is than in her room with the pacifier."

"I'll give it a try but if you hear someone screaming bloody murder from six miles away, you'll know it's Laura."

Within the next three months, Laura began to use her pacifier only at night, and by the time she was three she had stopped using it altogether. I believe Jean continued to carry one with her and will, at least until the day Laura graduates high school.

All parents seem to fall within the wide spectrum from trying to totally ban any form of attachment to pacifier, blankets, and stuffed animals to happily providing these items and going along with their children's wishes and whims.

At one end of the spectrum was Mrs. Schlade. She came in with her infant daughter, Annie, for her one-month checkup. Mrs. Schlade (she was one of those people you would never call by her first name) was tough, but elegant. Annie, a normal, healthy infant, was her third child. Her first two children from an earlier marriage were in their teens. They had only just recently become my patients, so I had no idea how Mrs. Schlade would mother an infant. My first hint was the fact that Annie's baby nurse, Eleanor, had not only come along for the exam, but was the one who held and comforted the baby.

"Dr. Weinberger, please tell Eleanor there is no need for the baby to have a pacifier. Eleanor is insistent on her having one." Eleanor looked shyly at the floor.

"Most babies have a need to suck. It's a reflex that's usually lost by six months. So, the pacifier can usually be gone by eight to ten months of age," I tried to explain tactfully to Mrs. Schlade. "With that in mind, what's wrong with a pacifier at this age?"

Mrs. Schlade looked up at me from her seat. She didn't look like she had given birth a month ago. Perhaps that was due to the fact that she had just returned from a week at a spa. Even her hair was perfectly done. It looked like it wouldn't move in the wind.

She thought for a moment. "My other children never had them, and they're just fine and, well, I just don't like the way they look."

"How do they look?" I asked. I had heard parents complain about how a pacifier looks in the mouth of a two- or three-year-old, but I couldn't imagine a pacifier looking anything but normal in the mouth of an infant.

"It looks like if you pulled the pacifier out of their mouths they would fly around the room, deflating like a balloon." She waved her hand in the air as if demonstrating the path Annie would take.

"I promise you she won't deflate," I said with a smile. But I knew, at that point, little Annie would never have a pacifier.

At the far other extreme was Lisa Fisher and her daughter, Reese. Reese had always been an unusually healthy child. I rarely saw her more than once or twice a year. But what made Reese memorable was from early on she always came in with her stuffed bunny. The bunny, known as Bunny, was always fully dressed in a coordinated outfit down to its underpants and socks. Bunny had accessories such as hats and jewelry Reese had made out of felt and construction paper and beads. If it was cold out Bunny wore a coat or sweater.

While Bunny was always perfectly put together, Reese was one of those kids who, no matter how well-dressed, always looked a little messy. Her knee socks would be at half mast. Her headband would almost be down in her eyes. Her jacket would be buttoned cockeyed. But Bunny was always immaculate.

After examining Reese I always took a minute to examine Bunny. Invariably, Reese was delighted when I would report that Bunny was also very healthy.

When Lisa and Reese came in for Reese's five-year checkup I couldn't help noticing Bunny was not with them. I debated whether or not to inquire about Bunny's whereabouts. I thought only a tragedy of some sort could make Reese come without Bunny. I knew Lisa would never make Reese leave Bunny at home. Should I ask or do I just keep my mouth shut? Finally I decided to go for it—Bunny's absence was so obvious—I had to know where she was.

"Uh, Reese, where's Bunny today?" I asked cautiously.

Lisa shook her head and looked worried. Reese's eyes filled

with tears. This was what I was afraid of. "It's so sad, Dr. Weinberger," Reese said in her high squeaky voice.

I sat down next to her and took her little hand in mine. "You don't have to tell me if you don't want to."

"No, I'll tell you," she said very dramatically. "You see we went on vacation and Bunny decided to stay on in Disney World." She sniffled and wiped her nose on the sleeve of her sweater.

"Bunny decided to stay on in Disney World?" I questioned.

Reese nodded. "I have a new Bunny. She looks like the real Bunny only cleaner. But she's not the same. She doesn't like to go out as much."

I gave her a hug. "I'm so sorry," I told her. What else was there to say?

I caught Lisa alone as she was paying her bill. "Bunny decided to stay on in Disney World?" I asked. "What happened?"

"Well," she explained, "we had to switch hotel rooms and I must not have realized Bunny was still in bed. The moment I realized she wasn't with us I was on the phone with the hotel manager, housekeeping, and the laundry. I would have called Walt himself if I could have, but Bunny was nowhere to be found. Believe me, I was more upset about this than Reese. And she's right, that other bunny is just not the same."

Then there is one of my favorite stories—one that I often use as an example when parents ask me what my position is on blankies, lovies, and binkies. Frank and Linda Pechette were returning from a long road trip with their two daughters, Christy and Carly. Traveling with a three-and-a-half-year-old and an eighteen-month-old is always a trying experience, but this was a particularly difficult trip for Frank.

Frank, a high-powered advertising executive, is a workaholic, but he had promised his wife, Linda, an overworked homemaker, that on this trip he would be more involved with the girls. He would help more, do more, and give her a much-needed break.

By the time they pulled into their driveway late at night in the pouring rain, Frank was nearing the end of his patience. He was relieved that eighteen-month-old Carly was asleep. He reached carefully through the McDonald's wrappers, empty juice boxes, and broken crayons that littered the car's back seat and slowly pulled the car seat strap over Carly's head, doing his best not to wake her.

Meanwhile, Linda had already led Christy into the house, slipped her expertly into her pajamas, put her into bed, and was already unpacking and sorting laundry in the basement by the time Frank came into the girls' darkened bedroom carrying the still-sleeping Carly.

Frank gingerly laid Carly in her crib. While he was removing her shoes she woke up. First she looked around her familiar room, bleary-eyed, then she started screaming, "My passie! My passie!"

"What, what? I can't understand you. Stop crying, will you?" Frank begged.

Christy's voice rose from her bed, across the room. "She needs her pacifier, Daddy."

"Where is it?"

"She had one in the car," Christy offered helpfully.

Frank went back out in the rain and started rummaging through the mess all over the back seat, throwing food wrappers and baby wipes as he plowed through. He imagined he could hear Carly's screaming through the rain. At last he found the pacifier wedged under the car seat.

He ran back inside leaving a trail of water behind him. He had the presence of mind to at least rinse the pacifier off before he stuck it in his daughter's mouth. She immediately quieted. He turned to leave the room, was almost out the door, when a loud scream hit him again.

"What? What is it now?" he pleaded.

Carly continued sobbing. Christy's voice floated through the darkness. "She wants Ruff." Ruff was an old dish towel Carly carried around with her.

"Well where the hell is it?" Frank was getting more and more exasperated. He could feel himself losing control.

"Hell's a bad word, Daddy," Christy reprimanded him.

"Fine, where the heck is it?"

"Maybe it's packed in a suitcase?" Christy was trying to help.

Carly continued to scream, pacifier in hand.

Frank rushed to the kitchen and returned to the girls' room with the whole drawer of dish towels. He dumped them out on Christy's bed. "Which one is like Ruff?"

"She only likes Ruff."

"Just pick a dish towel," Frank ordered her.

"All right," Christy said doubtfully, rolling her eyes. She carefully picked through the dish towels until she came to one that seemed to be the right color and texture. She handed it to her father. "But Ruff is ripped," Christy reminded him. Using his teeth, Frank quickly tore it. He rushed it across the room to Carly, who grabbed it hungrily in the dark and sighed. She put the pacifier back in her mouth and closed her eyes.

But Frank didn't even make it to the door before a scream once more pierced the silence, "Dis is not Ruuuuff!"

Frank lost his temper. "This is the only Ruff you're getting," he yelled. "I am not looking for any more pacifiers or dish towels at one in the morning. I have had enough. Now be quiet and go to sleep. I have had—" Frank yelled.

The whole time he was yelling, Christy was saying, "Daddy. Daddy! *Daddy!*," louder and louder until Frank stopped in mid-sentence and screamed, "What?" at her.

"Daddy, you're being way mean to Carly. You just don't understand."

"I don't understand what?" Frank asked angrily.

"You don't understand how hard it is. I'm three and all *I* have is my thumb and *I* can hardly get through the night."

So, when parents ask me about lovies and pacifiers, I tell them I basically share the same philosophy as Christy

Pechette: don't be mean because many of us need more than just a thumb to get through the nights—and the days as well.

Parents tend to forget that kids experience stress as much as adults. They think stress can only be caused by adult issues like mortgages and marriages and on-the-job demands. But as the everyday events of an adult's life can create tension and stress, so can the events of a child's life. My children certainly weren't immune to it.

"Hello, Dr. Weinberger. This is Mrs. Brown, the school nurse. I have Lisa in my office and I'm afraid she's not feeling too well."

"What's the problem?" I asked. Lisa was rarely sick.

"She's feeling chilled, and she's quite pale and clammy. She thinks she might vomit."

"I'll be right over to pick her up," I said.

Lisa was lying on the nurse's cot, pale and sweaty. By the time I got her into the car her color was improving. By the time we made the short drive to the office she was the picture of health. She spent the rest of the afternoon playing with the office staff and happily drawing in my office. There was no talk of nausea or throwing up. I was baffled. It just didn't make any sense.

The next day I got another call from the nurse. "Hi, Dr. Weinberger. It's Mrs. Brown. Lisa's feeling sick again."

"She was fine last night and this morning," I told her.

"Well, she's not running a fever, but she really doesn't look well."

"I'll be right there."

Once again I found a pale and sweaty Lisa. Once again she perked up by the time we got to the office.

On the way home I looked over at her. "Gee, Lisa, you really look terrific."

"I feel terrific, Dad. What's for dinner?"

When it happened the third day in a row, I knew something was up.

"There's something going on at school that's upsetting Lisa," I told Susan that night. "She's clearly not feeling well when I come for her, but by the time we get to the first stoplight she's miraculously cured."

"Do you mean she's faking it?" Susan asked. "That's just not like her."

"No, she can't be faking it. When I came to get her she was lying on that little cot in the nurse's office. She was so pale she blended right in with the sheets. There's something seriously bothering her."

"Well, I'll get to the bottom of it," Susan said, and went upstairs to talk to Lisa.

She came back down a half hour later with a smile on her face. "I know what the problem is now," she said. "Next Friday is the fourth-grade play and Lisa has a pretty hefty part in it. She's convinced that she's going to—as she says—'flub my lines and make a fool of myself in front of everyone.' "

"Poor kid. What can we do other than assure her everything will be fine?"

"Everything will be fine. I just went over her lines with her and she knows them cold."

The next morning we sat down with Lisa and had a long talk. We reassured her she had nothing to worry about; she knew her lines. We would be there as we always had, and she would do great.

"You guys don't understand. I know my lines now, but how can I be sure I'll remember them when I'm in front of everybody, or what if I trip or come on stage at the wrong time?"

She was turning pale at the mere thought of all that could go wrong. She looked down at her breakfast with disgust and pushed her plate aside.

"Lisa, none of those things are going to happen. But even if they did, what would be so terrible? The play will still be wonderful. You'll still be wonderful and we'll be proud of you no matter what happens, because you took the part and learned the lines and did your best and that's what's important," I told her.

"You would be proud even if I flubbed up?" Lisa asked in disbelief.

"Of course," Susan said. "But you're not going to. You could do those lines in your sleep."

"You really think so?"

"I know so," Susan reassured her.

"Well, will you still rehearse with me every night until the play?"

"Of course," Susan said, giving her a hug.

"Then Mom will know all your lines and she can be your understudy. If you won't go on, Mom can and *she'll* become the star!"

"Cut it out, Dad. You know I'll go on."

"Good, because Mom would look really silly up there with the fourth grade."

Lisa pulled her breakfast back in front of her and happily ate it. That was the end of the stomachaches and, as predicted, Lisa's performance was flawless down to the little wave she threw us from the stage.

"So, what's new?" I asked Keith Francis, who had come in with his mother, Lydia, and an earache.

"We're moving!" five-year-old Keith said excitedly.

"Moving! You're not leaving me, are you?" I asked him.

All of a sudden he looked concerned. "Mommy, are we leaving Dr. Weinberger?"

"No, we can still come see Dr. Weinberger. We're only moving to Stratford."

"When did all this happen?" I asked.

"In just the past two weeks—we weren't even planning to move. I was driving home from my dance studio and I saw the 'for sale' sign on one of my all-time favorite houses. It's three minutes from my studio, close to both the grammar and high schools, and it has five acres of land. I didn't think for a minute we could afford it, but I figured I'd call anyway. It turns out the owner's being transferred to London and is desperate to sell.

We made an embarrassingly low offer and he took it. We close the first of next month and move right in. The place doesn't even need any work."

"Well that's pretty exciting. You like the new house, Keith?"

"Uh-huh. My room is huge."

"How does Elise feel about moving?" Elise was Keith's fourteen-year-old sister.

"She's excited too, mostly because she gets her own bathroom," Lydia answered.

"Have you talked to her about changing schools and all that? Moving can be very stressful for kids."

"She says she's excited about the new school."

"Well, congratulations and good luck."

Six weeks later Elise Francis came in. "What's up with you, Elise?" I asked.

"It's really strange. I've been getting these stomachaches and vomiting a lot."

"Really. How long has this been going on?"

"For about a week."

"Does it happen after meals, or at any particular time?"

"Yeah. It always happens late at night or first thing in the morning. The rest of the time I feel fine."

I examined her thoroughly, but couldn't find anything physically wrong with her.

"We could line up a whole bunch of tests, because there is the possibility there's something organically wrong, but I'm wondering if this is a reaction to your move. I know how tough moving can be."

"Yeah, I was really excited to move into that huge house, and not have to share a bathroom with Keith, and have a huge yard and everything, but I really miss the old house."

"Tell me what you miss about it."

"Gosh, everything—I miss the colors of my room and the street we lived on and even the way it smelled. This house doesn't smell like *our* house. You know I always lived in that old house, and even though I was excited about the new house, deep down, I don't think I ever wanted to leave. I guess it's kind of silly with the new house being so big and beautiful and all."

"You know, Elise, I remember perfectly the house I grew up in. I lived in Homestead Park, Pennsylvania. I can still recall everything about that house—the lawn, the stone wall in front of the house and the steps that led to the street, the two trees on either side of the step. I can remember when I was little, standing on my tiptoes to look into these two little kitchen windows to see if my mom was in there.

"When I went to college my parents decided the house was too big for them, so they sold it. Their new house was fine, but to this day I never think of that house as ever being *my* house. My house is the house on Main Street where I grew up.

"Our first house is always part of us. That's because we associate the physical place with all the memories—good and bad—we had there, and it becomes part of who we are. I don't think you're being silly at all. I think it's very stressful and sad to move, even if it's to a bigger, more beautiful house. I think you have to give yourself time to get used to it. If you give it some time, and talk about how you're feeling, two things will happen: one is that slowly but surely the new house will start feeling like home, and two is that your stomachaches and vomiting will stop. What do you think? You willing to give it a try?"

"Sure. But what if the stomachaches don't go away?"

"Why don't you give it about a week. I want you to talk to your mom, or dad, or me, or a friend when you're feeling sad about the move. If the stomachaches haven't at least improved by then, then I want to set up some more tests for you. Okay?"

"Okay. You know I already feel a little better."

"Funny how talking about it helps."

"Yeah," she said and went on her way.

After two weeks I still hadn't heard from Elise or her mother so I gave them a call and reached Lydia.

"Hi, it's Dr. Weinberger, I'm just following up on Elise. What's happening with the stomachaches and vomiting?"

"They've stopped altogether. She told me what you two talked about, and we talked about the move as a family, and now she's doing fine. I think she felt like she wasn't allowed to feel anything but happy and excited about the move when she was really feeling anxious and sad. She felt much better when she realized we felt that way too—that there was some ambivalence on our part as well."

"Well, I'm happy to hear she's doing better. I don't think we can downplay how difficult it is for children to pick up and leave and go to a new place. It really opens the door for all kinds of fears and anxieties."

"Well, I think we have it under control now. At least everyone's talking openly about how they feel."

"That's what's needed to ease the transitions. Give me a call if there're any other concerns or problems."

"Of course. Thanks for the follow-up."

Moving is the kind of stress-trigger that's obvious. You can anticipate that your child will go through a tough time when you move. But as kids are constantly trying to navigate through and figure out their world, stress can be triggered by things you never thought of.

Nine-year-old Billy Gannon came into the office on an emergency. He was having trouble breathing. I hurried into the examining room.

"Hi, Billy, how're you doing?" I asked.

"I (puff puff gasp gasp) can (gasp) hardly (puff gasp) breathe." I quickly examined him but couldn't find any cause for his pained and strained breathing. I realized he was hyperventilating. I got him a paper bag to breathe into and sat with him until he had calmed down. Once he had settled down I sent him out to the waiting room with the nurse to look at the fish tank.

"What's going on?" I asked his mother.

"I don't really know," she replied. "The only thing I do know is lately he's always asking me if he's going to die."

"You know, younger kids sometimes go through a stage where they think they're going to die. But Billy's a little old for that. There must be something triggering this fear. Can you think of anything?"

She thought for a moment and then I could see the light-bulb go off above her head. "Oh my God, yes. About six weeks ago my aunt died and we went to the funeral and wake. I was surprised they had an open casket. I wouldn't have brought Billy had I known. But Billy didn't seem freaked out or anything at the funeral. He had a few questions, but he hasn't talked about it since then."

"I'm sorry for your loss." She nodded. "Do you remember what any of Billy's questions were?"

"He wanted to know what she died of and how she got it. He talked about what happens after you die, but we had discussed that with him a long time ago."

"What did she die of?" I asked.

"She had cancer. Do you think Billy thinks he has cancer?" she asked.

"Well, I think we should ask him."

We called Billy back in. "Hey Billy, I was sorry to hear your great-aunt died. That's very upsetting."

"Yeah, she had cancer. I saw her in the coffin."

"Your mom tells me you're asking a lot of questions about dying. Since I'm a doctor I was wondering if you had any questions for me?"

He thought for a moment and looked at his mother. She nodded at him. "You can ask Dr. Weinberger anything," she assured him.

"What if it's a stupid question?" he said.

"There is no such thing as a stupid question."

He thought for a moment longer. "Can you catch cancer from a dead person?" he finally asked, looking at the floor.

"I think that's a very good question. And the answer is no. You cannot get cancer from a dead person."

"You sure you can't get cancer from a dead person?"

"You know what, Billy? You can't even catch cancer from a live person. Cancer isn't like a cold or strep throat. It's not contagious."

"So for sure I don't have cancer?" he asked.

"You are one of my healthiest patients. For sure you don't have cancer."

"What about when I couldn't breathe today? That wasn't healthy."

"I think that was because you were thinking so much about being sick you made yourself feel sick. But you feel fine now, right?"

He thought for a moment. "Yeah, I really do."

"Good for you. Do you have any other questions?"

He thought some more. "No, I think that's all."

"Good. You know if you ever get worried like that again, don't wait. Ask your parents or me so you don't start feeling bad again. Deal?" I held out my hand to shake on it.

He shook my hand. "Deal!" he said happily.

In pediatric training we were reminded that our patients were children. But in today's world, advertising, radio, TV, music, parents, educators, and many other voices are saying, "Forget being a kid, you are a small adult." Kids are no longer allowed to be kids. Children are pushed through each phase of development at breakneck speed, being forced into the next stage before they have a chance to master the one they're in. The clothing, toys, media, and social pressure all scream for our children to act like little grown-ups.

Chloe Poole came in for her five-year checkup. She was sitting on the examining room table reading a book. "What are you reading, Chloe?" I asked as I sat down next to her on the examining room table.

"Oh it's just something for reading lab," she told me.

"What's reading lab?" I asked.

"It's like a little school I go to every Tuesday where they teach me to read."

"It's to help prepare her for first grade," her mother interjected.

"I thought that's what kindergarten was for," I said.

"Well, reading lab will help make sure she's successful in first grade," her mother explained.

"Do you have any reason to think she wouldn't be successful?" I asked.

"Well, no. Chloe's very bright, but so many of the kids go to this reading lab thing, I didn't want her to start out behind."

I thought to myself, but didn't say, "Reading lab—just another way someone figured out to separate parents from their money."

"What do you like to do other than read?" I asked Chloe as I began the exam.

"Well on Monday I go to Suzuki violin. On Tuesday I go to reading lab. Wednesday is tennis. Thursday and Saturday is soccer, and on Friday . . . let me think, what do I do on Friday? Oh yeah . . ." She put a finger in the air. "On Friday I get to be a little girl."

Her mother and I laughed, but later I thought how sad this was. I knew that Chloe's schedule was not uncommon and I wondered what had happened to afternoons of milk and cookies, and playing around the neighborhood until you were called in for dinner.

Larry Robinson had brought ten-year-old Nathaniel in for a checkup. "So what are you up to these days, Natty?"

"Oh not much. School and stuff."

"Yeah? What stuff? Do you take any lessons, play any sports? What do you like to do?"

"You play basketball," his father suggested.

"Yeah. I play basketball," Nathaniel said. "I want to be on the swim team too, but my mom and dad say just one activity at a time."

I looked at Mr. Robinson. "That's unusual," I told him.

"Well, you know, we just moved here a couple years ago

from a little town in Iowa. No one there had anything like the kids here have. I've never seen such schedules of activities. But that's not the way we do things in our family. Right, Nathaniel?"

"Yeah, right, Dad," Nathaniel said, rolling his eyes.

"You can see the support I get. We're struggling to keep our values the same as they were in Iowa. Part of that is limiting the outside activities the kids have. They can do one activity a week. That way they have time for their schoolwork, religious school, and chores that need to be done. I also want them to have some time each day to do nothing, so they can read a book, or take a walk, or just play."

"Tell me more." I was very impressed with the Robinsons' commitment to their personal values and lifestyle.

"We all sit down to dinner together every night. We take family vacations together. We closely monitor what they watch on TV—"

"Jamie Howard can watch whatever he wants," Nathaniel interrupted.

"That's fine for Jamie. But that's not how we do things," Mr. Robinson told him. "You can see what we're up against here.

"In theory it's simple—family comes first. But in practice it's getting tough. We get a lot of complaining from the kids. But we feel certain that down the line they'll really appreciate the foundation this way of life gives them."

"I got to tell you, Nathaniel, you're one lucky guy to have a dad like this."

"Yeah he's all right but I still want to be on the swim team."

I learned a lot listening to Larry Robinson. I realized the way to combat much of childhood's stress was to reestablish family values in the home. Along with that comes the challenge of saying no. I found when I began to discuss this with parents they loved to hear me say it was okay to say no. They were so swept up in the "gotta-do-gotta-have-gotta-buy" mentality they had forgotten about the simple things like staying home as a family, sitting and talking, and reading books.

They were relieved to hear from someone in something of a position of authority that their child wouldn't suffer if they didn't go to "moms and tots" or the most progressive nursery school at eighteen months of age. They were happy to hear their children wouldn't be left in the dust if they didn't start swim lessons at six months and piano at age two. But like Larry Robinson, I felt it was a tough battle. There are so many kids out there like Chloe Poole who only have one afternoon a week to be a little kid.

8

I Was Here First!

It's as if a husband said to his wife, " . . . I'm going to bring home a nice new wife because I have so much love in my heart that I have enough to share with two wives."

From the waiting room you could barely hear it. But it got louder and louder as I approached the closed door of the examining room—a cry. No, a wail. No, more of a screech. It was hard to define. The sound had an almost animal-like quality. I knocked on the door of the room and poked my head in. "Is someone slaughtering animals in here?"

Eight-year-old Steven Lewis was sitting, still as a statue, on one end of the examining room table, a strange, intense smile on his lips, his huge brown eyes wide and unblinking, his hands folded innocently in his lap. His six-year-old brother, Alan, was seated on the other end of the examining table, mouth open, tear-streaked face contorted, working up to another unearthly wail. Their mother, Judy, sat angry and frustrated in front of Alan.

"Alan Lewis, don't you dare make another noise like that," I warned, hurrying in and closing the door firmly behind me. "Now, why are you making those ungodly sounds?"

There was no response, but I followed his glance over to Steven, who remained stock still down to his disarming smile. "Did Steven do something to you?"

"He won't say," Judy muttered through clenched teeth. "This goes on all the time and I've had it."

Judy and I had talked about sibling rivalry before. In fact, Steven Lewis was the poster boy for sibling rivalry, a title he earned early on when he had, at age three, attempted to sell his infant brother to a neighbor child.

"Steven, I want you to go to the waiting room while I examine your brother. Then he can wait out there during your examination."

"Why does he get to go first?" Steven snarled. "He always goes first."

I thought fast. "Today he's first because his shirt is already off. Now get out of here."

Steven reluctantly obeyed me, making a big show of stomping angrily out of the room. I turned my attention to Alan. He had made a valiant effort to stop wailing, and now was just sniffing and wiping his nose and eyes on his shirt. I handed him a tissue, which he held tightly, while he continued to use his shirt as a handkerchief.

"Now, why don't you tell us what happened," I said, sitting down next to him.

"Can't," he mumbled into his shirt.

"Yes, you can. Steven's out of the room," Judy tried to reassure him.

Alan just shook his head. So I went ahead with the examination. I noticed bluish green bruises on the outside of both his upper arms. "What's this?" I asked him, pointing to the bruises. He shrugged.

"Let me guess. Could it have something to do with Steven?"

"I didn't say that," Alan said, a look of terror coming over his face.

"You didn't have to. I bet he slugs you every time he walks by."

"How did you know?" Alan asked in amazement, as he put his shirt back on. I noticed a fresh, bright green spot on the front of his shirt.

"The same way I know you had lime Jell-O for lunch. It's just magic."

He looked suitably amazed. "Wow!"

I finished the examination. "You're doing fine. Now go send Steven in, and you can play in the waiting room."

I decided against talking to Steven about using Alan as a punching bag. I knew that he would eventually take it out on Alan. So I performed the usual exam on Steven, who was also in perfect health, and sent him out to the waiting room with a stern warning to stay away from his brother. I wanted a moment alone with Judy.

"So, can I assume that the bullying and fighting have not improved?" I asked Judy.

"Not only has it not improved, but I found out something from my sister that's really disturbing."

"What's that?"

"She found out from her daughter that Steven has Alan in such a state of terror that he can make Alan cry just by pointing at him. That explains why he's always bursting into tears for no apparent reason. Just the other night we were out to dinner and suddenly Alan was sobbing. Steven was sitting right next to him and holding one of those big menus. I'm almost sure that he was pointing at him from behind the menu."

I couldn't help laughing. "I apologize for laughing, but the picture of the boys at the restaurant, with Steven pointing . . . Sorry. I thought I had heard every form of sibling torture, but this is a new one."

"I'm so happy to amuse and enlighten you," Judy said with a sarcastic grin. "When you're done laughing maybe you can HELP me."

"Okay, seriously now—did you ask Alan about this?"

"It's no use. He's too scared to tell on Steven. And if I say something to Steven he'll just assume Alan tattled and Alan will get pounded. I don't know what to do. I'm beginning to think they both need to see a psychiatrist."

"Let's try something else first. Steven is a very powerful kid. He's physically big for his age. He's very intelligent and he's good at sports, right?"

"Yes."

"Now, Alan is just average in height, was chubby until about a year and a half ago—"

"—which Steven still doesn't let him forget," she interjected.

"Right. And being two years younger, he's not as good at sports. I'm sure that in his eyes, he's completely powerless compared to his brother, and he'll never catch up. What we need to do is come up with something that will give Alan a sense of his power. We don't want him to get in the habit of using babylike behavior in response to Steven. He needs to excel in an area that Steven can't or won't compete in—any ideas? What are his strengths?"

"He's very musical. I was thinking of starting him on piano lessons. We were amazed to find that he can actually pick out some songs on the piano without ever having had a lesson."

"And Steven isn't interested in music?"

"Not even a little bit."

"Good. Go ahead with the piano lessons. Give him lots of positive attention for playing. You also might want to try giving Alan some strategies to use when Steven starts up with him."

"Like what?"

"Like ignoring him, walking away, looking for a friend from the neighborhood to play with, instead of Steven. You can continue to do the things we talked about before: even though they share a room, make sure they have their own space and insist that they respect each other's belongings. Assure and reassure Alan that you will protect him from Steven and then do it. And give Steven lots of positive one-on-one attention, especially for not picking on Alan."

"I don't know. It doesn't seem like anything works," Judy said doubtfully. I couldn't blame her. Steven had the most acute case of sibling rivalry that I had ever seen. I don't think that Judy Lewis had enjoyed a peaceful day since she brought Alan home from the hospital and Steven had realized that he would have to share his little world. She had worked diligently to diffuse Steven's anger and help him accept Alan as more than a punching bag, but, so far, nothing worked.

"Stick with it. It should improve when Alan starts feeling more powerful and capable. Then he'll be better able to brush off the attacks or ignore them altogether. Steven will probably start laying off a little as he gets older and busier with activities. Maybe you should think about getting Steven involved in some organized physical activity like soccer or swimming while Alan is doing his musical thing. He's a very physical kid and that might help him let off some steam."

"You know I'll try anything. Which reminds me—do you know where I can pick up a straitjacket in a child's size twelve?" she said with a tired smile as she got up to leave.

"I'm glad to see you've maintained a sense of humor," I responded.

"What sense of humor. I'm perfectly serious," she said over her shoulder as she headed toward the waiting room, where she hoped to find both boys alive and in one piece.

Few families with two or three kids born within a few years of each other are immune from sibling rivalry. And while Alan and Steven were an extreme case, being the Cain and Abel of modern times, sibling rivalry, to whatever degree, is a constant source of anxiety and uproar.

It's not surprising that sibling rivalry is such a fact of life when you think about what the existence of the secondborn means to the first. It's as if a husband said to his wife, "You are the love of my life and I will never stop loving you, but I'm going to bring home a nice new wife because I have so much love in my heart that I have enough to share with two (or three or four) wives. In the beginning I'll probably pay more attention to her, but don't worry, we will still do all the same family things, as always, together. Now, I want you to be nice to her and love her and share your things (including me) with her." Of course when you look at it that way, it's really no surprise that sibling rivalry so often rears its ugly head.

However, sibling rivalry should not be viewed as only negative. When it's in a healthy environment, sibling rivalry is an important way that children learn to get along, stand up for themselves, negotiate, and be social with other children. Often only children don't begin learning these skills until preschool.

Birth order, the number of years between children, and the sex of the children are all factors that influence the relationship between siblings and the intensity and form of the sibling rivalry. The term "sibling rivalry" is often used incorrectly. What we're really talking about is far more general—sibling interaction. To parents it can look like sibling rivalry but what's actually going on could be sibling reverence, sibling manipulation, sibling play, or sibling collusion.

I had been taking care of the Walstra family since Jenny was three and Brandon was five. In typical little-sister fashion Jenny adored, worshiped, and admired her older brother. Brandon agreed with her—he should be adored, worshiped, and admired. Their mother, Rebecca, was very aware of this relationship. It disturbed her and almost every time she came in she had a story about it.

When Jenny started preschool, the first thing she would do upon arriving at school each day was to run to the toy telephone and "call" Brandon. "Hi, Brand, this is Jenny. I just wanted you to know that I'm here at school and I arrived safely. I'm having fun, and I'm safe, and I knew you'd want to know. Bye-bye." Brandon, of course, wasn't the least bit concerned whether Jenny had arrived at school safely or whether she was having fun. In fact, he was fairly oblivious to the fact that she was even going to school.

"Brandon has been taking more notice of Jenny," Rebecca reported to me on a visit when Jenny was six.

"Well, that's good," I replied, knowing how important her brother's attention was to Jenny.

"Well, yes and no," Rebecca said.

"What do you mean?" I asked.

"Apparently he's figured out that Jenny can reach the kitchen cabinets, and he's proclaimed that slavery is not dead. He lies on his bed like King Farouk and bellows, 'Jenny— Cheetos—now!' And she, of course, is thrilled to bring them to him."

About a year later Jenny's grandmother took her to California for a week. No matter how busy she was or how much fun she was having, Jenny would take time each day to write her brother a detailed letter of her day's activities, and to tell him how much she missed him.

She couldn't wait to get home to him, and when she did she ran to him, gave him a huge hug, and shouted, "Oh, Brand, I missed you so much. Did you get my letters?"

"What letters?" he asked disinterestedly, squirming out of her hug. "Did you go somewhere?"

"I can't tell you how this hurts Jenny, but she always comes back for more," her mother reported to me shortly after the California trip. "She'll do his bidding no matter what he asks, and whenever he's in trouble she's always the one standing up for him. Even when he's catching it for being mean to her, she's still his little attorney."

"I know how you feel because it sounds a lot like what goes on in our house. Gordon and Lisa have a similar relationship to Brandon and Jenny. They too have that older-brother-younger-sister-she-worships-him-he-thinks-she-should thing going. The only difference is that Lisa can be pushed only to a certain point by Gordon, which he's tremendously fond of doing. Pushed past that point, she'll retaliate."

"I'd love to see Jenny retaliate. What does Lisa do?"

"Well, a typical evening in our home would include—but not be limited to—Gordon making Lisa wash the dinner dishes, even though it's his turn. This would be followed closely by

Gordon coming into Lisa's room, messing with her artwork and then wiping his dirty hands on her bedspread. This would push Lisa to her breaking point, signaled by her incredibly high-pitched scream. Lisa then will retaliate, simply by going into Gordon's room. Gordon is very particular about Lisa not being in his room. It's even posted on his door that she's to keep out. Lisa's entrance into the forbidden shrine is heralded by Gordon's bellowing. When Lisa lets out another high-pitched scream we know that Gordon has responded to her presence in his room by hitting her. Our evening deteriorates from there."

"Oh." Rebecca looked grim. "Maybe I don't want Jenny to start retaliating. But what can I do to help her?"

"This is a tough one. I'd just keep encouraging Brandon to be tolerant and even loving to Jenny. His approval is so important to her. You can give her ways to build self-confidence and self-esteem, so that she doesn't need to rely so much on his approval. But we both know he's always going to hold an important place for her."

Karen and Tony Glidden always seemed to be the perfect example of the older-sister–younger-brother combination. Karen was two and a half when Tony was born and she immediately took on the role of junior-mother-in-training. She would stand right by me when I examined him and provide color commentary. "What's you doing to my Tony now, Dr. Weinberger?" "I don't think he needs a shot today." "He's not growing fast enough, is he?"

Before their mother had a chance to fill me in on anything, Karen would give me all the news. "Tony has a tooth coming in and it makes him fuss." "Tony was up all night with a cough. He sounded like a dog barking and we didn't get no sleep."

As she got older she would offer her suggestions and remedies. "I think all he needs is to drink lots of water and take some pills." "I think he's allergic to ice cream because he barfed the other day after he ate some."

When Tony was just beginning to walk, Karen, curly red hair and freckled nose, just like her mother, would follow him around, guiding him away from the areas of the office that she felt were dangerous, and helping him up when he fell. She spoke to him in almost the same tone as her mother, with only a slightly more exaggerated, exasperated tone, "Now, Tony, how many times have I told you that you must stay away from those plugs. If you touch it, you will surely become electric."

When Tony was five and Karen almost eight I watched Karen automatically go to Tony to help him pull his turtleneck shirt off. "Kaareeen, I can take my own shirt ooooffff," he whined from inside the navy blue of his shirt.

"That's interesting," Karen said, turning away and sticking her nose up in the air, "because yesterday you sure couldn't."

After Tony had gone into the waiting room, so that Karen could have her check up in the privacy befitting a young lady of seven and three quarters, I asked her how she saw her little brother. "Well," she said, giving it plenty of thought, "now, he only sometimes listens to me, but I know just what to do when he gets in his bad moods."

"What's that?" I asked, amused by her whole demeanor.

"I go get him his bat and his ball and I tell him, 'You go out there in the yard and hit this around for a while and then you'll feel better.' It works every time."

As Karen and Tony got older, Tony occasionally resented the attention of his older sister, but at the same time you could see how much he adored her. In typical big-sister–little-brother fashion, she continued her role as the responsible caretaker in the family while Tony became more of an imp. Funny and a little wild, it was clear that he had no intention of competing with his older sister in the areas of school, organization, or overall maturity. He had Karen for all that.

When they were six and nine, Mrs. Glidden quietly watched them interact and then shook her head, a strange look on her face. "What?" I asked her.

"They remind me so much of me and my little brother, Everett."

"In what way?" I asked.

"Everett is a wonderful, competent man. He's an architect with one of the major New York firms. He builds skyscrapers, for God's sake, but he can't remember to pick up a pie to bring to Thanksgiving without my reminding him. And when I do he usually cons me into getting it for him. It's amusing, but at the same time I get a little tired of playing his mother. I don't want Karen to end up like that."

"Well, if I were you I'd want to make sure that Karen is valued for all the things she does and is, not just for her nurturing. Encourage her to excel in many areas. Now with Tony you want to encourage him to be more independent. Make sure he's got plenty of things he can do well—things that Karen isn't into, so that he doesn't always feel second best. But, let's face it, like you and Everett, Tony will always be Karen's baby brother whether he's building skyscrapers or performing heart surgery."

"I guess you're right," she responded, "but first he has to learn to take his shirt off all by himself."

Twins are no different than other siblings. One of them usually takes on the role of older, dominant sibling almost from birth. If both twins are healthy and the same gender, then it's usually the firstborn who takes on this role and the parents often perpetuate it.

I didn't know James and Timmy Morris until they were thirteen. They were identical twins, both bright, healthy, and athletic boys. James was only three minutes older but it might as well have been three years.

What first struck me was that James was always called "James," never "Jim" or "Jimmy," while Timmy was never called "Timothy" or even "Tim." It had been that way since birth, their mother told me. Although, she said, it had not been a conscious choice, that was just how it had evolved.

James and Timmy had the usual sibling rivalry and competition that brothers have, but one day they took it a step further. The Morris brothers, at sixteen, were both playing varsity soccer for their high school team. James was a fullback and Timmy was playing goalie. I wasn't there to witness what happened, but their mother, more than a little embarrassed, filled me in.

It was an important game against the rival school. Throughout the game Mrs. Morris could see James ordering Timmy around; positioning him here and there by pointing, yelling, and even shoving. Timmy responded by repositioning himself wherever his brother didn't want him to be. Shortly before halftime the score was tied 1 to 1 when a goal slipped by Timmy.

The gun went off signaling halftime and as the players headed for the sidelines, an irate James roughly grabbed his brother. Down they went onto the muddy field, James yelling at Timmy for letting the goal get by, and Timmy yelling right back at him that the ball had gotten by him too. Their teammates tried unsuccessfully to pull the twins apart. The spectators became silent watching, as the brawl turned into an out-and-out fistfight.

Mrs. Morris watched, mortified, from the stands. Finally the coaches and referees pulled the boys apart and ejected them from the game—which was won by the rival team.

"They've always been competitive," said Mrs. Morris. "But this is . . . this . . . I don't know."

"James and Timmy have always gone to the same schools, camps, played the same sports. Neither of them have ever had their own place in the sun, so to speak, have they?"

"No, I guess not. Being twins, they've always been in the same grade and they both have the same interests and strengths."

"I know it's a couple of years off, but you might want to give some thought to encouraging them to go to different colleges. It will be hard at first. They've always had each other to rely on, but I think it would be wonderful for each of them to develop a separate life from the other . . . to have a chance to be in the spotlight alone for a change."

"We've actually discussed that possibility already. We were preparing them for the fact that they both won't necessarily want to apply to the same schools, and, of course, they won't have control over where they're accepted."

"How did they react to that?"

"James had already given it some thought, but Timmy was shocked. I got the feeling, though, that he kind of liked the idea, after he gave it some thought."

"I bet since the infamous soccer game he's really taken a shine to the idea."

Female twins are no different. Brooke and Jamie Callner were fraternal twins, born five minutes apart. Brooke, the firstborn, was almost a half pound larger than Jamie at birth and she remained the bigger of the two and the leader. Brooke was well-known early on for bullying Jamie. They were often bickering and competing for the attention of their mother, Margie, a busy career woman who admittedly had not planned to have even one child, much less two. The girls were usually brought in by Margie and whoever the nanny-of-the-moment was.

The girls were in for their five-year checkup. Both of them were healthy and doing well. "How are they getting along?" I asked Margie, as the girls raced each other down the hall to the waiting room.

"We really have to keep an eye on Brooke, or frankly, she'll just beat the hell out of little Jamie. But that Jamie surprised us last month."

"Yeah, how?" I asked, expecting a blood-and-guts story of revenge and retaliation.

"The girls had just learned to write their names when we found BROOKE written in marker on the new wallpaper in the hall. I went after Brooke screaming like a banshee. She swore on the cat's life that she hadn't written her name on the wall. Of course I didn't believe her and she was punished—no TV. A few days later I was looking at an art project that Jamie had brought home from school and I noticed that she printed her E backward. The E on the wall was backward too. So I did a little detective work and checked out some of Brooke's more recent artwork, along with Jamie's. Brooke's E's were all printed correctly, while some of Jamie's E's were backward and some weren't. I didn't need to be Sherlock Holmes to figure out that Jamie had learned how to write 'Brooke' and purposely wrote her sister's name on the wall, to get her in trouble."

"She probably enjoyed watching Brooke get it."

"Oh yes. She's been having a grand time. Of course she's not so happy now. She was not only punished for writing on the wall, but for not speaking up when her sister got in trouble, as well."

Over the years the Callner girls continued their campaign of torture on each other, Brooke overtly hitting, pinching, or pushing Jamie, who loved to show off her "Brooke bumps" and bruises, while Jamie was sneaky and subtle, putting Brooke's beloved blankie in the trash when Brooke wasn't around, hiding phone messages or favorite articles of clothing.

When they were eleven, Brooke came in with a sore throat. When I looked in Brooke's mouth I noticed that the inside of her cheeks were cut up. "Brooke, have you showed these cuts to your orthodontist? He needs to adjust your braces."

"It's not the braces, Dr. Weinberger. It's Jamie. She grabs my face and rubs the inside of my cheeks against my braces. She thinks it's funny because nobody can see what she's done to me, but she's always showing everyone every little bruise I give her. What she doesn't know is that I can be sneaky too."

"What does that mean?" I asked, more than a little afraid to find out.

"I spit on her food whenever she's not looking. I've been doing it for years and she's never figured it out," Brooke stated proudly.

"Well, uh . . . good for you . . . I guess," was the only

response I could think of. "But since you have a strep throat we had better test your sister too," I added.

"Jocelyn's the sick one," ten-year-old Courtney Sanders informed me as I walked into the examining room. Nine-year-old Jocelyn just nodded up at me. There didn't seem to be a need for her to speak when her sister could so competently take care of everything. Courtney continued, "Leave it to Jocey to get sick with us going away next week. I hope this won't ruin everything."

"That's why we're here, Courtney. I'm sure she'll be fine," Mrs. Sanders said.

"Jocey, what are you doing? Get up on the table so that Dr. Weinberger can examine you," Courtney said in an exasperated tone. Jocelyn sort of sighed and scrambled up on the table.

"So what's the problem?" I asked, sitting down next to her.

"She has a sore throat," Courtney answered.

"Thanks, Courtney, but I was asking Jocelyn."

"Oh, sure," Courtney was quiet for a moment as I began my exam. I felt Jocelyn's glands and then took out my otoscope.

"Open your mouth and say 'ah,' " Courtney ordered before I had a chance.

I looked at her with what I consider my warning look. "Oops. Sorry," she said with an apologetic smile. "I just thought we'd get the show on the road."

I looked into Jocelyn's throat and took a throat culture. "Yuck," Courtney exclaimed as Jocelyn gagged slightly. "I hate that."

"Me too," Jocelyn finally spoke. "If I don't have strep, can I still take my tennis lesson?"

"We'll see," her mother responded.

"So how's the tennis coming?" I asked her as I continued the examination.

"Great. But I don't want to miss my lesson today. I want to be ready to play with my dad when we go to Florida next week. He promised to play with me every day."

"We'll see what we can do about that. What about you, Courtney, are you playing tennis too?"

"No, just Dad and Jocey play. I'm going to sit on the beach with Mom and read. We have two book reports due when we get back."

"Well, that's very diligent. How about you, Jocelyn? Are you going to do any schoolwork on vacation?"

"No way! I'll be too busy playing tennis and swimming and fishing with Dad."

I left the room briefly to check the strep test.

"It's negative," I said, coming back into the room. "Looks like you just have a cold."

"Okay," Courtney responded again before Jocelyn could.

"Okay, Jocelyn Sanders?" I asked again.

"Oookay," she said with a smile.

"Go on to the waiting room, girls. I'll be right there," Mrs. Sanders said.

"You want to go to the consultation room?" I asked her.

"No, this will just take a moment. I was just wondering if it's normal—you know—the way Courtney is always speaking for Jocelyn?"

"It's pretty typical of a big sister. Jocelyn'll start standing up for herself more as she gets older. Let me ask you a question. It seems like Jocelyn has become her father's little buddy and Courtney is yours. Am I reading that right, or am I way off base?"

"We're both close to both girls, but I think that's pretty true. Is there something wrong with that?"

"No, but you just want to be aware that both of you are being openly affectionate with both girls. Watch out for favoritism."

"I see what you mean. We'll be aware of that."

"Don't worry about Courtney and Jocelyn . . . they'll work out their own stuff as long as they both feel loved by both of you."

* * *

Georgie Schmidt was waiting for me in the consultation room. "What brings you here without the kids?" I asked her as I took a seat next to her.

"The kids of course. The house is in a constant uproar with the fighting. There is never a quiet moment." Not surprising— I didn't really think that there would be too many quiet moments in the Schmidt family. They had three children: Ben, thirteen, William, eleven, and Lauren, seven.

"Tell me what's going on."

"Take yesterday, after school. Ben was in his room doing his homework and Lauren was watching TV in the family room. William came home from baseball and went straight for the TV. He changed the channel without asking, even though Lauren was sitting right there watching one of her shows. She protested and he hit her. She screamed. The next thing I know William is off and running, Ben is chasing him through the house, William's trying to get away, and Lauren is still screeching from being hit."

"And this surprises you?"

"It doesn't surprise me. But I'm sick of it. I want to know what we can do about William's behavior."

"You see this as being about William's behavior?" I asked her.

"Well, he always seems to be in the middle of every conflict."

"Of course. He's the middle child. He's stuck between Ben, who's this great student, a high achiever, and who you and your husband rightfully think is wonderful, and Lauren, the baby, and the only girl in the family. She's sweet and lovely and good and is the apple of Ben's eye. Right?"

"Right," she agreed with my description of her children.

I continued, "William, who is very intelligent, has decided that he doesn't want to compete with his older brother in that arena. He will never be the little princess of the house. So, he has to make his mark somewhere, and what gets him more attention and could be more fun than picking on Lauren?"

"So what do I do about this?"

"Help him to find his own place and identity. Don't compare him to Ben or expect him to excel in the same areas and in the same way as Ben. Don't always automatically take Lauren's side against him. Little sisters have a way of provoking older brothers and then watching as the brother gets all the blame. Think about it . . . who told you what happened in the family room with the TV? Was it Lauren's story? William's? Or a combination?"

"Let me think . . . Lauren was yelling, and the boys were running around, but when the dust settled it was Lauren who told me what had happened. By then I had sent William to his room."

"Ah-ha. He didn't even have a chance to defend himself. Next time try listening to both sides of the story. I think you'll find that Lauren isn't without fault."

"And this will help?" Georgie asked in disbelief.

"If you mean, will the three of them stop fighting and bickering?—no. But if you help William find firmer ground in the family, he won't be as antagonistic, and Lauren won't provoke him so much if she knows that you're on to her game."

"It just seems that William is never going to get it together."

"He will. Middle children tend to be a little different, but they also tend to be the most skillful in handling people. They become the great negotiators. So don't give up on him."

"William, the great negotiator?" She shook her head in disbelief. "If you had seen him being chased around the house by Ben you wouldn't be able to picture it either."

As usual, Gracie Irving and her parents, Lynn and Bob, had requested the first appointment of the day to allow Bob to be at Gracie's exam and still get to work at a reasonable time. Gracie was always accompanied by both her parents at every checkup, exam, and consultation. She was an only child, and it was obvious that her parents thought she had hung the moon.

Gracie was a trip—running around the examining room like a maniac one moment, sitting sophisticatedly, legs crossed debutante style, having a serious discussion the next. Whatever mode she was in, the pure joy she gave her parents was evident.

Gracie and her dad were sitting on the examining room table, her mom in a nearby chair, when I walked in the room. Bob Irving immediately stood up and extended his hand. "Dr. Weinberger, good to see you." We shook hands. I greeted Lynn as well and then turned to Gracie.

"What's up, Gracie?"

"I go to school now," she announced proudly.

"Get out of town! You mean to tell me Mom and Dad let you out of their sight long enough to go to school?" Both parents laughed.

"I know you're joking, but leaving her at school that first day was so hard," Lynn said.

"How about you, Gracie? Was it hard for you?"

"Nah. It was easy," Gracie said, wrinkling her nose. "Amanda still cries when her mommy leaves, but not me."

"So you like school?" I asked.

"It's okay. There's just way too many kids there."

"How many is too many?" I asked her.

"Well, in the whole school there's about a zillion, and in my class there's seventy-three," Gracie told me confidently.

"I think it's more like twelve in your class, honey. And there are two teachers."

"Too many." Gracie insisted, turning her lips down in a pout.

"Miss Barnes, Gracie's teacher, is helping her learn to share," Lynn said, nodding at me. "Sometimes it's hard for her. She hasn't had to share very much."

"It's tough to share," I agreed with Gracie, "but if you share with other kids, then they'll share with you. Wait here, I'll be right back." I came back in with four Hershey's Kisses.

"Here, Gracie." Her eyes got big as I held out three kisses to her. "I want to share my candy with you."

"Thank you!" she said, enthusiastically grabbing all three kisses in her little hand. "Can I eat them now, Mommy?"

"Wait!" I said, covering her Kiss-filled hand with mine. "I have one Kiss. You have three Kisses, and Mommy and Daddy have no Kisses."

"Got any more for them?" Gracie asked, looking at me suspiciously.

"Nope, those are the last of my Kisses," I said, shaking my head sadly. I waited a few seconds, but Gracie did nothing except look longingly at her candy.

"I only have one Kiss, but I'd be happy to split it with you two," I said to Lynn and Bob.

"Why, thank you, Dr. Weinberger. That's so nice," Lynn said in a singsong voice.

"No, Mommy. Don't make Dr. Weinberger split that Kiss for three of you. I'll give you and Daddy one of mine to split."

There was a moment of mortified silence and then we started laughing. Gracie looked at us, confused.

"Whoa, Mrs. Barnes has her work cut out for her!" was all I could say.

Gracie, like many only children, found her first school experience to be something of a rude awakening. Spending your first three years not having to share the adults in your life, the toys on your shelf, or the candy from your pediatrician can make it tough when you're suddenly thrust into an environment where several children are vying for the attention of one or two adults, there's only one Big Bird puzzle, and you have to wait your turn for your snack or the bathroom.

It might have helped Gracie's social adjustment if, early on, she had been put in situations with other children on a somewhat regular basis. Having neighborhood children visit, playing with cousins, or being part of a play group are all relatively painless ways for preschoolers to begin learning to share and be social.

Mitchell Whiting was a typical only child. From his conception on, he was the focus of his parents' life. He grew into a bright, very mature boy who was given every advantage. At the same time, his parents had exceedingly high expectations of him, which he consistently strived to meet.

When he was eleven he came in with symptoms typical of hay fever. After getting him squared away, I asked him how things were going in general.

"Well, I'm playing Little League and my dad comes to every practice," he said as if his father was committing a major sin.

"Don't most dads go to the practices?"

"Not every single practice. Not all the time."

"Does it bother you?"

"Yeah! It makes me nervous because I feel like I have to perform for him. If I miss a catch or strike out, I feel like I let him down. And you know what? I'm not even good, but he wanted me to play because he said that it would make me more well-rounded. That's what they said about the piano lessons too. I think I'm plenty well-rounded by now."

"Can you talk to him? You know—ask him to not be at every practice? Hey, what would he say if you asked him to come only to the games?"

"God, Dr. Weinberger, I couldn't do that. He never got to play Little League, and he really loves it."

It's a common misconception that only children have it made. The fact is that it can be extremely difficult to be the sole recipient of two parents' love, discipline, standards, values, and expectations.

A few years later I sat again with Mitchell Whiting in the examining room. Unlike most fourteen-year-olds, he seemed to know exactly what the future held for him.

"I'll go to college, probably Ivy League, and then to med school," he said matter-of-factly, and without an ounce of bragging.

"When did you decide all this?" I asked him.

"It isn't like it was actually a decision. It's more like something I've just always known. My dad wanted to be a doctor, but he had to quit school when his father died. So, I've always known that I would be a doctor. Don't get me wrong. I'm not doing this just for Dad—it's what I want too."

"What's your specialty?" I asked him, half kidding.

"Heart surgery," he answered instantly and very seriously, to my amazement.

"And what if you change your mind?" I asked, playing devil's advocate.

"No way. It would be like asking my father to only come to the games," he replied with a smile.

9

Make Room for Daddy

It wasn't that long ago that a father's job was to bring home the bacon and dole out the punishments. But times have changed, and in many cases fathers are expanding their roles.

The first thing I noticed about Greta DeKlyn was her skier's tan, giving her the appearance of a raccoon. The second thing was that she was miserable. She had the harried and hassled look of one who was in desperate need of a vacation, despite the fact that she had obviously just returned from a ski trip.

The examining room was filled with her brood: Molly, five, three-and-a-half-year-old James, and two-year-old Samantha, all in various stages of minor maladies.

"What's happening?" I asked as I took a seat next to her.

"Marshall and I got back from Aspen late last night to find all three kids sick, the house a mess, and who has to deal with all of this?"

Obviously a rhetorical question.

"Me. That's who. Me and only me, and I just can't handle it anymore." The three children watched their mother's outburst intently.

"The housekeeper didn't let you know the kids were sick?"

"Marshall doesn't like to call home when we're away. He says that Magda is more than competent to take care of anything that might come up."

I knew their housekeeper, Magda. She often brought the kids in and she was competent and kind and obviously loved the kids, but it still seemed very odd that parents wouldn't have contact with their children while out of town.

"This really seems to be upsetting you," I said.

"It's an impossible situation." She struggled not to cry.

"Let me get the kids squared away. Then they can play in the waiting room while we talk."

Greta watched quietly as I examined each of her children, finding nothing more serious than a bad cold. They happily went to play in the waiting room, and Greta and I went into the consultation office to talk.

"Now," I began, "tell me about this impossible situation."

"Well, you know Marshall . . ." she began.

I shook my head. "I don't believe I've met Marshall. I can't remember him ever bringing the kids in."

"No?" She thought for a moment. "I guess not. Well, Marshall is twelve years older than me. He was married before and has two older kids. He never planned on remarrying, much less having more children. We started dating and fell in love, and I wanted to marry him. I gave him an ultimatum— either we get married, or the relationship is over. He agreed right away, but he told me that he didn't want any more children. He said that he had lived that part of his life and now he had the time and money to do whatever he wanted, and he didn't want that destroyed by children."

"But now you have three," I said.

"Well, shortly after we were married I realized just how much I wanted children. It was more than wanting kids—I needed kids. I told him how important it was to me and he reminded me of our agreement. I begged and pleaded. I promised him that he would never have to do anything, never have to lift a finger for the children. I promised him that I would not only do it all, but also that he would remain my number one priority, and that I would always be available for him."

"That's quite a promise," I said in disbelief.

"Well, at the time I had no idea what having children was really like. And now I regret it—not the children. I love them. I don't regret having them for a minute, but I'm sorry I made that promise. I'm one person living two lives. I'm a childless wife to my husband and I'm a single parent to my children." She started to cry. "I just can't go on like this."

"You're right. You can't. I don't know how you've lived like this for so long," I told her. "Do you think if we set up an evening consultation that Marshall will come in and talk?"

"I don't know, but I'll try."

Greta called me the next day, surprised and a little relieved. "Marshall agreed to come in and talk." Not wanting to give him a chance to change his mind, we set up a time for the next evening.

Marshall DeKlyn, a very elegant, well-dressed man in his late fifties, shook my hand warmly and sat down next to Greta.

"Obviously you agreed to come in because there's something upsetting your wife," I began.

He looked at me with the hint of a smile. "I know exactly what's upsetting my wife and I can't do anything about it. We had an agreement and I don't intend to change my lifestyle at this point. Greta has known this from the start. I've always been honest with her."

Greta hurriedly grasped his arm. "No, no, honey. No one expects you to change anything. I'm the one who's going to have to find a better way to handle all this myself."

"Wait a second," I said, not believing what I was hearing. "You are in an untenable situation. You can hire all the help you want for the house and the kids, but you're tearing yourself apart trying to run a separate life with your husband, and another life as the mother of three children." There was dead silence.

Greta looked down at her hands, now folded on the table in front of her. Marshall was still looking at me with a slight grin.

"What role do you play?" I asked him.

"Well," he said, sitting up straighter and adjusting his tie, "I see myself as the father figure," he said unconvincingly. "I provide materially for the children and of course I see the children each night." He thought for a moment, but couldn't seem to come up with any other sign of involvement with his children. "Look, I'm not the one who wanted more children. I've been that route. Greta, you're the one who wanted children, and now you have them."

For one of the first times in my professional career—actually in my life—I found myself speechless. We sat in shocked silence for several minutes. I finally spoke. "Tell me about your first go-around with children."

"Well," Mr. DeKlyn said, leaning back in his chair, as if preparing to tell a long story, "I was married very young the first time. I was only twenty-one—right out of college. We had two sons within the next five years and I was working my ass off trying to build a business. I readily admit it—I was never home—and that's what led to the divorce.

"My wife and kids moved to Ohio to be near her parents and I only saw the boys at holidays and for three weeks during the summer. I would do my best to be totally involved with them when they were visiting, but I was so far out of their lives that I always felt like a stranger to them.

"My whole life was work and I realized I felt empty." He paused and took his wife's hand. "Then I met Greta and, I know it sounds corny, but I knew I had found my soul mate." She smiled broadly at him. "Now I had someone to share my life and success with. I knew I didn't want more kids. In the first place they would be an encumbrance, and in the second place I knew I was a terrible father. All you had to do was look at my track record to see that. I think deep down I also felt like it would be a betrayal to my sons to have more kids."

"I never knew you felt like that," Greta said gently. Marshall nodded.

I felt way out of my league. There was nothing in my training that prepared me for anything like the DeKlyns. After some more discussion I suggested they see Maida Webster, patient mother, trusted friend, and wonderful family therapist.

With Maida they worked on Marshall's acceptance of the idea that his fathering his younger children was not a betrayal of his older children. Along with that they also talked a lot about Marshall's equating fatherhood with financial support instead of what was really needed of him—emotional support for both the children and Greta.

However, the feeling of not being able to do enough for them, within the practice, disturbed me. It was becoming ever more clear that if I was going to help these families, to give them all that they needed, and all that they asked for, I would need some help myself.

Strep throat and chicken pox were easy. It was the vastly different ways that families functioned and didn't function that was becoming my deeper concern. More and more I was being called upon to heal things that couldn't be cured with a trip to the pharmacy or bed rest. I knew that there had to be a better way to help these families. The answer was to put into practice what I had learned as a resident—but how?

Marshall DeKlyn was a very extreme example of one kind of father, but to be truthful, he probably wasn't that far off from what his father, his role model, must have been like. It wasn't that long ago that a father's job was to bring home the bacon and dole out the punishments. But times have changed, and in many cases fathers are expanding their roles.

Although it is different for each father and each family, it can't be denied that the more actively a father is involved with his children, the more the entire family benefits. It's also true that the father who becomes involved with his children when they are infants—feeding, bathing, playing with them, and, yes, changing their diapers, is the father who will be confident enough to continue his involvement with his children as they grow.

It's the father who waits until his child is old enough to play ball who will have trouble getting and staying involved in his child's life in any sort of meaningful way. Strangely enough, it can be the wife/mother who's the biggest stumbling block to that early father-child connection. Leslie Finch started out to be one of those mothers.

She brought her daughter, Margaret, in for her one-month checkup. "Margaret's doing great," I told her as she got the baby dressed. "Now, how are you doing as a first-time mom? Is it everything you thought it would be and more?"

"It's much harder than I thought. Boy, I'm tired."

"It goes with the territory," I assured her.

"No, I'm really deep-down-to-the-bone exhausted. I haven't had a minute alone without Margaret since the night in the hospital after I gave birth. I just assumed Roger would be helping more . . . you know, be more involved. But he just isn't. Once he changed her diaper and he acted like it was some sort of big deal. I know he loves Margaret, but he's just so . . . I don't know . . . hands off."

"That's not too unusual. Some dads need a kick in the butt to get into it. Here's what I want you to do. Tonight you tell him that you're going out for a few hours Saturday afternoon, so the baby will be with him. I don't want you to ask him, I want you to tell him, as if this is the most natural thing in the world. Be careful how you phrase it. Don't say you want him to 'baby-sit' with Margaret. He's not the baby-sitter. He's the dad and he is, at least in theory if not in practice, equally responsible for her." A slow grin spread over Leslie's face at the thought of her baby-free afternoon.

"Can you do that?" I asked, knowing that a lot of first-time mothers are reluctant to leave their one-month-old babies-even with the father.

But not Leslie. "You bet I can!" she almost shouted, sounding like a cheerleader.

The next time she came in, I couldn't wait to hear how her afternoon out went. "Tell me all about it," I said, before I even examined Margaret.

"It didn't work out at all. I got very upset and so angry. You know, I can't believe you would recommend I abandon my baby," she said, suddenly angry at me.

"I didn't recommend you abandon Margaret. I suggested you leave her for a few hours with her father. Now, tell me what happened."

"Well, he was fine when I told him he was going to take care of Margaret. No problem. Then, before I left, I went over everything with him. I showed him where the bottles were and how to heat them up. I showed him where I kept the diapers and the baby wipes and I even wrote out your number and put it by the phone—just in case. He seemed confident and in complete control when I left, and I did have a wonderful three hours. I felt like a prisoner set free."

"So what was the problem?"

"When I got home, there he was in front of the TV, and Margaret was in her crib. I went right in to see her, and, Doctor, I couldn't believe my eyes.

" 'Calm down, calm down,' he kept saying, which just made me more upset. 'I was just changing her and some of that lotion got on the little tape you close the diaper with. It wouldn't stay closed, and I didn't want to waste another diaper. So I figured I'd just tape her up. It worked great.' Ooh, I wanted to smack that silly smile right off his face. Her entire diaper was covered with duct tape and he didn't see anything wrong with it!" She looked at me, obviously expecting me to agree with her.

"Was Margaret in distress?"

She shook her head no.

"Was she crying?"

She shook her head no.

"Was she sleeping peacefully—you know—like a baby?"

She nodded her head yes, and even smiled, faintly.

"So what was wrong with the duct tape?"

"You just don't duct tape a baby. He treated her like she was some sort of do-it-yourself-fix-it project, not his daughter."

"You know when we had our first child, my wife told me she was going to leave me alone with him for the first time. I told her that was fine, I'd take care of everything.

"She got home and picked up our son and said, in amazement, 'You changed him?'

"I said, 'That's right. He had a BM so I changed him.'

"She said, 'Did you clean him off?'

"I said, 'Of course.'

"Now she was very suspicious. 'How did you clean him off?' She wanted to know.

" 'I held him over the kitchen sink and squirted some soap on him and then used that sprayer thing on his bottom. He got nice and clean.'

" 'What kind of soap?' she asked.

" 'Dishwashing soap.' She was very upset about that. You'd have thought I'd used Brillo on the kid. But to this day I still think I did a terrific job."

Leslie didn't say anything. It was clear she expected me to continue. "So, you see what's going on here?"

"Yes. You and Roger are clueless when it comes to changing babies."

"No, that's not it. Roger and I and probably your mother-in-law and maybe even your own mother, all have different ways of doing things. Granted, Roger probably used three diapers' worth of duct tape, but he did it his way and Margaret was fine. If you chastise him for not doing things exactly your way, he really won't want to be involved with Margaret's care at all."

"Let me get this straight; as a pediatrician you're advising me to overlook the use of hardware on my baby."

"Now you've got it! I assure you, if you just tell Roger what a great job he's doing when he takes care of Margaret—instead of correcting him—then he'll jump into this with both feet. Remember, there is no one right way to do things. I'm sure Roger was just trying to be thrifty when he used the duct tape. It makes perfect sense to me even if it doesn't to you."

"It *would* make perfect sense to someone who used dishwashing soap on their baby. But I'll try to be more flexible and understanding."

Leslie Finch did lighten up a bit after that, particularly when she saw that even little Margaret could benefit from having two parents involved in her life. Of course it didn't hurt that with Roger more involved, Margaret could get some rest and time to herself.

Tina and Patrick Wellman came in for a consultation. Tina was eight months pregnant and they were pediatrician shopping. A nice-looking couple in their early thirties, they asked all the usual questions, had the usual concerns, and decided that they would use our practice.

I started to take their histories. "What do you do?"

"I'm in public relations and Patrick is a graphic artist," Tina answered.

"Have you made any decisions about child care yet?" I asked.

They looked at each other and smiled. "I'm leaving my job in three weeks. I'm going to be staying home with the baby," Patrick said proudly.

"Do you see a lot of dads doing that?" he then asked, concern in his voice.

"To tell you the truth, I don't see that many, but I think it's great. You're a real pioneer," I told him. "Do you mind if I ask how you came to this decision?"

"Not at all," said Tina. "We always agreed that one of us would take care of the baby. Neither of us is comfortable with a full-time nanny or day-care."

"I admit, I just assumed that Tina would be the one to quit her job, but when we started talking about it, we realized that made absolutely no sense. Tina makes more money, she has more opportunity for advancement, and she's simply happier with where she's at now than I am."

"Also Patrick can freelance and work part-time as the baby gets older. There's no way I can do that. So, this just seemed to be the right answer." I could see how pleased they were with their solution to child care.

"I'm curious. How do your families feel about this?"

"Both mothers are amused by it, but my father's not so sure," Patrick said.

"Actually his father said, 'It's just not right for an able-bodied man to be sponging off his wife,'" Tina said in a surprisingly deep baritone.

"Thanks, Tina. Now Dr. Weinberger's going to think my dad's a chauvinist pig," Patrick complained.

"Not at all. I'd be surprised if you didn't get some of that. Remember this is a relatively new idea. Even you admitted that you assumed Tina would be at home. You better expect to get some of that attitude."

Tina Wellman went back to work six weeks after the birth of her son, T.J. I always looked forward to Patrick and T.J.'s visits. It was terrific to see the way he reveled in his son. He could barely take his eyes off the baby. But when Patrick brought T.J. in for his three-month checkup, I could tell that something was not quite right.

"Tina's really unhappy," Patrick told me as he held T.J. over his shoulder and gently patted his behind. "When she comes home from work she wants to be with T.J., but she insists that he prefers me and that hurts her."

"That's pretty much the way it is in all families. T.J.'s going to be more comfortable with his primary caregiver, and that's you. He doesn't know mom from dad. At this point, he just knows whose hold feels the most natural and whose voice and face are the most familiar. I'm going to tell you the same thing that I would tell the mothers who come in here and voice the same concerns for their working husbands. T.J. will not love her less, but she must understand that T.J. recognizes you as his primary and constant caretaker."

"You can be the one to explain that to her," he said.

"Don't be afraid to tell her. It's just a fact of life, and a fact based on the stage that T.J.'s in. Before she knows it, T.J.'s face will light up every time she enters a room, and the next thing she'll know, he'll be running to the door to meet her. Right now he's just more comfortable with the one who's more familiar—that's you."

Patrick Wellman wasn't my only house-husband and stay-at-home dad. Arnie Oppenheimer's road to house-husbandry was a lot more rocky than Patrick Wellman's. Through his three children's early childhood, Arnie was a disinterested, uninvolved parent. He was a workaholic in the high-pressure job of futures trading. Although his hours would have allowed him to be home in the late afternoon and evenings with his family, he was rarely home before ten or eleven at night.

Carole Oppenheimer often complained about her husband. But I was still surprised by what she told me when she came into the office one day. She had brought her middle child, Carly, in with a fever and sore throat. I noticed that Carole was not herself. She was very quiet and distracted.

I finished examining Carly and turned my attention to Carole. "We know what's wrong with Carly, but what's bothering you?"

"Hmm? Oh." She looked at Carly and I realized that she didn't want to talk in front of her six-year-old daughter.

"Carly, did you know we got five new fish for the tank? You want to go out and take a look?" I suggested.

"Yeah!" she said and happily ran out.

I looked at Carole, expecting her to speak, but she just looked back at me, her eyes so sad.

"What's going on? I can tell something's wrong."

"I'm . . . we're getting a divorce," she said. Her eyes instantly filled with tears.

"When was this decided?" I asked, handing her a tissue. I had seen Carole just six weeks ago and she hadn't mentioned divorce.

"Last week. Arnie's been fooling around. I suspected it for the longest time, but now I have proof."

"So you're going to separate and file for a divorce?"

"Yes, I just can't put up with this anymore."

"What did he say when you told him?"

"He doesn't want a divorce. But then why should he? He has everything he wants the way it is now."

"I know I've suggested this before, but what about counseling before you make a big move like this? You have nothing to lose and your whole marriage to gain."

"No. This is it. As far as I'm concerned it's over."

"Are you sure you don't want the name of a good counselor?"

"No, I'm sure about this."

"What about the kids? Do they know anything yet?"

"No. I'm not going to say anything to them until I talk to an attorney." She looked at her watch. I could tell she was getting anxious talking about all this. "I've got to get over to the park and pick Derrick up."

"Okay. You know I'm here if ever I can help you or the kids."

"Thank you," and she hurried out.

Two weeks later I was chatting with Mary Leigh, who had brought in her six-year-old, Tracey. "Carly Oppenheimer's your patient, isn't she?" Mary asked.

"Uh-huh." I waited for her to mention the divorce. I couldn't imagine why else she would be bringing up the Oppenheimers.

"Can you believe what that poor family's going through? How can someone so young have a massive coronary?"

"A massive coronary? What are you talking about?"

"Didn't you hear? Arnie Oppenheimer had a heart attack. He's doing all right now, but he won't be able to work anymore or do anything more strenuous than taking a walk. Can you imagine? He's only forty."

"Are you sure? Where did you hear this?"

"Carly and Tracey are best friends. We've all been helping with the kids so that Carole can be at the hospital with Arnie. I'm surprised you didn't know."

The following day I got a call from Carole. "I suppose you

heard about Arnie?" were the first tired words out of her mouth.

"Just yesterday. I was going to give you a call. How are you and the kids doing?"

"I don't know. I'm absolutely numb. It's all so unreal. It feels like I'm watching myself in a movie."

"I can only imagine. I'm glad you called. There must be something I can do for you and the family."

"There is. That's why I called. I think that now I'm ready for the name of a counselor. I've totally lost control of my life. I don't know whether I'm coming or going. Here I was about to divorce this man and now he's lying in the hospital. He was so close to death. There's no way that I can go through with a divorce. Now I'm just so confused."

"It's a tough time, I know. I'm going to give you a couple of names for yourself and then I'm also going to give you the name of someone for the kids." I gave her the referrals.

"Thanks, Dr. Weinberger. I've got to get back to the hospital."

"Will you promise to call if there's anything else I can do?"

"Absolutely, I need all the help I can get."

But I didn't see or hear from Carole for several months. Then she came in with eight-year-old Derrick. Carole looked great, not at all what I had expected.

"How's it going?"

"I don't want to jinx it, but I think things are starting to come together. Arnie's feeling better each day, but he will have to be on permanent disability. I went back to selling real estate full-time and that's going well. So well that I told Arnie that he would have to start taking more responsibility for the care of the kids. After all, he's the one who's home most of the time. At first he gave me a hard time, but now I think he's starting to enjoy it."

"That's great but what about the two of you?"

"I don't know. It's very strange, but Arnie has been a different man since the heart attack. He's more like he was when we first got married. He's sweet and attentive. He's trying so hard to keep us together. But I don't know if this is just temporary because of the heart attack, or if he's really changed."

"You still in counseling?"

"We're in counseling *together*. Right now we're just taking it one day at a time. But if things continue the way they're going now, then I could see us staying together."

It was six months before I saw any of the Oppenheimers again. When they finally came in I was surprised to see that it was Arnie with all three children. After I was done with the kids Arnie said that he wanted to talk to me alone. The kids went to the waiting room, and we went in the consultation room.

"How do you like being an at-home dad?" I asked, eager to hear how he was doing.

"I love it, and let me tell you, no one is more surprised than I am. I had no idea what I was missing. Did you know that lots of dads go to those assembly programs at school? I'd never been to one. It was hysterical. Derrick played a verb. He did a little verb dance with five other kids. He was cute as hell. I was so proud, I thought I'd burst."

"I try to get to those programs. There's nothing like seeing your kids up there," I agreed with him, remembering some of Gordon's and Lisa's stellar performances.

"I can't believe that there was this whole world going on that I had nothing to do with," he mused.

Suddenly he looked very serious. "Dr. Weinberger, Carole said she talked to you about our marriage—I was a bum, but I'm determined to make us work. But I've also been a lousy father. I wanted to ask you how I could make it up to my kids."

"Look at you! You've already begun making it up to them. You do it just the way you're doing it—by being there and being involved and loving and just enjoying them." His face broke into a huge, proud grin.

"Really, that's it?" he asked. I nodded. "Who would have thought that a heart attack would be a blessing, but if I hadn't had it I would never have gotten to know my kids the way I do now, and I would have certainly lost Carole."

"You could have had the heart attack, but not changed at all. Give yourself credit for heeding the warning of the heart attack, and turning your life around."

Another family I had been seeing had a very different reaction when tragedy struck. The Klein children were three and six and I had been seeing them both since they were born, but I had only seen Gary, the father, once or twice.

I was on my way into the examining room where both of the Klein kids were waiting for checkups, when I was stopped by Edith. "Can I talk to you for a moment?" she asked, and without waiting for an answer she headed for the consultation room. I followed her obediently.

"What?" I asked. She didn't sit down, so neither did I.

"It's not Sandy Klein in there with the kids. It's Mr. Klein and he looks like something's wrong."

"What do you mean?" I asked, surprised. Edith was not one for dramatics.

"I'm not sure. He looks really hassled and peeved. Maybe he's mad because he had to wait. He doesn't seem the type to wait for anything. Just wanted to warn you."

"Well thanks, Edith. I appreciate the warning."

I hurried to the examining room. The last thing I needed on this morning was to be yelled at by an irate father. I knocked on the door, took a deep breath and walked in. Edith wasn't kidding. Mr. Klein just didn't look right. His hair was disheveled, his suit was wrinkled, and his tie was askew.

"Hi, I'm terribly sorry to keep you waiting, but I got tied up at the hospital this morning. I've been running late all day, and I do mean running. I'm sorry." He didn't answer me. He just looked at me with a glazed look. I wondered for a moment if he was on some drug.

Looking at the kids, I realized they weren't themselves either. The six-year-old, Reed, was usually very high-energy, racing around the examining room, but today he was just sitting quietly on the examining table, next to his sister, three-year-old Whitney.

Something was not right about Whitney either. Usually Sandy had her dressed like a little doll. She always matched from the bow on the top of her head to her little socks. Today she didn't have a bow. I realized that I had never seen this child without a bow. Even before she had hair, Sandy had found a way to affix a bow to her fuzzy little head. Today, her clothes didn't even match. Actually they didn't even fit. She seemed to be wearing Reed's clothes.

"How's everything?" I asked, scared to hear the answer.

Gary let out a huge sigh, then looked over at his children. "Sandy, ah . . . Sandy had an aneurysm—a brain aneurysm. She died before they could get her to the hospital." Reed looked over at his father and his eyes filled with tears. Whitney immediately stuck her thumb in her mouth.

I couldn't believe what I was hearing. "Oh my God. Oh God. I'm so sorry. I don't know what to say. When did all this happen?"

"Last Friday. Thank God both kids were in school."

"Mommy went to heaven and she can't come back," Whitney said matter-of-factly.

"I know, honey, and I'm so sorry." I sat down next to her and put my arm around her.

"How you doing, Reed?" I said, reaching behind Whitney and grabbing his arm.

"I want Mom," he said choking back the tears.

"It's hard. Isn't it?"

He nodded his head. I examined both children slowly and gently. They were, understandably, quiet and withdrawn.

When I finished the exams, I turned my attention to Mr. Klein. "Do you have a minute to talk?"

"Just a minute," he said. So I turned the children over to Edith in the waiting room and took Mr. Klein into the consultation room.

"I want to give you the name of a good therapist. This is just so traumatic, and I think you all could probably use some help."

"I can't see myself talking to a therapist. We'll be all right. I just have to figure out what I'm going to do about the kids and all. Do I hire a nanny or have them go with their grandparents or what? I can't very well give up my job to be with them. You know Sandy took care of everything. I wouldn't have known that the kids were supposed to come in today, except I happened to look in Sandy's date book. You know when I went to pick Reed up at school that Friday, I didn't even know where his classroom was. Hell, I didn't even know what his teacher's name was. I'd never even seen the nursery school where Whitney goes. Now how do I go from that to full-time father?"

"Gradually and with help. Please take a couple of names. If it would make it easier for you I could call and let them know that you'll be calling and tell them a little about your situation."

"No really, I'll be okay. We'll be okay." He looked at his watch. "I've got to drop them off and get to a meeting." He stood up to leave.

"You're back to work already?" I asked incredulously.

"Just part-time. You know how it is. Some things can't wait. Thank you for your help." He offered a quick handshake as he hurried out.

I watched him walk out, his children sadly trailing him, trying to keep up with the rushed, grown-up steps of their father.

I waited a week before I called him to offer him help again and see how all three of them were doing.

"Things are starting to settle down," he said. "I've hired a live-in nanny. She'll take care of the house and the children. They seem to like her."

"And the kids, how are they?"

"They're all right—considering. They've been spending most of their time with my sister-in-law and her kids."

"Have you given any more thought to getting some counseling for you and the kids?"

"It's unnecessary. We all seem to be doing okay."

That was the last contact I had with Gary Klein. From then on the kids were brought in by their nanny, a very proper, but loving, British nanny. Mrs. Potter was authentic—the real thing. She always made me think of Mary Poppins. The kids even called her Nanny. She was apparently off on the week- ends, but it didn't seem like Gary was spending the weekends with Reed and Whitney either. Several times, on a Saturday, I got calls from their aunt, who lived in a nearby town, with concerns over one of the children.

There was no doubt that these children were well cared for and even loved by their nanny and aunt, but the tragedy of their mother's loss was greatly compounded by the inability of their father to make the necessary changes to become a con- sistent and important part of their lives.

John Much sat on the examining table—a larger but other- wise exact replica of his eight-year-old son, Todd. They were both wearing khakis and jean jackets and swinging their legs. Why is it, I wondered, that the few fathers who come in with their children sit on the examining table, when I rarely ever see one of the mothers up on the table? I guess it's just a dad thing.

John almost always brought Todd in. Todd's mother, Beckie, worked for an insurance agency and John worked at home as a freelance writer; a job that allowed him to be Todd's primary caregiver.

"What's up, Todd?" I asked, sitting across from him on a stool.

"I hurt my stomach, sliding at a baseball game, and the school nurse said that you had to look at it."

"I didn't think it was anything serious, but the nurse made a big deal out of it," John said. I had found that fathers were usu- ally pretty relaxed about things like scrapes and cuts.

"Pull off your shirt and let's have a look."

Todd pulled off his shirt. He had a good five-by-seven-inch

scrape on his stomach. "That's a good one, all right. Were you at least safe?"

"I wasn't only safe, I scored a run."

"Good for you. Well, it looks like you're keeping it clean but I think a scrape this deep and big should be covered. The school nurse could have done this for you. John, you watch. This dressing will need to be changed every day, until it heals."

John watched carefully as I bandaged his son. "Make sure you keep it nice and clean and dry so it doesn't become infected—and you"—I looked up at Todd—"no more sliding on your stomach until this is completely healed."

"But I can play, right?"

"Absolutely."

"So, what's up with you?" I asked John.

"Same old stuff. Actually there's one new thing in my life."

"What's that?" I asked, expecting an interesting new client.

"I'm going to be one of the room mothers—ahh—parents for Todd's class next year. Isn't that a kick?"

Rarely were fathers room parents. This was a job that was usually taken on by mothers. So much so, that although the official title was room parent most people called the job room mother.

"How did that happen?" I asked.

"Beckie was asked to do it, but she doesn't have time to do the job justice. On the other hand, I've been feeling a little bit at loose ends since Todd's been spending a full day at school, so I figured why not? We need to do our part for the school, and it doesn't really matter whether it's Becky or I who puts the time in."

It was refreshing to talk to a father like John Much. Sometimes I felt like he was one in a million.

"Good luck. I understand it's a hotbed over there," I said, teasing him.

"Well, it's a tough job, but somebody's got to do it," John replied.

The following fall John brought Todd in for his yearly checkup.

"How is the third-grade room parent?" I asked him.

"I had no idea." He shook his head. "I had absolutely no idea."

"What do you mean?" I asked.

"I thought it would be an easy job, but it's really tough. You've got to line up volunteers for about a million events and field trips and attend meetings and take phone calls from parents who have complaints and questions but don't want to talk directly to the teacher. You know, I can't stand in front of school anymore without being hounded and mobbed. And it's just the beginning of the year."

"You know I remember Susan was a room mother but she never complained."

"No? Well then she's made of sterner stuff than I am, because if I have one more parent come up and beg me to be the Halloween helper, I don't know what I'll do."

You don't have to be the primary caregiver to be a good and involved father. I know one father who when he can get a break in his workday is known to run over to school at dismissal time just to give his son a hug and kiss before he gets on the school bus to go home.

Another father always takes each of his children away once a year on separate weekend vacations. He says, "We do plenty of family stuff together all the time, but there's nothing like taking each of them away alone, without interruptions or the bickering and stress of everyday life. You really get to know your kids that way." This is a father who truly enjoys his kids—always has and undoubtedly always will.

I don't know of a home where the parenting can be split fifty-fifty, but it is important that parents act as a team. When the child is a baby, both parents can take responsibility for, and spend time with, the child. And when the child is in school, the school should know that both parents are interested and involved, that both parents are there for conferences, and that both share emergency duty, even if it means disrupting the workday.

By putting forth the effort and making the time, most fathers find that they enjoy their children and that the time they spend with them is valuable, memorable, and sure beats anything else they could be doing.

10

Reality Parenting

They deserve to be parented based on who they are, rather than on who we are, what we want, and how we were parented.

From the time of her son, Quinn's, birth, Rosellen Stauffer was always talking about how brilliant he was. For two years I thought she was joking. Then she brought Quinn in for his two-year exam.

"Look at this," she said proudly, handing me a piece of paper.

I looked down at the paper. It was covered with scribbles. "Yes?" I said, not quite sure why I was looking at scribbles.

"It's Quinn's first work of art. I saved it to show you. Don't you think it's brilliant? He did it over two months ago," she told me proudly and quite seriously.

I didn't quite know what to say. "It's uh . . . ah . . . umm . . . beautiful," I finally said.

"I knew all along. Remember, I told you from the beginning he was brilliant."

She stood firm in her belief that she was raising a genius until he turned four. When she brought him in for his four-year exam she brought with her a briefcase full of papers. It was a complete report on an extensive battery of tests. She had actually taken Quinn to the Geselle Institute to confirm her belief that her son was the next Einstein. However, she was crushed to learn he was only smart—not a genius, but smart.

"Can you look over these tests," she asked me, "and tell me what we can do to *make* him brilliant?"

Year after year, appointment after appointment she pursued this. There was no telling her that we couldn't make him brilliant. I could only predict trouble ahead when Quinn started school, where his performance would undoubtedly fall short of his mother's unreasonably high expectations.

It's not only important to understand where your child's at intellectually, but also to understand your child's basic temperament. Louise Bohn came in with her five-day-old son, Kent. He was screaming his little head off.

"What's going on with him?" I said loudly.

"You tell me. He's inconsolable unless he's on the breast. There's nothing I can do to make him stop."

I went ahead and examined the baby through the screams, and he was fine. He had even gained weight. I finished the exam. Louise put his clothes back on him and put him on her breast. Boom! He was quiet. Silence filled the room. It was such a relief. Kent had the highest-pitch scream I had ever heard, and when he cried he worked himself into such a state that sweat dripped off him, and his face became bright red.

"Woooo," I said, "this is going to be tough."

"You're telling me. I was going to go back to work in six weeks, but I can't if I have to have my breast in his mouth twenty-four hours a day."

"We'll have to try everything; different pacifiers, we'll express your milk and try different nipples. It might work to swaddle him. We'll just have to see how it goes."

Louise and Kent came in for his two-week exam. I knew the minute they came into the office. Kent loudly announced their arrival throughout the office—the whole building, I suspected.

"I can guess how things are going," I shouted over the din. His lungs had certainly developed over the two weeks. I examined him. He was fine and healthy. It was his mother I was concerned about. "Did bottle-feeding or the pacifier work?"

"No," she yelled back.

"What about the swaddling?"

"It only made it worse." She put him on the breast—silence. "Now we can talk," she said with a sigh.

"Let's discuss personality differences, because you have a baby here who has a very low threshold to stimuli and he wants what he wants when he wants it. He won't have it any other way. That's going to be a killer combination for you and your husband. So if you can understand him, at least we can start from there and work on it." She nodded.

I continued. "Now what do you do when he's inconsolable?"

"You mean like always?"

"Uh-huh."

"My husband, my sister, my mother, everyone tries to comfort him. We try the bottle or the pacifier, rocking, swaddling, but nothing works except putting him on the breast. We tried letting him get real hungry, hoping that would make him take the bottle, but that didn't even work."

"I'm sorry," I told her, "but I think you have a definite breast-feed baby here. I don't know if there's any way you'll be able to get him off the breast until he can feed himself and drink from a cup. I'm even going to go so far as to predict he's going to be a challenging kid. But I do think he'll be much happier as he gets older and can do things for himself."

"How can you predict this?" she asked, looking a little scared.

"Based on his temperament."

"What do you mean?" she asked.

"His temperament is basically how he comes to you, prewired, so to speak. There are nine characteristics of temperament as described by Alexander Thomas and Stella Chess."

She noticed that Kent had fallen asleep, but she didn't

move him. I didn't blame her. "What are they and how does Kent fit into all this?"

"You want to know what all the characteristics are?" I asked her. She nodded.

"Okay, let me see if I can remember them. There are nine. The first one is 'activity.' Activity relates to the amount of physical activity you see in him during sleeping, eating, and, later on, play. He seems to be a fairly active little guy from what I see so far. Next is 'rhythmicity'; this relates to the regularity of his physiological functions such as hunger, sleep, and elimination, and it seems he's very irregular. The next one is 'approach/withdrawal.' That deals with the nature of his response to new people, stimuli, and places."

"I can answer that one," she chimed in. "He doesn't like anything or anyone new. He just can't seem to deal with it."

"Right," I agreed with her. "Let's see." I thought for a moment. " 'Adaptability' is the ease or difficulty that his reaction to stimuli can be modified in a desired way. Well, he's clearly not very adaptable. Next is 'intensity.' That's the energy level of his response regardless of the stimulus."

"I'd say he rated high on that one too. Have you ever seen such intense crying?" Louise said, keeping her voice low so as not to wake Kent.

"I can't say that I have. Let me see." I thought for a moment. " 'Mood' is next, and that refers to how pleasant and friendly or unpleasant and unfriendly his behavior is in various situations. 'Persistence,' or attention span, is exactly what you'd think—the length of time an activity is pursued with or without obstacles, and that's directly related to the next one, 'distractibility,' which is the effectiveness of outward stimuli in interfering with his ongoing behavior.

"Now, 'sensory threshold' is one we should look at. It's the amount of stimulation, like light or sound, necessary to note a discernible response. Well, as you know, Kent is extremely sensitive to the least stimuli. Let me see . . . I think that's it." I counted them off to be sure. "Activity, rhythmicity, approach/withdrawal, adaptability, intensity, mood, persistence, distractibility, and sensory threshold." I looked up at her. "Have I totally confused you?"

"No, not at all. I know he's brand-new, but I can really see where he would fit into each of those categories. I have my hands full, don't I?"

"Yep. You got a tough cookie. But you'll see. As he gets older there's lots you can do to help him and yourself. Your job will be to respond appropriately to him and give him what he needs. We have a family in the practice who has a little girl—she's about four now—who was something like Kent as an infant. The other day I asked the mother how things were going. She said things were getting easier all the way around—that life was particularly smooth as long as she stayed on 'meltdown watch.'

"I asked her what that was, and she said if she pays attention, she can clearly see when her daughter is getting overstimulated or tired. This almost always results in a tantrum. She sees part of her job as a parent is to move her daughter to a calm and quiet place before she has a meltdown, as she calls it.

"As her daughter gets older she'll be able to both deal with the stimulation and being tired, but she'll also, hopefully, learn to internalize what her mother provides for her now, and learn to remove herself from a situation that's too much for her to handle."

"And I'll be able to do the same for Kent?" Louise asked.

"Absolutely, as long as you pay attention to who he is and what he needs. You'll be able to read the cues he gives you."

"And she did say it's getting easier?"

"It's gotten easier for her year by year. But you have to remember these basic characteristics won't really change. A lot of how difficult or how easy Kent is will depend on how you relate to him, and how you meet his needs.

"My two kids were temperamental opposites from the day they were born. Gordon, my oldest, was a very shy, cautious, slow-to-warm-up kid. We learned pretty quickly we needed to move slowly with him and that he would need lots of extra support and time when he was in a new situation—like the first day of school. We had to be very patient with him and let him take his time getting comfortable in these situations.

"On the other hand, our daughter, Lisa, was the most easy-going, accepting kid right from infancy. She went to sleep and woke up with a smile. If you gave her a warm bottle—fine, a cold bottle—dandy. I believe it could have been yak's milk in the bottle and she would have been fine. To this day she's the same way."

"So you didn't have any problems dealing with their differences?" she asked.

"Sure we did. For example, we made the mistake of sending them both to sleep-away camp. Lisa was crowned Miss Camp Timbertops, and Gordon spent the summer in misery. He was just beginning to adjust to camp when it was time to come home. To this day when Gordon needs to take his time adjusting to a new situation we'll say, 'Gordon's just not a camper.' The point is every child doesn't have to be a camper, and the parent who can understand who their child is, and make it easier for their child, is the parent who will enjoy raising that child, and it will be a happier child."

Just then Kent woke up with a startle and a scream. Louise looked at me with panic in her eyes.

"Remember it *will* get better. Just keep repeating to yourself, 'It will get better,' " I said to her, after reassuring her she could call me at any time. "And may God be with you," I thought as I heard Kent's screams trail down the hall and out the office.

What parent doesn't have preconceived views of who their children are and who they will be? It takes a lot to be realistic about who our children really are. We need to not only be aware of where they're at developmentally, but also must realize that to a great extent in the nature versus nurture balance, nature plays a tremendous part. As Louise Bohn found out, our children come to us prewired, temperamentally and genetically. So we must be intuitive, open, and realistic if we're going to parent our children as they need to be parented—as they deserve to be parented—based on who they are, rather than on who we are, what we want, and how we were parented.

Like Gordon, Monica Metheny had been a slow-to-warm-up kid from birth. Everything with her was a challenge. With children like Monica I became accustomed to taking my time, cajoling them, and playing games with them to get them through their exam.

That winter Monica had been in a lot due to a series of ear infections. She was in yet again with a double ear infection. The minute I walked into the examining room she jumped down from the table and climbed onto the little shelf under the table.

"Where's Monica?" I asked loudly.

Her mother played along. "She was here a moment ago, but she's seemed to disappear."

"Well, that's too bad because I had some special stickers for her today. Oh well, there's another four-year-old girl in the next room who I know will want them."

"Here I am, here I am." She stuck just her hand out from under the table and waved.

"Well, that's a relief! Come on out so I can look at those ears and you can look at the stickers."

"No. I don't want to."

"Monica, it's time to get on the table now," her mother said calmly but firmly. She was an expert at walking the fine line between respecting Monica's shy temperament and letting her know certain things were expected of her.

"No."

"Dr. Weinberger needs to look in your ears."

"No. I don't want him to."

"Well, what do you want?" I asked her.

"I want hamburgersandcreamedcorn for dinner." She pronounced her favorite dinner, her favorite foods in fact, like it was one word. Monica was a true creature of habit. Like many children with this nature she would find what she liked and not want to vary from that food or routine.

"She's still on the hamburger and creamed corn kick?" I asked her mom. These had been her favorite foods, practically the only foods she'd eat, since she started solids.

"I don't think it's a kick. I think it's a lifestyle. We'll have to find a college that serves it." She turned her attention to Monica. "We can have hamburgers and creamed corn for dinner—no problem."

"Hooray," she shouted, but made no move to come out.

"Now come on out," her mother said.

"I want Dr. Weinberger to come down here."

"Okay. Here I come."

"You don't have to do that," Mrs. Metheny said.

"No problem," I said as I tried to squeeze into the tiny space. Monica giggled.

"Let's see that ear," I said, and, surprisingly, Monica complied, turning her head. "This one's infected again," I reported to Mrs. Metheny.

"Okay, let me see the other one."

"You can see the other one the next time I come in," Monica said happily and she meant it. She had had enough and was finished with me.

The flip side of the coin, temperamentally speaking, was Hannah McCallum. There were three girls in the McCallum family. The two older girls, Haley, seven, and Heather, five, were the kind of children whom you could dress in the morning and in the evening their hair bows would still be in place, their shirts tucked in, and their knee socks up. But two-and-a-half-year-old Hannah was different.

"I can't leave her alone for a minute," her mother, Hope, told me.

"Why? What happens?" I asked.

"What happens?" she repeated to me. "Where do I begin?

Would you like me to tell you what happens in an average week?"

"Sure," I replied, watching Hannah try to remove the knobs from the drawers of the storage unit.

"Monday—I got Hannah dressed and I put her on my bed with *Sesame Street* on the TV, hoping I could take a really quick shower. I couldn't have been in the bathroom more than three minutes, but when I came out—no Hannah. I looked and dripped all over the house and couldn't find her. I happened to look out the window and there she was walking down the street with our new puppy in tow, wearing nothing but her underpants.

"Tuesday—we're trying to housebreak this puppy, so one of us gets up early to walk him every morning, but apparently not early enough. Now, Hannah has been warned not to take the puppy out of its crate in the morning, but she got up before dawn, took the puppy out of the crate, and put him on the white sofa in the living room. She goes back to bed, but leaves the puppy on the sofa, and he's too little to get down. By the time we woke up, suffice it to say, the sofa was no longer white.

"Wednesday—I'm busy getting all three girls ready to go to Haley's choir concert. I was drying Heather's hair and Hannah slipped away. She went down to the kitchen, got into the fridge where she found a bottle of amoxicillin. She opened the childproof cap and decided after drinking half the bottle, because of its pretty pink color, it would make a great finger-paint, and the kitchen floor would make a great canvas.

"After being reassured by your office that she was in no danger from the medicine, I mop the floor, and rebathe and redress Hannah. Then I made the mistake of leaving her to get myself dressed. When we went downstairs to find Hannah and leave, there was dirt everywhere, especially covering her. She had taken every plant in the house out of its pot. I dressed her in outfit number three—no time for another bath, and left the mess for later."

"You did all that?" I asked Hannah.

"Uh-huh," she responded with a big smile, then resumed ripping the paper that covers the examining table into tiny pieces.

"You want to hear more?" Hope asked.

"Absolutely," I responded.

"Thursday was the day of the great supermarket fiasco. Hannah was unhappy as we pulled into the parking lot. I knew, even then, that I should have just turned around and gone home, but I was determined to get the grocery shopping done. Hannah was sitting in the cart whining. What I didn't know was she had grabbed a bottle of laundry detergent and was hiding it by sitting on it.

"Suddenly Hannah, the groceries, and the floor were covered with sticky green detergent. The bottle had burst. People were slipping and falling all around us and Hannah was screaming. I knew it was time to leave, but I was determined to get the groceries. I toweled off Hannah and the groceries and finished up the shopping. We were almost done checking out when a can of beer spontaneously burst open, covering Hannah and the already bagged groceries. I couldn't help laughing. Hannah was crying, but gosh darn it, I had my groceries.

"Friday—the phone rings. It's one of my good friends and I start venting to her about my week with Hannah. About ten minutes into this I realize that I'm going to pay for this, because Hannah is no longer by my side. I get off the phone and go to the kitchen to find that Hannah has somehow climbed up onto the kitchen counter and found the Marshmallow Fluff in the cabinet. She has completely covered herself and her dolly in Fluff. I tried to hide my laughter as she gives me a wild explanation, and I get the camera so I can snap a picture. What's one more mess to clean up when I have this willful, spirited, but very funny and entertaining kid? Of course I called my husband later that day and told him to get home because I was resigning, but he reminded me that I can't quit. This job is for life."

Hope McCallum was the perfect example of a mother who made it so she and her daughter were a perfect fit. Instead of laughing about and enjoying Hannah's antics, she could have been constantly scolding and angry. She had realized early on she wasn't going to change this child, so she might as well learn to enjoy Hannah and treasure her for the outgoing, curious, active child she was instead of trying to change her.

One of the easiest-going children I saw was Adam Wright. Even when he was suffering with pneumonia he was still in a good mood.

"Does he ever give you any trouble?" I asked his mother, Pam.

"No, I have Philip for that." Philip was her older son. "They're like night and day."

"Tell me about it," I said.

"We go to the arcade and I give them each five dollars and tell them that's all they're getting. Philip spends it within the first ten minutes, and is back with his hand out for more. When I tell him no, he argues, cajoles, complains, pleads a case like Clarence Darrow, and has a fit even though you would think he would have learned from previous experience that when I said five dollars is all, I mean it. But no, he always has to push and push.

"In the meantime Adam is happily playing the games and when he runs out of money, he might try an occasional request for more quarters, but when I say no, he says okay and walks away. See—night and day."

"You definitely have two very different kids," I remarked. "What does Adam do when Philip has his fit?" I asked.

"He just watches or walks away. The other day about an hour after one of Philip's fits, Adam said to me, 'You know, Mom, I don't think I'd mind being a hostage.'

"I was a little shocked, but I said, 'Why do you think that?'

"He said, 'Well, hostages have to eat when they're told, and sleep when they're told, and do everything they're told to do, right?'

"I said, 'That sounds about right.'

" 'Well, that's pretty much how I have it now. Right?' he said with a big happy smile.

"I had to agree with him, even though I knew there was a flaw in his logic somewhere. I guess the thing is, he's so malleable and easygoing he *would* make a good hostage," she said with amazement and amusement in her voice.

Celeste Van Leer brought in one-year-old Linda and four-year-old Eddie. They both had mild colds—the sniffles really. I had been treating the Van Leer children since Eddie's birth. They were my best customers. It wasn't that they were sick more often than my other patients, it was just that Celeste brought them in for everything—stomachaches, colds, even the normal, everyday bumps and bruises all kids get on a regular basis.

She was a small, incredibly anxious woman who always flitted in like a little bird hovering over her kids. Her anxiety always seemed only slightly relieved after I had declared her children healthy and fine, and she would flit out until the next minor "emergency" came up.

Once again I tried to discuss the difference between minor discomforts and treatable illnesses with her. She just couldn't seem to get it. Finally, I asked her about her own childhood.

"Well, at the time I didn't think it was so strange, but looking back I can see how bizarre it was. You see when I was two, my older brother ran into the street and was run over—killed instantly. After that I wasn't allowed off the porch. The fear of death was literally put in me. My whole life was school and home. That's bad enough when you're six or eight but a whole other thing when you're in high school. I wasn't allowed to join any activities or go to parties or date. I had no friends. My first taste of freedom was when I went to college. Peter was the first man I ever dated and I married him."

I realized that without therapy, it would be impossible for Celeste to parent differently. Just having the children, just keeping them alive, must have seemed like such an over-whelming task to her.

As Linda and Eddie got older, Celeste continued to parent them based only on her childhood experiences, ignoring who her kids were and what *they* needed. Early on Linda developed her own way of dealing with her mother. She could constant-ly be heard saying, "Mom, just leave me alone." Eddie, on the other hand, became an expert at using his mother's fears and anxieties to get whatever he wanted.

Our model for parenting is invariably our own upbringing. Every parent will tell you how, when they were children, they decided, "When I'm a parent I'll never do *that* to my kids." Twenty-seven years later a similar situation occurs and they hear their mother's voice, tone, and words coming out of their mouth—suddenly they're channeling their mother. It's always a shock.

Although Celeste Van Leer was an extreme case, it is, regrettably, not that unusual. We probably all know a father who insists that his son, who is only mildly interested in sports, be the star of Little League, because Dad wanted it so badly himself as a child.

Some start with the best intentions but still miss the mark. There was the mother who told me she realized she was par-enting her daughter exactly opposite of how she was parented when she refused to let her three-year-old wear nail polish.

"My mom was always making me wear dresses and party shoes, and curling my hair when all I wanted to do was wear jeans and play baseball with the boys. So I was going to raise my daughter to be rough-and-tumble. I forgot to consider maybe she wasn't that kind of kid. Luckily a friend, listening to the whole nail polish debate, pointed out to me what I was doing. Now I really try to parent her for who *she* is, not for what *I* missed out on."

Along with parenting based on or in reaction to how we were parented is the pitfall of assuming your child is one way because you or a sibling or your entire family is that way.

Eight-year-old Skip Hardy had come in complaining of a sore throat and earache. I examined him, did the throat culture, and while we waited for the result I asked him how school was going.

"Don't ask," he replied.

"Too late. I already did," I said with a smile. "Come on. You can tell me. What's wrong with school?"

"I just hate it. That's all." Tears filled his eyes. This was one of the strongest reactions to this question I had ever seen.

"Why do you hate it?" I asked.

"Because it's so hard. I'm like the dumbest in the class. I can't do anything there except gym."

"You can't be the dumbest. You're not dumb at all," I tried to reassure him.

"Yeah, then why can everyone else in the whole class read, and I can't read at all? Aaron's been reading since kindergarten." Aaron was his older brother, a very bright kid, who never had trouble with school. "Even Logan Barnhart can read and he won't turn eight until August."

"Well, everyone learns to read in their own time. I'm sure you'll be reading soon," I told him, but I was concerned. Something didn't seem right. I caught his mother, Suzanne, as she headed out of the examining room. "Can I speak with you for a moment?"

"Sure. Skip, I'll be out in a minute," she said and then looked at me questioningly.

"Is what Skip said true? He's not reading at all?"

"He can read a few words, but other than that he's just not getting it at all. He told you the whole story. The only thing at school he excels in is gym."

"Has he been tested? Do they have any idea why he's having these difficulties?"

"They've been recommending he be tested since the beginning of kindergarten. But I assure you the problem is not with Skip. No one in our family has ever done poorly in school. His teachers just aren't doing their job."

"Talk about denial," I thought to myself. "Well, whether the school is doing its job or not, if I were you I wouldn't let this go on too long. This is clearly affecting his self-esteem. You know if you don't figure out what's going on, he's just going to fall further and further behind."

"I told you what's going on. It's the school's incompetence, so we're looking into private schools for Skip."

The Hardys put Skip in a school where the elite of the elite send their children—more a place for the advanced and even gifted than for someone struggling like Skip.

It didn't take long for the teachers at the new school to insist Skip be tested. The results: Skip had an average IQ coupled with learning disabilities in several specific areas. But Skip was now in a school where an average IQ was way below average. The wrong school, coupled with the parents' unrealistic expectations, made for a no-win situation. It was no wonder he was floundering. He was way behind in school and feeling very bad about himself.

It was obvious Skip needed special care, special attention, and a school that would serve his needs. I recommended this to the Hardys, but they wouldn't hear of it. Shortly thereafter they left the practice, no doubt because I wasn't telling them what they wanted to hear.

In some extreme cases, parents are called upon to accept the unacceptable, to deal with the extraordinary, and to find a level of strength in themselves that they probably never knew they had.

Henry Wall didn't look good. He was very pale with dark circles under his eyes. His right ear was draining, he had a fever, and his mother said he refused to eat. I had seen him a week earlier when his ear first started bothering him. I was very concerned that his ear infection hadn't responded to antibiotics. One month earlier I had seen him for his three-year checkup and he had been fine. The drastic change in him in just one month was really alarming.

"Not feeling too well, are you, buddy?" I said to him.

"My ear hurts. Can I go home now? I just want to go to bed," he whined. His mother and I exchanged looks. Henry was not the kind of kid who ever wanted to go to bed.

"Henry, I know you're feeling lousy, but I still need to do some tests so I can find out what's making you sick. Then we can fix you up." He sighed and nodded.

"We're going to need to do a blood test."

"NO!" he started to whimper. "It will hurt."

"You're right, it will hurt. But just a little, I promise."

"Why do you need a blood test?" his mother, Nikki, asked, looking very concerned.

"He looks pale and anemic. He has an enlarged liver and spleen and he didn't respond to the medication for the ear infection. We need to find out why."

As I suspected, his hemoglobin was very low. Henry's blood count showed he had many abnormal white blood cells.

I sat down with Nikki Wall and her husband, Hank. "I'm going to have to refer Henry to Dr. Sue Macintosh. She's a top hematologist at Yale. She'll run some more tests on Henry."

"What do you expect to find?" Hank asked.

"At this point I'm just not sure. Let's get Henry in to see this specialist as soon as possible and find out what's wrong."

A test on Henry's bone marrow revealed that Henry had acute lymphocytic leukemia.

There is nothing more horrible for parents to hear than their child has cancer. At first Hank and Nikki and their older child, Darcie, were devastated. They were in a state of shock and disbelief. But then they quickly realized that this wouldn't help Henry. They rallied themselves to his support and helped him through the painful process of fighting leukemia, which included radiation of the brain and nervous system, and a therapy of very toxic medication.

They were all there talking Henry through the most miserable and painful times, taking all the necessary and often difficult steps to bring him to remission and recuperation. This included putting the rest of the family and careers on hold.

With the help of his family, Henry responded well to the treatment and recovered fully from the leukemia. However, it became clear when Henry started school that the extreme amount of medication and radiation he had been exposed to had lasting effects on him. This took the form of severe learning disabilities.

Once again his parents rallied. Even though it was several towns away, they enrolled Henry in a school that specialized in learning disabilities. Every day they would take Henry to school and pick him up. It was a joy to see how his life turned around and how he flourished there.

Through all of this, Hank and Nikki have continued to be active, responsible, and supportive parents not only to Henry, but also to Darcie, who had taken a back seat during Henry's illness. They have been particularly successful in allowing Henry to be an absolutely normal child, despite all he had gone through. They have instilled in him the belief that he can be, and do, anything.

Hank and Nikki Wall rose to the challenge of coping with a seriously ill child. When parents are faced with this kind of misfortune they have two choices. They can handle these hardships, traumas, and tragedies with courage, optimism, and pluck, or they can cave in. From what I've seen, those that choose to handle these situations responsibly and head-on, grow from the experience. The sick child has a better chance of both surviving and reaching his or her full potential, and the entire family, including siblings, become stronger, more caring people.

I was making hospital rounds and stopped in the nursery.

"You have a new patient," one of the nurses said.

"Really? I don't recognize the name," I responded, looking at the papers.

"She was born last night. The mother gave the OB your

name as pediatrician," the nurse continued, as she changed a tiny newborn.

Generally we meet the parents long before the baby is born. That way they get to know us and we get to know something about them. But every now and then someone will get our name from a friend and just put us down as pediatrician of record.

My newest patient, Thea Kittlewell, was all of fourteen hours old. She weighed in at seven pounds, twelve ounces, and seemed to be doing fine. I looked further through the papers that came from the delivery room and found that the mother, Aimee, was eighteen years old and unwed. "This comes ready-made with its own set of problems," I thought to myself as I went down the hall to see Aimee.

"Hi, Aimee, I'm Norman Weinberger, the pediatrician." I held out my hand. She shook it.

"Oh," she said, looking me over, with typical teenage suspicion.

"How're you feeling?"

"Tired. But okay. Did you see the baby yet?" she asked.

"I just examined Thea. She's doing great."

She sighed. "That's good."

I sat down in one of the chairs next to the bed. "So, what are your plans, Aimee?" I asked cautiously.

"Plans? I guess I plan to take my baby home and raise her. Isn't that pretty much what all mothers do?" she said with an edge to her voice. I got the message.

"So, you're comfortable with all this?"

"Well, anyone can figure out I didn't plan on Thea, and I guess I do have other choices, but I've had nine months to get used to the idea and I don't know—I never could just give her up. I love her, and I know she'll love me. I know it isn't going to be easy but I can do it," she said determinedly.

Two weeks later Aimee and her mother brought Thea in for a checkup. I was concerned when I discovered the baby had decreased muscle tone in her arms and legs. But knowing I'd see Thea again in two weeks, and not wanting to alarm Aimee, I decided I'd wait and see if anything developed. When Aimee and her mother brought Thea in for her next exam, the muscle tone was even more decreased. I suspected that Thea had cerebral palsy.

"Aimee, I'm going to give you the name of a pediatric neurologist. I want you to take Thea to see him."

She looked down at her baby, and then back at me, then at her mother. The color drained out of her face. "Why? What's wrong?"

"Well, we can't be sure until the neurologist runs some tests, but I suspect Thea has cerebral palsy."

"Cerebral palsy? That's serious, isn't it?"

What I said suddenly seemed to hit her. Her eyes filled with tears, and she hugged Thea tightly. "Oh!" She sounded like she'd been hit. "Is Thea going to die?" She started to sob. Her mother put her arm around Aimee's shoulder, but didn't say anything. It was clear she was going to let Aimee handle this.

I slid my stool over to where she was sitting. "No, Thea isn't going to die. But yes, this could be serious. If she does have cerebral palsy the neurologist will be able to determine how severely she's affected. Do you know what cerebral palsy is?" I asked gently.

She shook her head.

"Cerebral palsy is a condition that results from damage occurring to the motor center of the brain during pregnancy or delivery. People who have cerebral palsy, or CP, have coordination problems. They often have speech problems as well. These problems can range from very slight to quite severe."

"Why do you think Thea has it? She seems fine to me."

"I know she looks fine, but what tipped me off was the muscle tone in her arms and legs." I took Thea from her and showed her what I meant. "See, her muscle tone is very lax. If she was a few months older we would see an increase in her muscle tone, which would eventually lead to some spasticity," I explained. Aimee looked baffled.

"Look, why don't we just wait and see what the neurologist says," I continued. "If she does have CP we'll see to it you get all the help you need. I promise you, you won't be alone in this. Right, Mrs. Kittlewell?" I was trying to get Aimee's shocked and very quiet mother to offer some comfort.

"That's right," Mrs. Kittlewell offered halfheartedly.

"I'm really scared. I never thought anything like this could happen."

I wrote out the name and number of the neurologist for her. "Do you want me to call him first? I could tell him a little about you and Thea, and let him know you're calling?"

"Yes, thank you."

"I'm going to call him later today. I know you're scared, but I don't want you to wait on this. Give him a call tomorrow, and I bet he'll see you and Thea next week."

"Okay. Thank you," she said, and sadly left the office.

I sat down for a moment and sighed. She had come into the office never suspecting anything but a normal checkup, and she left scared and devastated. This was the side of pediatrics I hated.

After the diagnosis was confirmed, Aimee brought Thea in. Something about her had changed. She seemed more grown up, and fired up as well.

"Okay, my daughter has CP. Now what do I do first?" Aimee, in the span of a week, had begun to accept her daughter's condition, and she had mobilized. She was ready for action.

We set up physical therapy at the hospital. Aimee and Thea attended it religiously. As Thea got older Aimee took her to various specialists. Aimee also realized she would have to spend all her time with Thea if she was going to meet her very special needs. She went on welfare in order to do this. She completely educated herself on CP, and learned how to use the system to get what Thea needed, even going all the way to the governor to get a wheelchair for her daughter.

When Thea reached school-age Aimee fought for her to be

in a regular classroom and won. So, Thea would spend most of her day in class with an aide, being pulled out only for speech therapy. Being a very bright child, Thea did well in school.

In the meantime, with Thea now in school all day, Aimee was able to not only go back to work, but attend nursing school with the ultimate goal of becoming a pediatric nurse. Even with the strain of working and going to school, Aimee's priority remained Thea. Surgical procedures at Newington Children's Hospital allowed Thea to walk with the support of braces. Through Easter Seals, Aimee got Thea into summer camp. Aimee found a speech therapist in a neighboring town, and a physical therapist as well, to supplement the work being done in school.

It was an incredibly rough road, but Aimee got her nursing degree and went on to become a registered nurse. She continued to meet all Thea's needs, whether it was finding the best doctor and best hospital for a necessary surgery, or working with the school to make sure Thea's special educational and social needs were met.

The last time I saw Thea, she was a bright, outgoing nineteen-year-old. She had graduated high school at eighteen, right on schedule, and was attending college with plans to become an administrative assistant.

I'm often awed by the abilities of some people to rise to the challenge of having a child with spectacular needs. Not everyone can take on this massive responsibility and few can do it in the grand style of Aimee Kittlewell.

Going through experiences like this builds people like Lee Hamel, the mother of a multichallenged child, ten-year-old Zoe. Zoe's disabilities include multiple organ problems, mild mental retardation, speech difficulties, and extremity problems for which she's had several surgeries.

From the get-go Lee kept a diary of all of Zoe's problems, doctor appointments, surgeries, setbacks, and triumphs. She was always an advocate for Zoe. This included driving the school system crazy on several occasions. One of the battles she fought was for the right for Zoe and other physically challenged children to ride the school bus. The school officials were concerned about liability.

"What if Zoe fell?" they objected.

"She would get back up," was Lee's reply. She finally compromised with them. She would sign a release form, and Zoe would ride the bus. Now she rides the bus every day with her friends from the neighborhood, who happily help her on and off. This allows her to feel normal, independent, and competent.

In the meantime Lee has taken her fight to a bigger arena. She has become a national advocate for the rights of the disabled. She is helping millions, and it all started with her wanting what we all want—the best for our children.

11

Breaking Up (And Coming Together) Is Hard to Do

Her parents were willing to put their differences aside and put their child first. With divorce a given, they made the best of the situation for their daughter.

This kid couldn't be Chelsea Hart, I thought to myself as I walked into the examining room. The last time I saw Chelsea, for her fourteen-year exam, she was cheerful, animated—joking with me about what she thought high school would be like. She was a normal, happy teenager. Now, almost fifteen, she sat in front of me, quiet and withdrawn. She wouldn't crack a smile.

"Chelsea Hart! What brings you in today?"

"Sore throat."

"Has it been hurting long?"

"A couple of days."

"Well, let's take a look," I said, wondering what happened to the bubbly, chatty kid of ten months ago.

"What's new?" I asked as I looked in her throat and ears.

"Nothing," she responded in a monotone.

"Really? Nothing's new? What about high school? How's that going?"

"It's okay."

"Looks like strep. I'm going to take a throat culture," I told her. She looked back blankly at me.

"You know I've been wondering, since the last time we talked, if you made the basketball team. I know you were looking forward to trying out."

"I decided I didn't want to play," she answered quietly. Could this really be the same kid who had told me she was practicing her basketball three hours a day so she would be sure to make the team?

"Did your mom bring you today?" I asked. If I couldn't find anything out from her I would have to try her mother, Kathy. A dramatic change like this was just too alarming to ignore.

"She's in the waiting room with Bennett." Bennett was her seven-year-old brother.

Chelsea did have strep, so I gave her a prescription and walked her out to the waiting room. Kathy was flipping through a magazine. "Hi, Kathy," I greeted Chelsea's mother.

"Oh, hi. Let me guess—strep throat, right?" she asked, standing up.

"Right. She should feel better after starting the antibiotics. Kathy, do you have a minute? I'd like to talk to you."

"Sure. It's just strep though, right?" she said, looking at Chelsea with concern.

"Right." She followed me to the consultation room. "Have a seat," I said.

"What's wrong? You're making me very nervous," she said, fidgeting with the strap on her purse.

"Except for the strep throat, Chelsea is physically healthy, but I'm wondering what's going on with her emotionally. She's just not herself. Last time I saw her she was a happy, talkative kid, and now I can't get more than a one-word answer out of her."

Kathy sighed loudly. "Well, right after Christmas, Kenneth left."

"What do you mean—he left?" Kenneth was her husband. I had only met him a few times, even though I had been seeing the family since Chelsea was a baby.

"He left. That's all. He decided he didn't want the responsibility of a family, and he supposedly moved to Hawaii. We haven't heard from him. He hasn't even sent the kids birthday cards, much less paid a penny of child support. My lawyers are trying to find him to serve him with divorce papers and get child support.

"I'll tell you, it's been hell. We're all taking it hard, but I think Chelsea feels, since she's the oldest, she should be more responsible for helping with the finances and taking responsibility for her brother. I tell her she doesn't need to, and I had to forbid her from taking an after-school job, but I can tell she still feels like a lot of this is on her shoulders."

"You didn't see any of this coming?" I asked, still unable to comprehend her husband just walking out.

"I was completely blindsided. I knew he was having some business problems, but his desertion came as a total shock. I couldn't even get out of bed for a week. Then I didn't have a choice. I had to find a job and take care of the kids. It's been a nightmare."

I knew Kathy hadn't worked outside the house since Chelsea's birth. I remembered her saying at Bennett's six-year checkup that she was just beginning to think about going back to work.

"What kind of work are you doing?" I asked her.

"I'm doing some bookkeeping and accounting for several small businesses, and I just got my real estate license. So I do feel like things are starting to look a little brighter."

"Have you or the kids had any help—you know—counseling?" Between the loss this family suffered, the pain they had endured, and the drastic changes they had gone through in such a short time, I knew they would all need more help than I could possibly give them. I hoped Kathy was open to the idea of counseling.

"No, I really couldn't afford it right after Kenneth left, but now I'm feeling more financially secure, and I can see how badly we all need it. Maybe you could give me some names."

"Of course I can. I only wish you had called me sooner.

There are a lot of places I could have recommended that wouldn't have been costly."

"Well, give me the name of those places to begin with," she said with a weak smile. "It's not exactly like I've sold my first mansion."

I wrote down the names and numbers of some family services, independent social workers and psychologists, and gave them to Kathy. "I can see how Chelsea's doing, but I'm wondering about Bennett. How's he holding up?"

"Actually I'm more concerned about him than Chelsea. She talks about how angry she is. She sees that everything is different now, but Bennett acts like nothing has happened. He never even mentions his father. I talked to his teacher to let her know what happened, and asked her to tell me if there was any change in his behavior, but there hasn't been. It's almost spooky."

"Do you try to talk to him about it?" I asked.

"Sure. But he clams up, or changes the subject, or leaves the room. It's like he just won't accept what's happened. If there's any change at all it would be that he's too good—too well-behaved."

"Uhhm. You know it's very common for kids his age to feel like a separation is their fault—like they must have done something to cause their parent to leave. I sure wouldn't put off calling someone. You've all been through a lot and you deserve all the help you can get."

Kathy left, promising to make arrangements for counseling. I sat for a minute with an overwhelming feeling of sadness. While the Harts' story was very unusual—the husband just walking out and disappearing—divorce was becoming more and more an issue we had to deal with. It seemed like every day I learned of another one of our families going through a separation or divorce.

While Connie Harris was always a very quiet and reserved woman, the last few times she was in, she looked downright depressed. With three kids under seven, she certainly had her hands full, and she seemed to be doing it all alone. I had taken care of the family since the oldest, Jessica, was born and I had never laid eyes on the father.

It seemed like she was also becoming more and more anxious about the children—bringing them all in every time one of them had a cold or complaint. After the fourth visit of that kind, I suggested we talk alone, without the children running around the room, demanding her attention.

"What's up?" I asked. "How's everything going with you?"

"Well, you know how it is. I'm busy with the kids, and they're always coming down with something. You know . . ." Her voice trailed off.

"I wanted to know how things are going with *you*. I know how the kids are. How are things with you and your husband?"

She looked down at her folded hands and then back up at me. "It's obvious, isn't it?" she said in a small voice.

"What's obvious?" I asked.

"That things aren't good—that my life is a mess."

"It's obvious that you're very unhappy," I told her.

"My husband and I . . . we uhh . . . we . . . we haven't gotten along in years. It just gets worse and worse. I feel so trapped. I've tried to get him to go to a marriage counselor with me, but he says he's not a clock who needs adjusting. I swear I would just leave, but what am I going to do with three small children and no job?" She started to cry. "I'm trapped," she sobbed. I got a box of tissues for her.

"Have you considered counseling for yourself, even if he won't go?"

"I don't think it would make any difference."

"Oh, I think it would."

"You do?" she said, dabbing her eyes.

"Absolutely. If you're this unhappy you have to do something about it, whether your husband will go or not."

She thought for a long moment. Then suddenly she got a

242 • *Norman Weinberger, M.D., with Alison Pohn*

panicky look on her face. "I've got to go see what the children are doing."

"They're fine," I assured her. "What's wrong? You look like you just saw a ghost."

"Nothing, nothing. I was just thinking if I went to counseling alone . . . well . . . what if the doctor, or therapist, or whatever thought I should get a divorce?" Her voice became a whisper on the the word "divorce."

"It wouldn't be a matter of what the doctor thought. It would be a matter of what you thought. No decent therapist would push you to do something you didn't want to do."

"Really, I have to get back to the kids," she said, suddenly flustered.

"Will you think about what we talked about?"

"I'll think about it."

"Will you call me for referrals if you decide to get some help?"

"Yes."

It didn't take Connie Harris long. She called the next day, and I gave her a couple of names. From there it didn't take her long to figure out that despite her fears she would be better off getting a divorce.

I didn't see her for several months after the divorce. Then she brought one of the kids in with a rash.

"I don't have to ask you how things are going. You look wonderful!" It was true. The depressed woman who spoke only in emotionless whispers was replaced by a confident, smiling, energetic woman.

"Everything's working out better than I ever imagined," she said.

"Tell me about it." Her enthusiasm was contagious and I found myself excited to hear her good news.

"Well, I got a job substitute teaching at the grammar school, but then one of the teachers had to start her maternity leave early because she was put on bed rest. I guess I must have been doing a good job, because they gave me her classroom, and they said I would be—and this is a direct quote—'a highly regarded candidate for a position in the fall.' "

"That's great. So Ricky and Jessica go to school with you?" She nodded. "Who takes care of David?" David was only four and in a half-day preschool.

"My sister has a three-year-old in the same school as David, so she takes him in the afternoon. She was so relieved I finally left my husband she was thrilled to do it. Everything really fell into place, and I love what I'm doing. The days just fly by."

"That's wonderful. I'm thrilled for you. How about the kids? How have they adjusted?"

"They're doing okay. I think they see their father more now than they did before the divorce. Of course they don't like the little house I rented as much as the big house we lived in before, and the boys fight more since they have to share a room, but they're all doing well."

"I'm sure the fact that you're happy makes them feel a whole lot better. Kids know a lot more about what's going on than we give them credit for. Seeing you so unhappy must have been very stressful for them."

"I can see that now, but when I was in the middle of that mess I couldn't see anything clearly."

"Well, I'm glad things are working out for you."

"I do want to thank you for recommending the counseling. It's made all the difference."

Of course along with divorce comes a myriad of problems. While the children of divorce are going through their difficulties, the parents are dealing with their own stress—not only from the divorce, but from custody issues, finances, and moving. It's a rare family that can handle all this gracefully.

The Laxton family had been through a particularly nasty divorce. Marty, the father, was a very successful banker, but somehow his wife, Joanie, and their children, Neal, fifteen, and Brent, thirteen, ended up with little financial support. To make matters worse, Marty started playing mind games with the boys: promising he'd show up and disappointing them, demanding he be able to see the boys when they had made other plans, and bad-mouthing their mother whenever they did get together. The boys finally decided they didn't want to see their father. The father countered by saying if the boys didn't see him—on demand—he wouldn't pay the child support. It was an ongoing struggle.

Often the worst casualty of divorce is the relationship between the child and the noncustodial parent. This happens when the parent either uses the child by venting their anger against the ex-spouse to the child, withholds child support, doesn't respect the visitation schedule and the needs and wishes of the child, or simply makes no effort to continue the relationship.

There is no doubt that it's extremely difficult to maintain a parent-child relationship when the parent no longer lives with the child, but with dedication and respect for the child and their changing needs it can be done.

Bridget Lange brought in her youngest, Peter, for his six-month checkup. In tow were her two older children, Heather, four, and Ali, six.

"What's new with the Lange family?" I asked as I came into the examining room.

"Well, Daddy's not staying at home anymore. That's new," Heather said. I stopped dead in my tracks.

"Oh, Heather," Bridget groaned.

"What happened?" I asked, stunned.

Bridget nodded at the two older children, meaning she didn't want to talk in front of them.

"Would you like to talk in private, after I examine Peter?" I asked.

"Yes, actually I would," she responded.

With Ali and Heather occupied in the waiting room, Bridget, little Peter, and I went into the consultation room.

"About four months ago Art said he didn't want to be married anymore, that he was moving out. I pretty much demand-

ed we go to counseling and it came out that he had been having an affair for some time, and he wanted to be with this
other woman," she said with an edge of anger in her voice.

"You must be devastated," I said.

"I am, and I'll tell you, he can have his divorce. I don't want
anything to do with him anymore."

"What about the kids?" I asked her.

"I have to admit he's always been a wonderful father. In fact,
I believe that's what held us together for as long as it did—we
were married almost eleven years. Anyway, he's still a great
father. He has all three kids every other weekend and he has
the girls two nights a week. He calls them every night. He was
at school for conferences and parents' night. I can see that he
plans to stay as active in their life as he can. As angry as I am,
it would be a terrible thing to do to the kids to not allow that
to happen. So we're both trying to amicably work out the
divorce agreement. In fact, we're in arbitration, and it's going
fairly smoothly."

"Well, I give you a lot of credit for putting the children first.
Particularly in a situation like this it must be very difficult," I
told her.

"It is, but I see how happy the girls are to see him . . . even
Peter lights up when his dad comes to pick him up. I can't
jeopardize that. How could I live with myself if I did?"

"You would be amazed at how many people do jeopardize
that relationship and live with themselves and the loss that
their children suffer because of it."

"How sad," Bridget said. "You'd think that since the children
usually end up bearing the consequences of their parents' failure, that most parents would put them first."

Bridget Lange certainly had the right outlook on how
things should be, but the families who could put this in action
were, sadly, few and far between.

The Schwartz family was one of those rare families that
were able to work out both the divorce and the custody
arrangement amicably. Ben and Sandy Schwartz decided they

would do everything they could to make joint custody of their two-year-old daughter, Celia, work.

They looked ahead to her school years, and both bought houses within walking distance of each other and the school. They decided that Celia would alternate her weeks between parents. Since both parents worked, Celia's nanny alternated houses as well. When Celia turned six she was given a dog for her birthday. So, each Sunday evening Celia, the dog, and the nanny switched houses.

In order to make the joint custody work, it meant Ben and Sandy would have to communicate on a regular basis and be flexible in terms of each of their and Celia's schedules. When Celia was in third grade, Sandy's job suddenly demanded she travel more. Ben was there to pick up the slack when she needed to be away.

Although the arrangement sounds a little crazy, it's hard to argue with success. Celia is now fifteen and a very happy, healthy, and well-adjusted child. And she has had the benefit of both her parents being regular and loving parts of her life. She's like this because her parents were willing to put their differences aside and put their child first. With divorce a given, they made the best of the situation for their daughter.

Of course children will have different reactions to divorce, and the age they're at dictates what some of that reaction will be. For preschoolers, like Celia, the issues are basic care, clothing, and feeding. They might not seem very aware of what's going on, but they can sense the stress and unhappiness around them. They might react by becoming lethargic, having sleeping or eating problems, or regressing in toilet training or speech. They might be feeling fear or guilt. They will need extra attention and reassurance that their needs will still be met despite the changes that are taking place.

Children ages six through eight often feel the divorce was somehow their fault—if only they were better behaved, daddy or mommy wouldn't have left. They often feel angry at the custodial parent and have loyalty conflicts.

Children of this age will also feel a tremendous amount of fear and grief. They need to be reassured that both parents still love them and always will, even when they misbehave. They will also need to be told and retold that they were in no way responsible for the split.

Children ages nine to twelve have more coping techniques, but they also can be feeling denial and/or anger. They often feel they should be exclusively loyal to one parent or the other, and might have psychosomatic stomachaches, headaches, and other ailments. They need to be reassured that they can continue to love both parents, and they need a safe place to express their anger.

Teenagers have greater independence and maturity, but they'll also be carrying a lot of anger. They might become depressed and withdrawn. Their parents' divorce often causes them to worry about their own future relationships and they will also worry about their financial future if money is an issue in the divorce—and it usually is.

Whatever the age of the children, the parents need to recognize that single parenting amid a background of emotional upheaval will inevitably change the way they raise their kids. Some parents become too close to their children, treating them more as confidants and friends than children. Other parents may become too hard-nosed and authoritative, trying to make up for the loss of support from the other parent.

Most divorces result in a decline of income. In the healthiest of circumstances the children aren't made aware of this, and both parents work together to provide for the children.

The parents must learn to balance their emotional needs with the needs of their children. It's important for both the children and the parents to have some form of outside support during this difficult time. This could be in the form of therapy, family, friends, or peer support groups at school.

While divorce is an incredibly difficult time I often see people like Connie Harris, who are able to emerge from the stress and depression of divorce, blossom, and see the world again as a wonderful place. In almost all cases, children in these situations bounce back quickly both from the divorce and from the stress and problems that led to it.

Hand in hand with divorce is the issue of single parenting. The most difficult aspect of this is that all the responsibility falls on one parent. There is no buffer, no break, no chance to say, "I'm going out for a walk, you take over."

It's particularly difficult for single parents who work full-time. After the stress of a full day of work they still have to handle the household chores and the kids all by themselves. It becomes difficult to keep rules in place and fight the battles that need to be fought when you're constantly exhausted and stressed. It's even more important, however, for children in this situation to take comfort in the consistency of rules and structure in the home.

As difficult as single parenting is, it can also be incredibly rewarding and fulfilling when the results are a happy, healthy child.

Rachel Resnick had been a single parent since her daughter was six months old. At that time she and her husband divorced and he moved out of the country. She was a single parent in the purest sense of the word. She had no family, and her in-laws also lived overseas and had no interest in the baby, Callie.

I started seeing Callie when she was six, and I talked with Rachel about what it was like to be a single mom.

"The early years were very difficult," she said. "You know how it is with a baby? It's a twenty-four-hour-a-day job. If I wasn't at work, I was with Callie. There was nothing else and really no one else. Callie would do something cute or funny, and I didn't have anyone to share it with.

"At the same time, though, I realized there were pluses to single parenting. I got to make all the rules and decisions. I never had to compromise with a spouse over how Callie should be raised.

"Looking back from this point, I think the hard part is not

so much in raising Callie, but in how being a single parent affected the rest of my life. I felt so alone—so isolated. I didn't fit into any group. I was single, but I couldn't do the things my single friends did like go to a movie or dinner on the spur of the moment. I always had to worry about getting a sitter.

"At the same time I didn't really fit in with my married friends either. Most of them only wanted to do things with other couples. I was also really reluctant to ask for help. I would be exhausted between working and taking care of Callie, and friends would even offer to give me a break by taking her, but I was too shy or—don't know—proud . . . maybe stupid, to take the help.

"Then around the time Callie started kindergarten I realized she would really benefit from the input of other people. I started reaching out and making friends and I decided going out once a week would be a priority. I made some great new friends through Callie's school."

"At that age Callie was becoming more independent. That must have made your life easier," I noted.

"Definitely. But that was a time where I had to really be conscious of keeping our relationship a mother-daughter one. I didn't want to drift into a buddy-buddy thing with her because she's such a strong personality. She could easily have ended up running the show."

"So how do you think Callie's doing, having only a mother?"

"Well, I'm a little prejudiced, but even according to her teachers she's a great kid—well-adjusted, bright, well-liked by her classmates. I know she wishes for a daddy, and I hope someday she has one, but I think she's doing fine the way things are now." I agreed with Rachel's assessment. She had done a wonderful job raising Callie. She was an outgoing, sweet, and confident kid.

I first met Andrea Ross when her son, John David, was six months old. She had been unhappy with their pediatrician, and on the recommendation of several friends had come to us.

"How did you happen to choose this practice?" I asked her, as she gently bounced John David on her lap.

"Part of the decision had to do with the fact that everyone said you spent a lot of time talking to your families, but it was also important that you had the early hours. I'm a working mom and it's hard to take time off work to bring J.D. to the doctor."

"So what do you do?" I asked, taking her history at this first appointment.

"I'm an attorney," she responded.

"And your husband?" I asked.

"Don't have one of those," she answered casually.

"Okay . . ." I said.

"You should probably know we don't see J.D.'s father. We don't even know where he is."

I nodded.

"We were living together when I got pregnant. He wanted no part of it, and when he realized I was one hundred percent committed to keeping the baby, he left, never to be seen or heard from again."

"I'm sorry," I responded.

"Nothing to be sorry about. I think it's healthier to raise J.D. without a father than with one who's not committed to him and nuts about him," she said, holding John David up and giving him a big kiss.

"I have to agree with you. But I also know how difficult it can be to raise a child alone. How's it going?"

"It's going pretty well. I've had to completely change my work schedule, and my social life is pretty nonexistent, but we have found a wonderful nanny, and so far the people at work have been very understanding, so I can't complain."

Over the years, Andrea maintained this attitude. Despite a full-time job she stayed tremendously in tune to John David's needs, changing his child care situation as he got older, making sure there were other people in his life who loved and treasured him, always letting him know he was number one in her

life. The happy, well-behaved, confident little boy he grew
into reflected this.

She made sacrifices in order to put J.D. first. She came off
the fast track at work and gave up the opportunity to be a partner in her law firm. Her lifestyle changed, as money that
would have gone to vacations, entertainment, clothes, and all
the extras went to child care, John David's needs, and his college fund.

"So, how do you feel about these sacrifices?" I once asked
her.

"Where's the sacrifice when this is what you get in return?"
she asked, nodding toward John David, who was intent on listening to his heart with my stethoscope. I had to agree with
her.

Richard Hughes was the father of four girls. When the girls
were seven months, three, six, and eight their mother tragical-
ly died of cancer. Richard, who was an executive at an insurance agency, took some time off, hired a full-time, live-in
housekeeper, and slowly started to rebuild his life.

Amanda Wilkens's sons were eight, ten, and twelve when
their parents were divorced. She returned to work in advertising, hired a baby-sitter for after school, and set about rebuild-
ing her life.

Two years after Richard's wife died and three years after
Amanda's divorce they met while working together on a charity board and began dating. Despite the challenges of dating
with seven kids between them, or maybe because of this challenge, they fell in love and decided to get married.

Sounds like the *Brady Bunch*, doesn't it? Even their closest
friends commented on the similarities. But real life seldom
works out that way, and Richard and Amanda had many issues
and obstacles to face.

There were constant struggles between the four girls on
one side, who now ranged in age from three to ten, and the
boys, now ages eleven to fifteen, on the other. The fighting

between the two factions seemed almost constant. There was always a full-blown feud going on in their home.

Finally, able to take it no longer, Amanda and Richard sat all the children down and told them that they must respect each other. They didn't have to love each other. They didn't even have to like each other, but respect for one another would be demanded at all times, and strictly enforced. And then they did just that. Amanda disciplined her boys and Richard disciplined the girls. And when there was a problem with a family interaction, they handled it together.

The children learned quickly what respect meant—that each child and each parent had a right to be in that house and be treated properly. It wasn't an overnight change by any means, but over time civility became second-nature. Respect eventually turned to like, and like turned to love, and within the span of a couple years a truly blended family and a happy one, at that, was born.

Five-year-old Trevor Hill's mom, Mindy, was getting remarried. His parents had been divorced since he was two and he saw his dad, who lived out of state, once or twice a year. I was delighted when Mark Henry, his new stepfather-to-be, came in to discuss how to handle his new role with Trevor.

"I think it's terrific that you're taking the time to really look at what your role with Trevor should be," I told him. "What's your relationship like now with him?"

"I think we have a pretty strong, comfortable relationship, but I'm sure things will be different when I move in with them, and actually become his stepfather."

"You're right," I told him. "You moving in changes things, particularly in Trevor's eyes."

"So, what do I do and what don't I do?" he asked.

"Well, basically you should be supportive of Mindy and her decisions on how to handle things with Trevor. If you do disagree with anything that's going on, and you probably will (because we all have our own ideas on raising kids), then you should discuss that with Mindy in private. You don't want to step into the role of disciplinarian," I explained, knowing a lot of stepfathers do just that, and it backfires on them.

"So, what do I do?" he asked, looking a little nervous.

"You just move slowly. Now that doesn't mean you let him walk all over you either. If he's acting up and Mindy's not around you have to respond, but you do it in the style that he's used to, that's already been set up. Other than that you let Trevor set the pace and allow your new relationship to evolve naturally into whatever it will become."

Apparently Mark did just that because he and Trevor formed a loving, very tight relationship. It was so close, in fact, that a little over a year later Trevor announced he wanted to change his last name to Henry so that it would be like Mark's, his mother's and Mark's extended family, whom he had become close to.

This was discussed first between Trevor's mother and father and then between Trevor and his father. Out of love for Trevor, his father agreed that he could take Henry for a last name so that he could feel more a part of that family. This was an amazing sacrifice for Trevor's father. Trevor was a lucky boy to be so loved by two dads.

"Should you tell him or should I?" Rachel Resnick asked Callie, who was now almost nine.

"I want to tell," Callie said, literally jumping up and down with excitement.

"What? Tell me what?" I asked, jumping up and down in imitation of her.

"You're not going to believe it," she warned, grabbing my arm.

"I will, I will believe it, if you'll just tell me," I whined in mock frustration.

"We're getting married!" she announced dramatically.

"No!" I responded.

"Yes, we are, and I'm going to walk down the aisle with

Mom, and be the maid of honor, and I get to wear gold shoes, and a beautiful white dress that goes all the way out to here when I dance," she said, holding her hands straight out to the sides.

"A white dress, and gold shoes, and maid of honor, and you know what you forgot to tell me?"

"What?" said Callie.

"Who are you marrying?"

"Oh, Nathaniel," Callie said offhandedly.

I turned my attention to Rachel. "So, tell all. Who's this Nathaniel? Where did you meet him? What's he do?"

"Well, don't you want to know about my shoes and dress and what we're serving at the wedding?" she teased, and then got down to business. "Okay. We met at work and we've been friends for a year and then he finally asked me on a real date about six months ago. We both just seemed to know from that point on that we would get married."

"So, it's all happened pretty fast," I said.

"Absolutely."

"And Callie seems pretty happy. They get along all right?" I asked.

"They get along great," Rachel said.

"That's wonderful. I'm thrilled for all three of you," I told her.

About a month after the wedding Rachel called. "Callie's really been acting up lately. She's way out of control. I was wondering if you think I should take her to see a psychologist or something."

"Tell me what her behavior's been like."

"Well, she just seems to say no to everything. If I tell her to wear this skirt or that shirt she refuses. If I tell her to eat her dinner, or go to bed, she refuses. And everything is high drama all the time. Also she's constantly rude to Nathaniel and me."

"It sounds to me like a couple of things are going on here. Number one is that she's having to adjust to sharing you with your new husband, and that's got to be a shock to her, but I also think that we're seeing the beginning of adolescence here. Why don't you lay off of some of the control issues a little and see if that helps."

"What do you mean, control issues?"

"Well, let her pick out what she's going to wear, and she can certainly decide if she wants to eat or not. You know, Rachel, Callie's just turned nine and it's time to let her have more of a say in these things or you're going to have a rebellion on your hands."

"I can do that, but what about getting her used to Nathaniel and sharing me?"

"That's a matter of time. Keep reassuring her that you're there for her and keep some special time for the two of you. I would also insist on politeness. Try these things and then let's talk again in a few weeks. All right?"

"Sounds good."

Rachel called me three weeks later. "I think you must be the Amazing Kreskin because everything happened just like you said. I laid off her about her clothes and some other things and the change in her behavior was immediate. I only wish that I had seen the signs of that myself, but the best is what happened with Nathaniel."

"What?" I asked.

"Well, even after we insisted on civil behavior, she was still kind of standoffish with Nathaniel, but I decided to do what you said and just give her time. Then the other night I was getting ready to go out with some of my friends and Callie came in wanting to know where I was going.

"I told her I was going out and Nathaniel was staying with her, and she freaked.

"She was crying and saying, 'I hate Nathaniel, Mommy, I hate him!'

"So I sat down and took her in my lap, even though she's kind of big for that, and I asked her why she hated Nathaniel.

"She stopped crying and said, 'Cause, well, 'cause, well you know, he's just too . . . too, too, too . . . *nice*.'

"I looked at her and said, 'Too nice?' and she looked at me and started to laugh.

"I said, 'You know, Cal, I think I know why you're mad at Nathaniel. Remember all those years you wished for a daddy. Every time there was a wishing well, or a fountain to throw a penny in, or birthday candles to blow out, or a star to wish on, every time since you were three, you wished for a daddy. But what you didn't realize was that your having a dad meant that I would have a husband, and now you have to share me and that's probably kind of scary for you.'

"Callie just looked at me with those big green eyes and nodded and I said, 'But if you trust me on this one and open your heart to Nathaniel you'll realize in no time that there's a lot more love for you now than ever, and that I'll have even more to give you, plus you'll have Nathaniel, who loves you too.'

"She didn't say anything but she cheered right up and when I got home from my dinner out, Nathaniel said they had had a wonderful time. Ever since our talk Callie's really into Nathaniel. She's holding his hand when we walk down the street and she wants him to help her with her homework. They're just going great guns."

"That's wonderful!" I said. "Once you let her talk it out and then helped her express her feelings and fears, she realized there was, in fact, nothing to be afraid of. Like she said, she realized he was just too, too, too *nice!*"

12

Parent Power

"Discipline means to teach and that's really all we're talking about here—teaching your children to be responsible, conscientious, respectful, and respectable people."

Our practice continued to flourish and it became obvious it was time to expand. After much discussion we decided the solution was to bring in another doctor. Reflecting on what our practice needed, we realized the addition of a woman physician would be a tremendous benefit to our young adolescent girls. Understandably, at that age, many girls are more comfortable seeing a woman doctor.

After talking to many candidates we offered the position to Katherine Holden, a doctor with an excellent education and background. We were thrilled when she accepted.

It didn't take long to realize that our office, designed for two people, would not work for the three of us. Another expansion was out of the question, so we decided to open a second office in the nearby town of Darien. We set up a rotation schedule so all three of us worked at both offices. With the help of Dr. Holden, we quickly settled into the new office and began to build our Darien practice.

*   *   *

Jeff and Judith Brown decided to get married about a month before their son, Cody, was born. They were a very arty-kind-of-hippie-stuck-in-the-sixties couple. They worked in New York at their art galleries during the week and had a weekend house in Connecticut.

Cody was a little cherub of a baby boy and they doted on him, making him the complete and total center of their lives. Susan and I went to a party at the Browns' weekend house when Cody was three. He was still running around after midnight, singing songs and dancing and having a marvelous time being the center of attention in this room full of adults.

Susan and I talked about how, when our kids were little and we had a party, we would let them come in and say hello to the guests and visit a little, but when it was their bedtime, back upstairs they went. We wondered if the whole world had changed or if it was just these people.

Cody grew into a very outgoing, talkative, and bright boy, but when he started kindergarten Judith and Jeff began getting calls about his behavior. His teachers thought he was wild, out of control, and smart-alecky—pushing other kids around and talking back to the teachers. The mother and father told me all this with big smiles on their faces. They thought it was very amusing that their son was, what they perceived to be, this little counterculture character. I tried to talk to them about getting some help as a family so they could learn to discipline Cody but they wouldn't hear of it.

Then one night at about 7:30 I got a call from my service saying there had been a terrible accident and the family was on the way to the emergency room. Apparently the whole family had been out shopping and the kid was running in his usual wild fashion through the store, when he ran through a plate glass window.

He was badly cut up. I hurried to the emergency room. We had to call a plastic surgeon in to suture him up properly. Jeff and Judith were terribly shaken and they finally began to realize they were giving him too much leeway. But they found it difficult to change, and he continued to have difficulties at school.

These difficulties escalated when he got to first grade, and more mature behavior was expected of him. I had been suggesting they get help even before the window incident and finally they seemed a little open to it.

"What can we do to change him?" asked Judith.

"First you should understand that there are three basic styles of parenting. The first is the restrictive style. This is the old puritanical style. Children should be seen and not heard. It's very strict and structured. Children are treated like the serfs of the parents. These days, I don't see too many families like this anymore.

"On the other end of the spectrum is the permissive parent. These are, frankly, parents like you, who are concerned about the child expressing their creativity without being stifled. There's not much structure in these children's lives, and although they may grow up to be very creative adults, they may have no concept of responsibility."

"Do you see a lot of families like that?" Jeff asked.

"Absolutely. You know the fish tank in the waiting room?" They nodded. "You would be amazed what children do to that tank of fish in plain sight of their mother or father. I've had a child turn the thermostat up, and when I came in the next morning the fish were boiled. I've had children throw trucks and magazines in the tank, and just the other day I watched a child pull a chair over to the tank, lift the top off, and lean in with both hands, trying to catch a fish. I was watching the mother watch the whole thing.

"I went over to this little boy and said, 'Get down from that chair. This is my house and here we just look at the fish. We don't touch them.'

"The child just stood there looking at me, and the mother said, 'Don't speak to him like that. We never talk to him that way.' I just thought to myself, 'Lady, you're in for some real trouble!' "

"And that's what you think when you see Cody?" Judith asked, more serious than I had ever seen her.

"There are times when I've been concerned about Cody," I responded as tactfully as I could.

"So can parents change their parenting style?" Jeff asked.

"Yes, but it's not easy. I saw another family who had one son, Danny. They were very permissive and Danny was always the kind of kid who clearly needed a more structured environment.

"When he was fourteen, I got a call from his mother. He had been having a lot of behavioral problems at school, fighting and talking rudely to the teachers, not doing his work. The school gave him a warning—the next time there was a problem he'd be suspended. That afternoon he got in a fight and they suspended him.

"So the mom called me and the whole family came in the next evening for a consultation. I asked them what was going on, and got a whole song and dance from Danny about those blankity-blanks at school not knowing what the hell was going on, and then his father chimed in about Danny not knowing what the hell was going on, and the two of them were going at it—verbally, not physically.

"I turned to the mother and said, 'What do you think about all this?'

"Danny jumped right in. 'Why would you think she had anything to say? She never has anything to say.' All I could think was, 'If this was my mother she would have smacked me, if my father didn't get to me first—and I would've deserved it.' This woman just sat there. I felt so ashamed for her.

"I'm sure she sensed it, because she finally said, 'We want him to be able to express himself in all ways.'

"I said, 'But not that way, not by being disrespectful and just plain rude.'

"But there was no way this family was going to change their style and therefore there was no way they were going to change their child's behavior and attitude."

"So you're saying the permissive parenting style is always bad," Jeff said.

"No, not at all. These are extreme cases and I do want to stress that there is no good or bad style. On the other side of the spectrum, the child who's raised strictly but with two-way communication and tons of unconditional love can turn out very well. But Cody is telling you by his behavior that he wants and needs more structure. Your parenting style has to be the right style for the child, as well as the parent."

"So, you're saying we should be following the restrictive style?" asked Judith.

"Not at all. There's a third style, the one I see most often, and that's the authoritative style. This has become the most common and traditional parenting style of this generation. In this style there are rules and children know it, and they understand if they don't follow these rules there'll be consequences. But in the meantime there's a wide area in between where children can be creative and learn and grow. This is the style where you see time-outs for the younger children and contracts for the older ones." Jeff and Judith nodded, looking somewhat relieved that there was a middle ground.

I continued. "I see one family where this system is working well. Their eight-year-old, Cara, went through a phase where she would get very angry when things weren't going her way. She would lose control and try to hit or kick her mom and dad. But no matter how angry or frustrated she got at school or with her friends, this hitting thing would never happen in those situations. So, her parents knew, if she wanted to, she could control this.

"They picked a time when it was calm and quiet, and they explained to Cara that physical violence was totally unacceptable and in this society people who couldn't control their urges to hit and kick have to be isolated from other people. They told her next time she tried to hit or kick she would get one warning to stop. If she didn't stop, she would have to be isolated.

"The next time it happened they warned her, but she didn't control herself. It was almost dinnertime so her mother set one place in the kitchen for Cara while the rest of the family ate in the dining room. Cara couldn't stand it. She was sure she was missing out on something wonderful in the dining room.

"Her mother said it was a long time before Cara even got close to hitting again. The next time it looked like she was going to hit, her mother quietly warned her of the consequences and suggested she go to her room to cool off until she could use her words and not her hands or feet to express her anger. To her mother's surprise and delight Cara controlled herself. She learned how to handle her anger, and they haven't had any more incidents of hitting or kicking.

"This is a good illustration of how the authoritative style can work—Cara was disciplined, rather than punished. The reasons her behavior was unacceptable were explained to her in a calm and nurturing way. The consequences of her behavior were made crystal clear, and these consequences made total sense in the context of her behavior. She was told there would be a warning and there was, and when she was unable to control herself, the parents followed through with their plan. Cara needed only once to learn they meant business and she needed to find another way to express her anger. Note that her mother was completely open to her expressing her anger in an appropriate way. Letting your child know you want that two-way communication, even if they're angry, is a very important part of raising healthy kids."

"And we can do this with Cody," Judith said, more as declaration than as a question.

"Absolutely, but I think you could all benefit from some help in the process," I suggested.

Jeff and Judith were open to taking with a psychologist. The psychologist worked with them as a family, and at home. Cody began to realize his parents meant business. They were not going to put up with his wild antics and there would be consequences for his behavior. His behavior slowly but surely improved. But he continued to have trouble at school. The parents felt he'd been pigeonholed as a troublemaker. So they put him in a private school where he could start with a fresh slate.

The Browns picked a very traditional, strict school. From the get-go Cody did well there. He knew what was expected of him and he knew the consequences if he didn't meet these expectations. He became, in every way, a happier, more well-adjusted child.

When Cody was seven the Browns had a little girl, Mackenzie. At one of Mackenzie's earliest appointments Judith looked up at me and said, "We're not going to make the same mistakes twice. We're definitely raising Mackenzie with structure and discipline," she said passionately.

Alexandra Belford came in without her six-year-old son, Blake. She had requested a consultation because she felt that, in her own words, "Blake was a very disturbed little boy."

"Why do you feel Blake is disturbed?" I asked, recalling the chatty but well-behaved youngster whom I had seen at his last visit.

"He has such a short fuse. He just flies off the handle and into a rage at the slightest thing," she said.

"How do you handle that?"

"When he's in one of his rages there's really nothing I can do. So I just leave the room. When he calms down, he comes and finds me and starts raging all over again because 'I never listen to him.' "

"What do you do then?" I asked, picturing the scene and how frustrated she must be.

"I don't know what to do. I'm ashamed to say that more often than not he ends up sucking me in and I start yelling at him, like I'm the six-year-old."

"You're right. You need to remain calm, especially if he's so out of control. Is he doing this at school or when he goes to visit relatives and friends?"

"No, it's just the opposite. I'm always getting reports about what a little gentleman and delight he is."

"He's not disturbed. He's just testing you. He wants to see who's running the show, and he's doing it at home because it's safe. Because he knows you so well, he can push your buttons."

"That's for sure. He knows exactly how to get to me."

"So stop letting him do it. You're bigger. You're older. You're smarter and more experienced. You should be the one in charge. This is called *parent power*."

"So, what do I do?"

"When he's calm and collected I want you to explain to him that if he flies into another rage he will have to stay in his room until he's calm. Tell him you will not tolerate that behavior any longer, and if he's having a problem he is to calmly tell you about it and then you'll be happy to help him."

"What do I do if he won't go back into his room when he's in a rage?"

"Then you ignore him or walk away. You can occasionally remind him that you would love to help him as soon as he's calm. When he does speak calmly and control himself, heap praise and attention on. Positive reinforcement can work wonders at this age. If he stops getting attention for the negative behavior and gets lots of attention for behaving appropriately, he'll have no use for the wild behavior, and every reason to start learning self-control."

"You make it sound so easy," Alexandra said.

"I know it's not easy to ignore a screaming, raging child, particularly when it's your own, but it's the only way you're going to help him stop this negative behavior. The praise and attention part will be easier, and when you start seeing some results it will get even easier."

Another six-year-old with a will of iron was Taylor Faludi. Taylor was the last of five children and the only girl. She was pretty used to having things her own way, since not only her parents thought she was the center of the universe, but her four older brothers clearly felt that way as well.

Taylor had had an uneventful year in kindergarten. She had gone off contentedly every morning to happily participate in the various kindergarten activities. But first grade was not to her liking—not at all.

About a week after school opened I started getting calls from Mrs. Faludi. "I can't get Taylor to go to school. She says she won't go and she means it. I have to physically get her dressed, carry her to the car, and drag her into school. Then she'll run right back out the door," she said, sounding angry and frustrated.

"Have you asked her why she doesn't want to go to school?" I asked.

"Of course. She says she just doesn't like it. It's not fun like kindergarten was."

"So, how did you respond to that?"

"I told her if she would give it more of a chance she would like it, but she says she's given it enough of a chance and she's not going. We have this argument every morning."

"Have you talked to her teacher?"

"Yes. She says some children have difficulty with the transition to first grade and that each day after Taylor gets involved with their activities she's fine. But then the next morning it's hell all over again. She seemed to feel it was just a matter of time until Taylor happily went to school. But she's not the one trying to dress a child who's lying on the floor like a sack of potatoes."

"How about this—try explaining to Taylor that this is her job. Dad's job is to go to the office. Mom's job is to take care of the family. Her brothers' and her job is to go to school."

"I'll try," she said doubtfully, "but I really don't think that will work."

"You could also try some positive reinforcement techniques. When you pick her up from school tell her what a good job she's doing. Praise the littlest thing she does when she's getting ready in the morning—that kind of thing."

"I'll try, but I'm really at the end of my rope here," she replied.

"Call and let me know what happens."

A week later she called. "Nothing works; if anything the situation is getting worse."

"Why don't you try letting Taylor bring a transition object to school with her—a favorite stuffed animal or toy that she can keep in her desk."

"Okay, I'll try it."

"Call and let me know what happens," I reminded her.

"We're still having to literally drag Taylor into school," Mrs. Faludi reported a week later. "I think she's starting to enjoy all the attention she's getting for carrying on like this."

"You're probably right, in which case I would just as calmly and quietly as possible keep doing what you're doing. Don't start giving in to letting her stay at home or we'll really be in trouble."

"Well, I sure don't know what else to do," she said.

"Keep me posted," I said, but I didn't hear from her for three weeks. Then she came in with one of the boys.

"What's happening with Taylor and school?" I asked.

"Oh, I got that whole thing settled over the weekend," she said with a triumphant smile.

"How?" I asked.

"Well, on Friday it was the usual struggle to get her dressed and into school and I had really had it. When she came out of school all smiles and giggles something in me snapped.

"She got into the car and I just looked at her and said, 'I've had enough of this now. There is no reason in the world that you shouldn't be going off to school each day with the same smile you have coming out of school. I'm putting an end to this little act of yours right now.

" 'You, young lady, are not leaving your room for the entire weekend except to use the bathroom. You will even eat in your room. I want you to think very seriously about your morning routine while you're in your room because if it continues on Monday—in other words if you don't get up, get yourself dressed, get into the car on your own steam, and walk happily into that school, under your own power—then you can forget soccer practice which starts on Monday. And the same goes for every morning you give me trouble going to school. You'll come home and stay in your room—period!' "

"How did Taylor respond to this?" I asked.

"Her eyes got huge and teary but she didn't say a word."

"And did she stay in her room all weekend?" I asked.

"We didn't hear a peep from her, and when I went in and woke her up on Monday morning she jumped out of bed and got herself dressed and went off to school with a smile on her face."

"That's great, you really took charge and set down the rules in a way she could understand. You know good parenting really boils down to three things: (1) unrestricted love, (2) open communication, and (3) a solid structure of clear guidelines and rules.

"In this instance you had the first two. There's no doubt that Taylor feels you love her infinitely and you were doing your best to listen to her reluctance to go to school. But once you set down guidelines and a very clear rule—not only was Taylor going to school, but that she was going to school under her own power—then it all came together.

"It is my deep and true belief that children are happiest when they have this kind of clear understanding of the rules. It's something solid and consistent they can count on," I told Mrs. Faludi.

"Well, in this case Taylor certainly pushed me to be crystal clear about what the rule was. I could have saved both of us a lot of time and anguish if I had done this sooner."

"We all know what to do in hindsight. You did great. You hung in there with Taylor until you found what worked and didn't let her get away with missing any school."

"I guess I did okay," she admitted with a proud smile.

Jill Chandler called. She wanted me to have a talk with her son, thirteen-year-old Eli. "He's out of control, and I don't know what to do with him," she said on the phone. "If he doesn't get his way he throws a fit."

"Why don't you all come in and we'll see what's going on."

Jill and her husband, Eric, had been divorced for about five years. Jill had custody of Eli and his fifteen-year-old sister, Kristen.

Jill, Eli, and Kristen came in—my last appointment on a cold night. We sat around the table in the consultation room. I started the ball rolling. "Eli, your mom called because she was concerned about your behavior. She told me you were out of control."

I was surprised when Kristen jumped right in, "Eli's just spoiled. Mom always gives in to him," she said in her quiet, intelligent way.

"What do you mean?" I asked. "Give me an example."

"Mom says we have to eat together as a family at the dining room table, but every night Eli takes his plate into the living room and turns on the TV and Mom does nothing about it."

I looked over at Jill. "What's the story?" I asked

"It's the end of a long day and I just don't have the strength to fight him. He makes such a fuss at the table if I don't let him go that I just give in. Then, at least, we can have our dinner in peace."

Eli sat back silently with a little grin on his face. "Eli, why do you think your mom wants you to all eat together every night?" I asked him.

"Because it's the only time of the day when we're not all going in different directions. It's the only time we can do something as a family," he said in a fair imitation of his mother's voice, obviously having heard the reason many times.

"That makes sense to me," I said, ignoring his tone of voice.

"Well, I'd rather watch TV," he said stubbornly.

"Yeah, and your mother thinks family time is important, and I agree," I replied.

Eli gave a snort and looked away.

I turned my attention to Jill. "If I were you, I'd say, 'Fine, go watch TV, but dinner is going to be eaten in the dining room, not in the living room. If you want dinner you sit down and eat with the rest of the family.' What would he do if you said that?"

"I still don't think he'll eat with us," she said, looking right at Eli.

"If he doesn't, it's only because you don't stick to your guns. Remember, you're still the parent and he's still the child. I know it's not easy doing it alone, but the fact that you're a single parent only makes it more important that there be structure and discipline."

I turned my attention to Eli. "What do you think of all this?" I asked him.

"I just want to watch my shows," he said in a sullen voice.

"Jill, the ball's in your court," I told her as they got up to leave.

The next day Jill called. "I just have to tell you what happened last night," she said, clearly excited. "We were in your parking lot and I commented that it was past dinnertime, so maybe we should just stop on the way home and get some dinner. Kristen suggested we stop for pizza and Eli said he wanted McDonald's. I said, 'This time we'll go for McDonald's. Next time we'll get pizza.'

"Kristen gave me a look that said, 'See, he always gets his way,' and suddenly it was so clear. I *was* giving in to him just to avoid an outburst—and I wanted pizza too.

"So I said, 'You know what? I changed my mind. I want pizza. So we're going for pizza.' Sure enough Eli started one of his fits. I looked at him really calmly and said, 'You can get home any way you want, but if you get into this car you better understand that we're going for pizza.' He got into the car and everything was great."

"Yeah! You stuck to your guns!"

"I sure did." I could hear how thrilled and happy she was.

"Keep it up. Don't let him have dinner in front of that TV tonight."

"He'll be at the table with the rest of us. You can count on it," she said with such power that I knew I could.

* * *

"No, you may *absolutely* not serve beer to your friends in this house," I said for the third time to Lisa, "and not only will there be no beer in the house, but there will be no beer in the driveway, or the yard, or in any cars, or down the street, or around the corner, or anywhere within walking distance of this house."

"But Dad, all the parents let us have beer at parties," Lisa begged.

"Then maybe you shouldn't be going to these parties," I responded.

"No, Dad. Mom, tell him."

"Tell him what? I completely agree with him. Furthermore, I can't believe you would think for a minute we would serve alcohol to tenth-graders," Susan responded.

"I can't believe you guys. You're making it so no one will come to my party."

"The only reason you and your friends go to a party is to drink?" I asked.

"No, you . . . you . . . just don't understand!" She dropped onto the sofa in a dramatic heap, arms crossed in front of her.

"Hey, I have an idea," I said, trying to save the day. "We'll give you and ten of your friends a real dinner party—a sit-down dinner party. I'll cook something real elegant, and we'll get all the china and crystal out. It will be like nothing any of your friends have ever seen before. What do you think?"

"God, Dad. That would be so embarrassing. Why can't you just let me have my party, my way—with chips and dip and beer?"

"Lisa, stop it now. The discussion's over. You can have an alcohol-free party or you can have no party. It's your choice." I was losing my patience.

"Then I choose *no* party," she said—stubborn thing—as if that would really hurt us.

"Well gee, Lisa, put an arrow through my heart," I told her with a chuckle.

"You're cutting off your nose to spite your face. It's you who wants the party, not Dad and I," Susan added.

"Don't you think *I* know that. But I'm not going to have a party no one wants to go to."

"Suit yourself. Both of my offers stand. You can have the elegant dinner party or you can have the regular beerless party anytime. Just say the word."

"Great. Thanks a lot," the Queen of Sarcasm said and stomped off to her room.

Susan and I looked at each other with a smile and a shrug. I know a lot of parents find this difficult, but not me. All I had to do was imagine the pressure that Lisa was under from her peers. We had just had a firsthand look at the pressure she felt over serving alcohol. There were similar pressures over the issues of drugs and sex.

Lisa had known for a long time that we didn't condone drinking alcohol. This had been the subject of many discussions. She knew, even when she asked if she could serve alcohol at her party, that we wouldn't allow it. She also knew we didn't want her drinking at other people's homes. But we knew we couldn't be with her all the time. So we just had to hope the values and standards we had raised her with would help guide her when she was in tempting situations.

Values and standards aside, we recognized the fact that Lisa was human and there probably would come a time when she would drink. So we put into effect an agreement between us and Lisa—if she was ever out and had been drinking and needed a safe and sober way to get home, all she had to do was call and one of us would be there anytime, day or night, to pick her up—no questions asked, no punishments or retributions given.

Still, I found it hard to believe many parents would not only allow beer to be served in their homes but would, in fact, be the ones who purchased it for their underage children and their friends. One of my patient families continued to serve their son and his friends alcohol despite the fact that his

younger sister had been in an alcohol treatment center. It bog-
gled the mind. Where had the whole concept of parental responsibility gone? I had noticed, with some alarm and for some time,
that many parents were giving up their power. They were, without realizing it, turning over the reins to their children.

Sam and Nancy Hoch had grown up poor. Now they were
self-made millionaires, several times over, and whether it was
about schoolwork, behavior, or buying things, they couldn't
say no to their kids. There was Ellen, who was fourteen and in
danger of having to repeat eighth grade, twelve-year-old
Jeremy, who was demanding the best new ski equipment for
his very first ski trip, and Jared, eight, who was simply a holy
terror.

Nancy had brought Jared in for a throat culture when she
shared all this with me. "Not a week goes by that I don't get a
call from one of Ellen's teachers and Jared's principal. And
Jeremy is always trying a new sport or activity and has to have
the latest and best equipment. Then he loses interest. His clos-
et is so full of the stuff, it looks like a sporting goods store. We
try so hard to be there for them, to give them what they want,
to be their friends—and look at where we're at."

"I think you just gave yourself the answer to the problem,"
I told her.

"Did I miss something?" she asked.

"You just said you try to be their friend. They don't need
you to be their friend. They have their peers for that. They
need you to be their parents."

"Well, of course we're their parents, but we can be their
friends too."

"I'm not so sure about that. A mother of one of my patients
was telling me she doesn't think she's doing a good job as a
mother unless her eleven-year-old daughter tells her she hates
her at least once a week."

"Well, that's fine for her, but I don't want my kids hating
me."

"Her daughter doesn't hate her either. She just gets angry when she can't have everything her own way."

"Well, so do my kids."

"Yeah, but the difference is you give in to them when they get angry. You said it yourself—you give them whatever they want. The mom I'm talking about doesn't give her kid what she wants. She gives her what she needs."

Nancy looked at me with a mixture of confusion and irritation. "It's all about responsibility and parent power and discipline," I went on."It's easy to give them what they want. They all know what they want. They see it on TV and hear it from their friends every day. Few kids know what they need, and that's where parental responsibility comes in. You've given the kids too much power, and not enough limits. That's why you're getting calls from the school. You need to give them discipline—set some clear limits and expectations, and then you need to be firm—no waffling later on."

"You know as far as discipline is concerned, we just don't believe in strict punishments or spankings or anything like that. That's just not our style," Nancy said defensively.

"Discipline doesn't mean punishment. It actually is derived from the word 'disciple,' meaning student. Discipline means to teach and that's really all we're talking about here—teaching your children to be responsible, conscientious, respectful, and respectable people. You do that by being involved in their lives, not by giving them everything they want and letting them always have their own way.

"Trust me. If you can do this, you'll feel more valuable as an involved parent than you would by trying to get your worth from giving them material things or by giving in to them every time they want to do something."

"So how am I supposed to do all that?" she challenged me. "Give me an example."

"Okay," I thought for a moment, "here's your example: you said Jeremy wanted ski equipment even though he's never skied before. Call me crazy, but going out and buying new ski equipment for a kid who you know doesn't stick with anything is nuts. Frankly, buying new ski equipment for *anyone* who doesn't yet know if they love skiing is nuts. So you say no to him. You tell him you'll rent equipment for him, but you say a firm no to buying it."

"But it seems so important to him to have his own equipment."

"In the first place, it might be important to him, but that doesn't mean you have to supply it. Secondly, you could find out just how important it is to him by telling him he can earn the money to buy the skis himself. My guess is having his own equipment won't be quite so important to him then."

"What if it is? What if he agrees to work for it?" she asked, as if working would be a horrible thing.

"Well then good for him. If he worked for those skis, believe me, he would treasure them a million times more than if you and Sam just shelled out the money for them."

"I just can't see telling him he has to earn the money for the skis."

"But you can see buying them for him?" I asked.

"Well, that's how we operate," she said with a shrug.

"But you were just complaining to me about the results of operating like that," I reminded her.

"I know. Do you really think we could just turn things around?"

"Sure. The kids will give you a hard time about it, and you and Sam have to be in this together—a united front—and it won't be easy, but you definitely can do it."

"I'll talk to Sam about it."

"You know this isn't just about buying them things. It's also about getting on them and staying on them about schoolwork and household responsibilities and respecting you and Sam and each other. It's a whole new way of life. It's no one-shot deal."

"But it can start with the skis?"

"It's as good a place as any to start."

She left, mulling all this over.

I didn't see any of the Hoch family for almost five months, then Nancy brought Jeremy in for his camp checkup.

While Jeremy was waiting in the examining room, I caught Nancy alone in the waiting room. "To ski or not to ski, that is the question?" I said to her with a smile. She immediately blushed a bright shade of red and shook her head, not able to even look me in the eyes.

"I'll take that to mean I can ask Jeremy how his new skis were on his very first ski trip."

"We just couldn't do it. We talked about it, but when it came right down to it, Sam said he wanted Jeremy and the other kids to have all the things we couldn't have as children."

I shook my head. "You're not doing them any favors by giving them everything they want," I reminded her—gently, I hoped.

"I know, but we can't seem to help ourselves."

I left her in the waiting room looking a little uncomfortable and embarrassed. I thought of what a disservice they were doing their children. What their kids needed was not sports equipment and total freedom. What they needed was structure and discipline and their parents to have some high but attainable expectations for them to meet. Giving them everything they wanted obviously filled a need in Sam and Nancy but it was detrimental to Ellen, Jeremy, and Jared.

I was browsing in a bookstore when I saw a mother and little girl at a nearby rack. The mother kneeled down in front of the little girl and said, "Mommy needs to find a book, so I want you to stand close by."

"Okay, Mommy," the little girl said, but a moment later she was running madly through the store.

The mother calmly led her back. "I told you that I needed you to stand near me for just a few minutes. If you run off again, you'll have a time-out."

The child, eyes wide, nodded at her mother. But once again

it only took seconds before she shot off. This time the mother returned with the child in one hand and a small chair from the children's section in the other.

"I told you that if you ran off again you would have a time-out," she said as she put the chair down facing the opposite bookshelves and firmly sat her daughter in the chair. "You are in time-out for three minutes."

The little girl sat facing the bookshelf, arms folded across her chest. The mother turned toward the other shelf, checking her watch. After three minutes the mother said, "Your time-out is over," and gave her daughter a hug.

I applauded from down the aisle. The mother looked up, a little startled.

"Well done! You did exactly what I advise. You gave her a warning and then another one with the consequences attached to it, and then you said, 'That's it.' Now she knows that she can't push you very far and that you're the boss. That has to make her feel pretty secure," I said.

"Why, thank you," she said, looking confused at this stranger's proclamation.

"I'm a pediatrician, Norman Weinberger," I introduced myself. "I enjoyed seeing in action the advice I often give," I explained.

"Well, it's certainly nice to have an expert's seal of approval," she said, looking less confused.

"No, it looks like you're the expert!" I said as she found her book and left, her daughter in tow.

13

With a Little Help from My Friends

I had been striving to keep up with and meet the ever more complex needs, demands, and struggles of the families in my practice ...

With all the changes and craziness going on in the world I started thinking again about how we could help our parents navigate the treacherous waters of balancing careers, marriages, and kids. I wondered if parenting groups might help. I took the idea to my friend, Maida Webster. If I were to do this I wouldn't want it to be without Maida. She had a solid background in family therapy, plus a natural warmth and openness that I knew would help our families and make the parenting groups successful.

We talked about how best to run the groups: couples or just moms? six participants or twelve? once a week or once a month? how long would we run the groups? We only got as far as deciding to hold the group in the evening in the Darien office when Val Hawkins came in with her new baby, her third child. She lost no time in telling me how difficult her life was with three children and a husband not very involved, between his job and his commute. She mentioned that she had lots of friends in the same situation and the lightbulb went on over my head.

"Do you think you could get together a group of four or

five couples who would want to be part of a parenting group
that meets to discuss these and other issues?" I asked her.

"I could have ten couples for you by tomorrow, I bet," she
said excitedly.

"I think for this first time out we should stick with four or
five."

So Val got the group together and Maida and I decided we
would meet once a month for six months. We started to get
excited about this finally, really happening. We thought long
and hard about what kind of format we wanted to follow and
decided to devote each meeting to a specific topic, like discipline or sibling rivalry or birth order. We would kick off the
meeting with a didactic speech about the topic and then open
the floor for questions and discussion.

For the first two meetings we had full attendance, but after
that the fathers started dropping like flies, until very few
fathers attended. It also became clear that the issues we would
discuss needed to come from the participants themselves.
They needed to talk about their husbands working too much,
and the stress of living in a community where they felt pressure to live up to a certain lifestyle. They all were young families—their oldest children being five or six, and it was difficult for them to hold it all together.

At the end of six months the group wanted to continue for
another six months, and as a result we developed a professional, yet at the same time very close, relationship. One of
our members had a miscarriage and the whole group grieved
along with her. Another spoke of her concern over leaving her
baby in the care of her mother, whom she loved but knew was
an alcoholic. Everyone, not just Maida and I, shared their
experiences and information. The group had really bonded.
Our experiment was a success.

At the end of the year they still wanted to continue but we
changed the schedule to meet only every other month. By the
end of the second year they still wanted to continue, but
Maida and I felt we had given this group of people a lot (and

received a lot in return) and it was time to move on and try a different group, a different format. We weren't quite sure what was needed next. We knew we were on the right track, but we felt the concept could use a little fine-tuning. And so we started looking at all the different possible criteria for our next parenting group.

"The three areas all parents want to control—but can't—are food, sleep, and elimination," I told our second parenting group. They were a group brought together by Maida Webster and me, having one criterion in mind—they were all dual-career families—lawyers and bankers and commodities traders who spent a chunk of each day commuting to and from New York City. We had brought this group together to meet once a month for a year.

As Maida and I imagined we would, we dealt with issues of child care, guilt over not spending enough time with their children, the difficulties and stress of juggling career and family. But these parents also wanted to tackle the most universal issues of parenting, including nutrition, toilet training, and sleep.

"At this point I'm starting to think little Gregory is going to be toilet-trained before Morgan," Linda Small said with more than a little frustration in her voice. Morgan was three, and not the least bit interested in being toilet-trained.

When Linda and her husband, Barry, made the slightest move to get him trained, he would point out that no one was trying to get his brother, Gregory, out of a diaper. This was true, but Gregory was only eighteen months old. "I can see it now—Morgan going off to first grade wearing Depends," Linda moaned.

"There are three things needed for successful toilet training," I told the Smalls and the rest of the group. "You need muscle and nervous control—to hold and let go. You need a vocabulary to communicate your need, and you need to want to. Obviously at age three, Morgan has the first two. It's the third you need to work on. I suggest you make a game of it.

Barry, you can put some Cheerios in the toilet and show Morgan how to sink them, or take him outside and let him water the grass or find north on the wet side of the tree. Show him this is fun and he's in control."

"Oh yeah, sounds like a great time," Barry replied sarcastically.

The following week I got a call from Linda. "I couldn't wait a month to tell you this," she said. "On Saturday I handed a box of Cheerios to Barry and said, 'The toilet training is in your hands now—so to speak.' He went reluctantly into the bathroom with both boys. About ten minutes later they all came out.

"I thought, 'Wow, that Dr. Weinberger is a miracle worker.' I said to Barry, 'That was fast. What happened?'

" 'Well, I sprinkled the Cheerios in the toilet and I look down and there's Morgan on my left, and Gregory on my right, and I start to uhhh . . . sink the Cheerios and I felt this little hand patting my calf. I look down and Morgan smiles up at me and says, "Good boy, Daddy, that's a good boy," and I look down at Gregory and he's got this very perplexed look on his little face, like he's wondering what the hell I'm doing, and I just suddenly got performance anxiety. It's not easy peeing with an audience . . . not to mention how stupid I felt shooting down Cheerios.'

"I don't think either boy will ever be trained," Linda told me with a laugh.

"Yes they will," I told her. "Have him try again. This time use Cocoa Puffs," I said jokingly.

Before we even had a chance to officially start the next meeting, Linda spoke up. "I'd like to announce that, at last, Morgan Justin Small has joined the ranks of those wearing big-boy pants. He is officially toilet-trained." A cheer went up from the group.

"It was the Cocoa Puffs, wasn't it?" I asked.

"No. Actually we had nothing to do with it. Last weekend we went to my sister's house and Morgan went into the bathroom with his cousin Luke. Luke is six months older than

Morgan and has been toilet-trained for almost a year. They stayed in the bathroom for about twenty minutes. When they came out Morgan was toilet-trained—just like that," she said. "He hasn't worn a diaper all week."

"It's like I said. He just needed to have the desire to be trained, and watching his older cousin do it made him want to do it too."

All children eventually become toilet-trained. This is a fact that parents of a three-year-old in diapers have trouble believing, but Morgan was not unusual in that boys often do not have an interest in being out of a diaper until they are in their threes. The Smalls were not unusual being driven crazy by a three-year-old still in diapers. Often the solution is to back off and wait for cues from the child that he's ready.

Nutrition was another hot issue.

"Tyler is trying to kill me," Joan Rashkow informed the group.

"How, exactly, is Tyler trying to kill you?" I asked, as the other parents exchanged confused looks, wondering, no doubt, how a two-year-old was trying to kill his mother.

"He's trying to kill me by not eating," she responded. "He eats nothing. He's existing on air." Now they understood. Several of the mothers nodded in agreement.

"Then it would seem more like he's trying to kill himself, not you," I teased. "If I remember correctly, Tyler is in the same percentile for his age group he was in a year ago, which means he's growing at a perfectly normal rate. I assure you he's not existing on air. Tell me, what does he eat?"

"I told you. He eats nothing," Joan said defiantly.

"I know he eats something," I gently coaxed her.

"Well, he does eat peanut butter sandwiches, sometimes, but only on white bread, no jelly, and he won't touch the crusts."

"None of them eat crusts," Lindsey Fleming remarked.

"It's a rare and wonderful child who eats crusts," I agreed. "What else will he eat?"

She thought for a moment. "He eats chicken nuggets and French fries. Oh, and that boxed macaroni and cheese."

"Uh-huh." I gave her an encouraging nod. "Any fruits?"

She thought for a moment and then somewhat reluctantly told me, "He'll eat apples, but only if I peel them, and bananas if I slice them on his cereal."

"Ah-ha! He eats cereal," I pointed out to her.

She smiled. "Okay, so he does eat some things, but he won't touch his vegetables."

Vegetables—it always comes down to vegetables. I've found that almost all parents think vegetables are the staff of life, despite the fact most parents won't eat *their* vegetables.

"He can stay perfectly healthy without vegetables."

"That's not what I was taught."

"The scale doesn't lie. Tyler is a normal, healthy two-year-old. He is absolutely flourishing. Wait until he's thirteen and eating you out of house and home. Then you'll be beside yourself worrying he has a tapeworm."

"He's so picky. That day will never come."

"Trust me. It will."

"Our problem is having the time to prepare a decent meal," Corinne Petrak said. "By the time we pick the kids up at day-care and get home it's almost seven. I'm embarrassed to say how often we stop at fast-food places. But it takes too much time to make dinner, and everyone's so hungry—I don't know what else to do."

"We cook several meals on the weekend, stick them in the freezer, and then nuke them as we need them," Lindsey Fleming offered.

"That's a great idea," I said, "but you can also use some quick and easy recipes. I have one that will work for almost any kind of fish or chicken. It's fast and tasty, especially if you have a grill."

"Whose kid will eat fish?" asked Joan Rashkow.

"Mine will," said Lindsey. "You just tell them it's chicken."

Terry Weber was already getting paper and pen out of her purse. "Let's have that recipe, Dr. Weinberger."

Dr. Norman Weinberger's Quick and Easy Twin Grilled Chicken Breasts (in honor of my wife and her twin brother)

4 skinless, boneless chicken breasts, halved

3 cloves garlic, minced

3 tablespoons minced fresh rosemary or
    1 and 1/2 teaspoons dried

1 tablespoon Dijon mustard

1 tablespoon fresh lemon juice

3 tablespoons dry white wine

1/2 teaspoon salt

1/2 teaspoon fresh ground pepper

2 tablespoons olive oil

Prepare grill or grate. Rinse the chicken and pat dry. Place in nonmetal bowl. In a small bowl mix together garlic, rosemary, mustard, lemon juice, wine, salt, pepper, and olive oil. Blend well. Pour mixture over chicken. Make sure chicken is well coated with the marinade. Cover and marinate at room temperature, turning once or twice for 15-30 minutes.

Coat grill with cooking spray or olive oil. Grill chicken, turning once and basting with reserve marinade, until chicken breasts are white throughout, but still juicy, approximately 3-4 minutes.

Serve with salad, rice, or pasta of choice—ahhhh.

You can substitute any firm-fleshed fish, such as swordfish, red snapper, halibut, or shark. You don't have a grill? Then broil for 8-10 minutes, turning once.

"My problem is what to say at dinner," said Perry Fleming.

"What do you mean?" asked Maida.

"Well, when I was a kid, we didn't eat with my parents. My mother would feed us early and then she and my dad would eat after we went to bed. I don't want that for my kids. I want dinnertime to be a family time—meaningful and important for them, and I worry about what words to say, what ideas to put out there, how the kids will interpret what I say and how it will all affect them later."

"No offense, Perry, but you're nuts," said Richard Weber. "We just try to get them fed and the kitchen cleaned up before midnight." A murmur of agreement went through the group. He continued, "At our house it's feeding time at the zoo. The chance of a meaningful conversation happening is zilch."

"I don't think you need to worry about mealtime being meaningful," I told Perry. "The fact that it's important to you to sit down as a family every night is meaningful in and of itself. Meaningful and silly and boring and interesting conversations will all eventually evolve out of your just being all together."

"But as they get older it will be more difficult to hold to a family dinner every night. So you really have to stick to your guns about this," Maida added. "Your instincts are right—the family dinner is an important and meaningful time. So stick with it even when they're running to music lessons and Little League and soccer."

The second parenting group was a tremendous success. We learned a lot about a generation of working parents and their stresses, both real and imagined. We were now ready to launch our new parenting groups, yet there was a fly ready to spoil the ointment. The fly in this case was the lease for our Darien office. It was about to expire and the landlords were being difficult in negotiating a new contract. We needed to find a new space in Darien. We were fortunate enough to locate a building around the corner from the old office, which was specifically designed for professionals. It was a larger, open office with more adequate parking. We quickly drew up the plans, and in short order moved to our new space.

While the office was being constructed, Maida and I reassessed what we were doing and where we could be most effective. We immediately agreed the most important group we could reach were first-time parents and their babies.

We decided to offer first-time, new parents entering the practice the opportunity to join a first-time parents' group. We had learned much from our previous experience, and used this knowledge to develop a six-session course lasting one and a half hours each. We would focus on areas such as child development, behavior, individuality, birth order, and nutrition. We would attempt to help husbands and wives make the adjustment to being fathers and mothers. We would talk about mothers returning to work, day-care, time constraints, personal time, husband-and-wife time, and many of the complexities of parenting in the '90s.

Our first group consisted of ten mothers and their infants, ages two to eight weeks. Fathers were invited but, from our previous experience, we knew not to stress the fathers attending each session. Instead we set aside one session when fathers were specifically invited to come and deal with their issues and questions. This group was a heterogeneous mix in many respects: economically, racially, and ethnically, and included mothers who would return to working outside the home, as well as those who would not.

At the first meeting of the group, after a short talk about what to expect in the first weeks of parenthood, we asked each mother to share with us how things were going so far.

Deborah Carter, an executive with a large cosmetics company who expected to return to work when her baby was three months old, spoke up first. "How are things going . . . how are things going?" she repeated thoughtfully, as if it were a tough test question. "Just let me think a second. I can't really think straight anymore. I've never been more exhausted. I used to have twenty people reporting to me. I was in charge and I could make split-second decisions. Now I can't answer a simple question. This is by far the toughest job in the world. I've worked for a lot of bosses and this is the most demanding boss I've ever had," she said, pointing to her infant son, Maxwell. "And I can't even quit this job."

"I know just how you feel," Gerry Sampson agreed. "The

other night we had my brother and sister-in-law over to see the baby. I was sitting at the table, eating and breast-feeding at the same time, when I caught a glimpse of myself in the dining room mirror. I didn't recognize myself. My hair was uncombed, I had no makeup on, my breast was hanging out, and I was shoving this greasy piece of lamb into my mouth with my hand, because I was starving and it was impossible to eat any other way and breast-feed at the same time.

"I was both repulsed and fascinated by my reflection. Then all of a sudden I started to cry, 'I used to be so elegant, what's happened to me?' My whole family just stared for a moment, and then my husband came over and gave me a big hug, but no one could say I was still elegant."

"I agree. I don't feel at all like myself," Sharon Herzig said. "My problem is between being exhausted all the time, my hormones being out of whack, and my breasts leaking every two minutes, I haven't felt very sexy, much to my husband's dismay. He asked me when I thought I would feel like making love again, and I told him I figured I'd be ready around the time Zach goes to college.

"Anyway, last week my mother called and she said, 'Why don't you bring the baby over to spend the night on Saturday. You and Paul get dressed up, go out to dinner and have a good time, and go home and . . . you know.'

"I said, 'What's you know, Mom?'

"And she said, 'You know—be . . . together.'

"All I could do was groan. It seemed like everyone was interested in sex but me. So the big night came and we got dressed up and dropped the baby and all the equipment off at my mother's, and went out for a lovely dinner, and Paul had a couple of drinks and we had a bottle of wine. Paul fell asleep on the way home and I thought I was off the hook.

"Anyway, we got home and he got his second wind and he's Mr. Romantic. I thought, 'Oh nuts,' I'm really going to have to go through with this, and the thought actually made me shudder, which, believe me, is not at all like me.

"So, I went into the bathroom and brushed my teeth and hair and put on something sexy to try to get into the mood. I came back into the bedroom and there's Mr. Romantic sound asleep and snoring and—*yes*—I'm off the hook. I put my flannel nightgown on and happily went to bed, sleeping through the night for the first time in seven weeks.

"The next morning my mom calls with this teasing singsong voice, 'How was last ni-i-ght?'

"And I could honestly tell her, 'It went great, Mom!' "

"It's so frustrating that our husbands don't get it," said Teresa Kinney.

"What do you mean?" asked Maida.

"Well, Jackson is only two months old and Jim is already pushing to have another kid. I don't even know if I want to have any more kids at all—ever—and he wants another one *now?*"

"What does he say when you tell him you're not ready to think about more children?" asked Maida.

"He gets sort of angry. He says that we had discussed this all before we were married, and we had. We were going to have three kids right in a row. But he's not home with the baby. His life hasn't changed much, but my life sure has and I'm just not ready for any more changes right now.

"I'm taking care of Jackson and the house and he's just not supportive at all. He says, 'What's one more child when we've already got Jackson?' but he has no concept of what it's like."

"Why don't you try to get him more involved with Jackson or the household chores so he can get a taste of what your life is like?" suggested Maida.

"I'll try, but he's pretty traditional when it comes to household chores and taking care of Jackson."

"So, what are you going to do? Are you going to have another child now?" asked Gerry Sampson.

"No, there's no way, and he can't very well do it without me."

"Why don't you tell him you'll have another one if he agrees to be responsible for the children every weekend," Deborah suggested.

"He would laugh in my face. He just doesn't see child rearing as his job," Teresa said. "But I guess it could help make my point clear to him."

I delighted in hearing the way the mothers supported each other—helping with suggestions and empathizing with each other. There weren't always solutions to every problem, but it was clear these women felt better just knowing there were others with similar problems who were willing to listen to them, help them, and support them.

To breast-feed or not to breast-feed? That was the nutrition question of this parenting group, along with most new parents.

"Well, you believe in breast-feeding, don't you, Dr. Weinberger?" asked Sharon Herzig.

"I believe in giving you the facts about breast-feeding, but it's your baby and your breasts and it's up to you whether you breast- or bottle-feed. The only person I ever told to breast-feed was my wife. I gave her all the information on the immunological benefits of breast-feeding, and all the statistics on how breast milk has everything our baby would need. I really campaigned for her to breast-feed. She told me, 'Norman, if you want to breast-feed, you go ahead and do it, because I'm not going to.' "

The group laughed. "I'm here to help you and your baby. If you want to breast-feed I'm here to help you with that. If you want to bottle-feed, then I'll help you with that too."

"Well, I'm just about ready to give up on breast-feeding," said Julie Rosati. "I'm having a lot of trouble with it, and I don't think Mary is getting enough food."

"I know how you feel," Gerry said. "Dr. Weinberger will tell you—I had a lot of problems too, and I was ready to give up after the third day. I couldn't get Betsy to latch on. I didn't think my milk would come in. I was a wreck. I went back in to see Dr. Weinberger and the nurse gave me some tips, but it still wasn't happening. So I gave her an occasional bottle, because, like you, I was afraid she wasn't getting enough to eat.

"Then finally by the sixth day I decided I really was committed to breast-feeding and I was going to make this work, and I did. I felt like Mother Earth after that. If I could do this, you can too. You just have to stick with it."

"That's right," I agreed with Gerry. "It's not at all uncommon to have some problems breast-feeding at the beginning. A lot of women do. After the meeting we'll have the nurse give you some pointers and suggestions and with perseverance and practice you should be an expert in no time."

The parenting groups were going well, and I felt like we were helping more and more parents launch their families with confidence and knowledge, but at the same time I was seeing many families in crisis and many children at risk.

"How old is their mother?" I asked Mrs. Utley. She was the paternal grandmother of two-year-old Ricky and four-year-old John. Their parents were going through such a messy divorce that the judge had given temporary custody of the boys to their grandmother. She had been unhappy with their pediatrician and had switched to our practice. I was trying to get a family history, but it was impossible to get a straight answer from Mrs. Utley.

I repeated my question, "How old is the mother?"

"Oh, she's just a terrible person. I told my son not to marry her. Now he knows he should've listened to me."

"I was just asking her age," I tried to get her back on track.

"I don't know. In her late thirties, I guess."

"How's her health?" I asked.

"I think she just got out of the psychiatric hospital because she's clearly crazy."

I took a deep breath and decided I'd take a different approach. "I see in John's chart that he saw an endocrinologist at Yale Hospital, because he had failure to grow. It says here the doctor thought it was psychosomatic."

"Those doctors didn't know the facts. That's the trouble with you doctors—you never bother with the facts. You would rather just make something up."

Uh-oh, I thought to myself. These kids are headed for disaster.

"Ahh . . . maybe you could give me the father's phone number. I'd like to talk to him," I said, thinking it had to be easier to deal with him.

"What do you want to talk to *him* about?" This was unbelievable. I had never run into anything quite like this before.

"Well, I just wanted to get some facts," I said pointedly. "And I know some people who can help me to help you."

"What kind of people—psychiatrist people? I don't trust them. They make things up."

Now it was clear why she left the last pediatrician. He was probably asking the same kinds of questions I was asking, and trying to help these children who were so obviously at risk. I knew she would eventually leave our practice and try to find a pediatrician she would be comfortable with—one who didn't ask questions.

Another family who wouldn't accept help, but desperately needed it, was the Price family. They had three children: Kimberly, Tad, and Lucy. When Lucy was three she was diagnosed with leukemia. At the time Kimberly was ten and Tad was six. Although most children today survive leukemia, Lucy just didn't respond to any of the treatments or medication. Eighteen months after her diagnosis she died.

Throughout her illness, and after her death, I continually tried to offer support to the entire Price family. I strongly recommended professional counseling, consultations, and support groups, but the family would have none of it. I even wondered if there was something going on in the family that counteracted the treatments Lucy was getting, because how families view a child's illness seems to have an impact on the illness itself.

Following Lucy's death the family spun out of control. The

parents got a divorce and the father moved away, eventually losing all contact with the rest of the family. Kimberly became a bizarre character who only wore black. Tad started acting out and was always in some sort of trouble.

It seemed to me that this family must have been just barely balancing their seesaw of a system when this tragedy struck. They didn't have the inner resources to deal with it, nor were they able to accept the help that was offered to them. It's sad and frustrating to see families that so clearly need help, but they view this help as messing with their system and their system is so fragile they're terrified to allow the intervention.

Throughout this time our family was going through many changes. Gordon was busy applying to college. He had done well in high school and was determined to go to a good college, so he applied to a ton of schools. It was a very stressful time. The minute he walked onto the campus of Bowdoin College in Maine he knew that was where he wanted to go. Knowing how difficult it could be for Gordon to adjust to a new situation I suggested he go to a school closer to home. But his heart was set on Bowdoin and luckily Bowdoin felt the same about Gordon.

At the same time Gordon was applying to colleges, Monty, the dog who had barked his way across the country twelve years earlier, died. I came home from the office that night to find my whole family sitting in the dark, mourning Monty.

I turned on the lights. "Everyone up and we'll pop the cork on a bottle of champagne!" I said. My family looked at me like I was an ogre. "I know you're all sad. I'm sad too. I loved Monty every bit as much as you all did. But I'm not going to sit shiva for a dog who lived a full rich life like Monty. He was fourteen years old, for God's sake. That's ninety-eight to you and me, and luckily he went without pain. Now what we need is another dog."

"Another dog!" Susan said increduously, no doubt thinking about another fourteen years of dealing with a crazed and volatile animal. "No way, Norman. It's out of the question."

"Come on, Susan. We're a dog family. We definitely need a dog."

"Dad's right," said Lisa, "there'll never be another Monty . . ."

"Thank God," Susan muttered.

"But we do need another dog," Lisa finished.

The next day at the office I asked everyone who came in if they knew of anyone with puppies for sale. Sure enough some-one did. Lisa and I went to see them. All puppies are cute, but these were adorable little white fluff-balls. We picked out a girl, hoping it would have a more relaxed disposition than Monty, tied a red ribbon around her neck, and took her home to Susan.

"Hey Sus," I yelled when we walked in the house.

"I'm in the kitchen."

"We have something to show you, Mom," Lisa said and put the little fluff-ball on the kitchen floor.

"No! I said no more dogs."

The ball of fluff skittered across the kitchen floor and went straight to Susan and licked her toes.

"Oh, she's the cutest thing I've ever seen," she said, reach-ing down and picking the dog up. "She's a girl, isn't she?" she asked, checking to see.

"Yep. Since Monty was named for Montana I thought she could be Connie for Connecticut."

"It fits her perfectly," Susan said, nuzzling Connie's little face. Yes, we definitely were a dog family.

Gordon went off to Bowdoin and the astronomical phone bill was proof of his difficult adjustment. We did everything we could to help him, and part of this was phone calls back and forth every time anything of consequence happened, whether it was four in the afternoon or four in the morning. By the beginning of his sophomore year, however, he felt com-fortable with the school, and his new group of friends, and started to really enjoy college.

Lisa looked at a few schools and decided quickly and easi-ly that Trinity College was the one for her. She applied early decision and by November everything was set. The next fall she went happily off to school and that was that: first child—stressful, second child—a breeze.

There was no empty-nest syndrome for us. Susan was busy with her career. She had worked hard and earned a doctorate in education. She was now a public affairs officer for the Norwalk school system and was busy developing the Norwalk Mentor Program, designed to match companies with schools. Individuals from the companies were teamed one-on-one to help children at risk of dropping out of school.

With more and more women involved in their careers, the empty-nest syndrome, as it was called in the 1950s and 1960s, was becoming a thing of the past. While we missed Gordon and Lisa, we enjoyed concentrating on our lives and on our careers, our extra activities and each other. I especially enjoyed cooking all the dishes I was interested in without having the kids there to make faces and gagging noises.

With the kids returning from college for occasional weekends and vacations we entered a new era of parenting. Gordon would go out with his buddies and come home at one or two in the morning. Susan and I would wait up for him, and it was making us crazy and exhausted. We finally told him he would have to tell us when he was coming home.

"But Dad," Gordon said, "when I'm at college you don't know when I'm coming home. No one does. I'm an adult now, and I have to be responsible for myself."

I realized he was right. My son was no longer a boy. He was a young man—a responsible young man. And knowing this, we would just have to learn to go to sleep and try not to worry.

Changes were going on at the office as well. Dr. Katherine Holden got married and moved out of town, and Dr. Jeanne Marconi joined our practice. She shared my vision of a practice complete with a family therapist, psychologist, and other support staff; a practice where we would meet all the needs of our families. We were about to make this vision a reality.

After a long search for the perfect location, the Norwalk office was moved to an ideal new spot—just down the street from our original office. It was a five-thousand-square-foot building, with lots of parking. The front of the building, facing the street, had large windows above which, protruding from the facade, was a frieze of trees, with a 1957 Plymouth depicted, as it drove along a road. I painted the car a bright red. It was perfect!

Because he was planning to retire in a few years, Bert decided to forgo financial responsibility for this new project. This clearly became, in Bert's terms, "my little red wagon." And this little red wagon turned out to be what I'd always wanted. There were individual waiting areas for sick and well children, and adolescents were given their own area as well. We had adequate examination rooms, a conference room, staff space, and offices we sublet to Maida Webster, our family therapist, and psychologist Dr. Jeffrey Lerner.

We brought in a part-time nutritionist, speech therapist, occupational and physical therapist. Finally, my dream practice was a reality. We would now be able to meet the complete needs of our families—medically, mentally, and emotionally.

Having Maida and Jeff as part of the practice meant our families would be able to get their help when they needed it, on site. They wouldn't have to make the uncomfortable leap of having to look outside the practice every time a problem or issue arose. I knew there would always be families like the Utleys and Prices who would be unable, for whatever reasons, to accept help, but I also knew with help down the hall, instead of across town, we would have a much better chance of reaching even the most guarded and reluctant families.

In the twenty years I had been in private practice I had watched the entire structure and fabric of family life change. I had been striving to keep up with and meet the ever more complex needs, demands, and struggles of the families in my practice as well as those of my own family, as we all made the journey through the cycles of life. So far it had been quite a trip. Now, with the new office, and being better equipped professionally, we were ready and excited to face the challenges of the next twenty years.

EPILOGUE

We have found a way to give our families the support and care necessary not just to launch a family but to guide and sustain it.

Life is a series of cycles. And our family was about to begin a new one. Gordon was getting married. He had met Cynthia Ann Carron at the end of his sophomore year at Bowdoin College. The attraction was immediate and mutual and they dated throughout college.

After his graduation he moved to Boston to be closer to Cindy, who still had two years left at Boston University. At this point we could see where their relationship was going. Sure enough, in the middle of Cindy's senior year at B.U., Gordon came home to tell us he was about to propose and planned to marry Cindy in June.

I couldn't help feeling Gordon wasn't ready for this. In my most fatherly voice I said, "Gordon, you just started a new job. Cindy is graduating and will be looking for a job herself. Don't you think you should wait?"

He looked at me with a big smile. I had the sense he knew this would be my reaction. "Dad, I am twenty-three. Just remember—when you were twenty-three, I was seven months old." Touché. He definitely was prepared for my response. He had even done the math. I guess no parent is ever completely ready for their child to get married. Marriage is the lifetime event that truly means your child is an adult.

On June 25, 1989, Susan and I escorted Gordon down the aisle. It was the best wedding ever. The newlyweds moved to Londonderry, New Hampshire. And they both took on the stressful daily commute to their jobs in Boston.

Gordon conceived the idea of manufacturing and marketing an old family recipe for apple pie. To our delight Gordon's Top of the Tree Apple Pies was not all that was conceived—on March 1, 1993, our first grandchild, Emily Carron Weinberger, was presented to us. This little creature totally captivated us. I began to appreciate that being a grandfather was far different and far more enjoyable than being a father. I also began to appreciate how difficult it is for a family to raise a child without the support of grandparents in close proximity.

After the birth of Emily, Cindy went back to work, taking a job closer to home, and our grandchild became one of the millions of children in day-care. Cindy showed all the natural loving and caring instincts of a nurturing mother. On October 23, 1995, our second grandchild, Jack Harrison Weinberger, was born. Gordon's skill, patience, and love for his wife and children constantly amaze me—I could write a book.

In the meantime Lisa graduated from Trinity College and went to the University of Pennsylvania to pursue a master's degree in fine arts in painting. I am proud to say that our home is a Lisa M. Weinberger gallery. After receiving her advanced degree Lisa moved back to Philadelphia and conceived her own "baby"—Masters Group Design, a graphic design business.

As my children pursued their new lives, I began to expand the function of our practice. Jeff, Maida, and I not only ran new-parent groups but we also started a group on discipline, and developed a multifaceted approach to children with attention deficit disorder and learning disabilities. Recognizing that good communication is key to informed and conscientious parenting, we developed a newsletter, designed by my daughter, Lisa, to keep our families informed of what was happening in the practice and in pediatrics in general. We continue to work to sharpen our skills to help families in crisis.

I see the future of pediatrics focusing on early prevention and intervention. So we continue to develop innovative ways to meet new problems. We have expanded our hours. Now a nurse is on staff as ombudsman and educator. She is available to talk to new moms about problems they would not "bother the doctor" with. We have a part-time pediatric nurse-practitioner and a physician's assistant who make home visits to our newborns and their mothers shortly after discharge from the hospital to ensure they're doing well. They assist with feeding problems, answer questions, and allay concerns.

Using all these methods, we have found a way to give our families the support and care necessary not just to launch a family but to guide and sustain it. In short—not only to raise happy, healthy children but also to raise happy, healthy families.

When I walked into the examining room Susan Walsh was leaning over the examining table getting her six-month-old, James, ready for his exam. Her three-year-old, David, was standing on a chair by her side, and as she undressed the baby she spoke quietly to David, making sure she was including him, answering his questions, explaining what I was going to do during the exam.

I was touched by the peaceful scene. The love with which Susan interacted with her children seemed to fill the room, and I felt like an intruder. I said a quiet hello so I wouldn't startle them.

"Hi, Dr. Weinberger. We're all ready for you," Susan said.

"I see that," I told her. "I was watching you with your kids and I have to tell you—you do such a wonderful job. You treat your boys with such gentleness and love and joy. It's a pleasure just to watch."

"Thank you, Doctor. That's a wonderful compliment. I was worried about how I would be as a mom, but I really find it so easy and natural. It was just clear from early on what my job as a mother was."

"And what was that job?" I asked.

"I see myself as a guide for my children. It's my job to help them on the path to adulthood. I'll know I've done a good job when they realize they alone are creating the course of their life, and my presence was only necessary to help nurture and support their innate instinct to explore the world and be themselves."

I was bowled over by her incredible view of what parenthood was. The more I thought about it, the more I realized it was also an apt description of what I was striving for as a pediatrician. I too had always hoped that I could be a guide, helping these families along the sometimes treacherous journey families go through, as their children and the entire family change and evolve.